Analyzing Data with Microsoft Power BI and Power Pivot for Excel

Alberto Ferrari
and Marco Russo

DISCARD
Courtright Memorial Library
Otterbein University
Courtright MemorialLib
Otterbein University
138 W. Main St.
Westerville, Ohio 43081

PUBLISHED BY

Microsoft Press
A division of Microsoft Corporation
One Microsoft Way
Redmond, Washington 98052-6399

Copyright © 2017 by Alberto Ferrari and Marco Russo

All rights reserved. No part of the contents of this book may be reproduced or transmitted in any form or by any means without the written permission of the publisher.

Library of Congress Control Number: 2016931116

ISBN: 978-1-5093-0276-5

Printed and bound in the United States of America.

1 17

Microsoft Press books are available through booksellers and distributors worldwide. If you need support related to this book, email Microsoft Press Support at *mspinput@microsoft.com*. Please tell us what you think of this book at *https://aka.ms/tellpress*.

This book is provided "as-is" and expresses the author's views and opinions. The views, opinions and information expressed in this book, including URL and other Internet website references, may change without notice.

Some examples depicted herein are provided for illustration only and are fictitious. No real association or connection is intended or should be inferred.

Microsoft and the trademarks listed at *https://www.microsoft.com* on the "Trademarks" webpage are trademarks of the Microsoft group of companies. All other marks are property of their respective owners.

Acquisitions Editor: Devon Musgrave
Editorial Production: Polymath Publishing
Technical Reviewer: Ed Price
Copy Editor: Kate Shoup
Layout Services: Shawn Morningstar
Indexing Services: Kelly Talbot Editing Services
Proofreading Services: Corina Lebegioara
Cover: Twist Creative • Seattle

Contents at a Glance

Contents

Introduction

Excel users love numbers. Or maybe it's that people who love numbers love Excel. Either way, if you are interested in gathering insights from any kind of dataset, it is extremely likely that you have spent a lot of your time playing with Excel, pivot tables, and formulas.

In 2015, Power BI was released. These days, it is fair to say that people who love numbers love both Power Pivot for Excel and Power BI. Both these tools share a lot of features, namely the VertiPaq database engine and the DAX language, inherited from SQL Server Analysis Services.

With previous versions of Excel, gathering insights from numbers was mainly a matter of loading some datasets and then starting to calculate columns and write formulas to design charts. Yes, there were some limitations: the size of the workbook mattered, and the Excel formula language was not the best option for huge number crunching. The new engine in Power BI and Power Pivot is a giant leap forward. Now you have the full power of a database and a gorgeous language (DAX) to leverage. But, hey, with greater power comes greater responsibility! If you want to really take advantage of this new tool, you need to learn more. Namely, you need to learn the basics of data modeling.

Data modeling is not rocket science. It is a basic skill that anybody interested in gathering insights from data should master. Moreover, if you like numbers, then you will love data modeling, too. So, not only is it an easy skill to acquire, it is also incredibly fun.

This book aims to teach you the basic concepts of data modeling through practical examples that you are likely to encounter in your daily life. We did not want to write a complex book on data modeling, explaining in detail the many complex decisions that you will need to make to build a complex solution. Instead, we focused on examples coming from our daily job as consultants. Whenever a customer asked us to help solve a problem, if we felt the issue is something common, we stored it in a bin. Then, we opened that bin and provided a solution to each of these examples, organizing them in a way that it also serves as a training on data modeling.

When you reach the end of the book, you will not be a data-modeling guru, but you will have acquired a greater sensibility on the topic. If, at that time, you look at your database, trying to figure out how to compute the value you need, and you start to think that—maybe—changing the model might help, then we will have accomplished our goal with this book. Moreover, you will be on your path to becoming a successful data modeler. This last step—that is, becoming a great data modeler—will only come with experience and after many failures. Unfortunately, experience is not something you can learn in a book.

Who this book is for

This book has a very wide target of different kind of people. You might be an Excel user who uses Power Pivot for Excel, or you may be a data scientist using Power BI. Or you could be starting your career as a business-intelligence professional and you want to read an introduction to the topics of data modeling. In all these scenarios, this is the book for you.

Note that we did not include in this list people who want to read a book about data modeling. In fact, we wrote the book thinking that our readers probably do not even know they need data modeling at all. Our goal is to make you understand that you need to learn data modeling and then give you some insights into the basics of this beautiful science. Thus, in a sentence if you are curious about what data modeling is and why it is a useful skill, then this is the book for you.

Assumptions about you

We expect our reader to have a basic knowledge of Excel Pivot Tables and/or to have used Power BI as a reporting and modelling tool. Some experience in analysis of numbers is also very welcome. In the book, we do not cover any aspect of the user interface of either Excel or Power BI. Instead, we focus only on data models, how to build them, and how to modify them, so that the code becomes easier to write. Thus, we cover "what you need to do" and we leave the "how to do it" entirely to you. We did not want to write a step-by-step book. We wanted to write a book that teaches complex topics in an easy way.

One topic that we intentionally do not cover in the book is the DAX language. It would have been impossible to treat data modeling and DAX in the same book. If you are already familiar with the language, then you will benefit from reading the many pieces of DAX spread throughout this book. If, on the other hand, you still need to learn DAX, then read *The Definitive Guide to DAX*, which is the most comprehensive guide to the DAX language and ties in well with the topics in this book.

Organization of this book

The book starts with a couple of easy, introductory chapters followed by a set of monographic chapters, each one covering some specific kind of data model. Here is a brief description of each chapter:

- Chapter 1, "Introduction to data modeling," is a brief introduction to the basic concepts of data modeling. Here we introduce what data modeling is, we start speaking about granularity, and we define the basic models of a data warehouse—that is, star schemas, snowflakes, normalization, and denormalization.

- Chapter 2, "Using header/detail tables," covers a very common scenario: that of header/detail tables. Here you will find discussions and solutions for scenarios where you have, for example, orders and lines of orders in two separate fact tables.

- Chapter 3, "Using multiple fact tables," describes scenarios where you have multiple fact tables and you need to build a report that mixes them. Here we stress the relevance of creating a correct dimensional model to be able to browse data the right way.

- Chapter 4, "Working with date and time," is one of the longest of the book. It covers time intelligence calculations. We explain how to build a proper date table and how to compute basic time intelligence (YTD, QTA, PARALLELPERIOD, and so on), and then we show several examples of working day calculations, handling special periods of the year, and working correctly with dates in general.

- Chapter 5, "Tracking historical attributes," describes the use of slowly changing dimensions in your model. This chapter provides a deeper explanation of the transformation steps needed in your model if you need to track changing attributes and how to correctly write your DAX code in the presence of slowly changing dimensions.

- Chapter 6, "Using snapshots," covers the fascinating aspects of snapshots. We introduce what a snapshot is, why and when to use them, and how to compute values on top of snapshots, and we provide a description of the powerful transition matrix model.

- Chapter 7, "Analyzing date and time intervals," goes several steps forward from Chapter 5. We cover time calculations, but this time analyzing models where events stored in fact tables have a duration and, hence, need some special treatment to provide correct results.

- Chapter 8, "Many-to-many relationships," explains how to use many-to-many relationships. Many-to-many relationships play a very important role in any data model. We cover standard many-to-many relationships, cascading relationships, and their use with reallocation factors and filters, and we discuss their performance and how to improve it.

- Chapter 9, "Working with different granularity," goes deeper into working with fact tables stored at different granularities. We show budgeting examples where the granularity of fact tables is different and provide several alternatives both in DAX and in the data model to solve the scenario.

- Chapter 10, "Segmentation data models," explains several segmentation models. We start with a simple segmentation by price, we then move to the analysis of dynamic segmentation using virtual relationships, and finally we explain the ABC analysis done in DAX.

- Chapter 11, "Working with multiple currencies," deals with currency exchange. When using currency rates, it is important to understand the requirements and then build the proper model. We analyze several scenarios with different requirements, providing the best solution for each.

- Appendix A, "Data modeling 101," is intended to be a reference. We briefly describe with examples the basic concepts treated in the whole book. Whenever you are uncertain about some aspect, you can jump there, refresh your understanding, and then go back to the main reading.

The complexity of the models and their solutions increase chapter by chapter, so it is a good idea to read this book from the beginning rather than jumping from chapter to chapter. In this way, you can follow the natural flow of complexity and learn one topic at a time. However, the book is intended to become a reference guide, once finished. Thus, whenever you need to solve a specific model, you can jump straight to the chapter that covers it and look into the details of the solution.

Conventions

The following conventions are used in this book:

- **Boldface** type is used to indicate text that you type.

- *Italic* type is used to indicate new terms.

- Code elements appear in a monospaced font.

- The first letters of the names of dialog boxes, dialog box elements, and commands are capitalized—for example, the Save As dialog box.

- Keyboard shortcuts are indicated by a plus sign (+) separating the key names. For example, Ctrl+Alt+Delete mean that you press Ctrl, Alt, and Delete keys at the same time.

About the companion content

We have included companion content to enrich your learning experience. The companion content for this book can be downloaded from the following page:

https://aka.ms/AnalyzeData/downloads

The companion content includes Excel and/or Power BI Desktop files for all the examples shown in the book. There is a separate file for each of the figures of the book so you can analyze the different steps and start exactly from the point where you are reading to follow the book and try the examples by yourself. Most of the examples are Power BI Desktop files, so we suggest that readers interested in following the examples on their PC download the latest version of Power BI Desktop from the Power BI website.

Acknowledgments

Before we leave this brief introduction, we feel the need to say thank you to our editor, Kate Shoup, who helped us along the whole process of editing, and to our technical reviewer, Ed Price. Without their meticulous work, the book would have been much harder to read! If the book contains fewer errors than our original manuscript, it is only because of them. If it still contains errors, it is our fault, of course.

Errata and book support

We have made every effort to ensure the accuracy of this book and its companion content. Any errors that have been reported since this book was published are listed on our Microsoft Press site at:

https://aka.ms/AnalyzeData/errata

If you find an error that is not already listed, you can report it to us through the same page.

If you need additional support, email Microsoft Press Book Support at *mspinput@microsoft.com*.

Please note that product support for Microsoft software is not offered through the addresses above.

We want to hear from you

At Microsoft Press, your satisfaction is our top priority and your feedback our most valuable asset. Please tell us what you think of this book at:

https://aka.ms/tellpress

The survey is short, and we read every one of your comments and ideas. Thanks in advance for your input!

Stay in touch

Let's keep the conversation going! We're on Twitter: @MicrosoftPress.

CHAPTER 1

Introduction to data modeling

You're about to read a book devoted to data modeling. Before starting it, it is worth determining why you should learn data modeling at all. After all, you can easily grab good insights from your data by simply loading a query in Excel and then opening a PivotTable on top of it. Thus, why should you learn anything about data modeling?

As consultants, we are hired on a daily basis by individuals or companies who struggle to compute the numbers they need. They feel like the number they're looking for is out there and can be computed, but for some obscure reason, either the formulas become too complicated to be manageable or the numbers do not match. In 99 percent of cases, this is due to some error in the data model. If you fix the model, the formula becomes easy to author and understand. Thus, you must learn data modeling if you want to improve your analytical capabilities and if you prefer to focus on making the right decision rather than on finding the right complex DAX formula.

Data modeling is typically considered a tough skill to learn. We are not here to say that this is not true. Data modeling is a complex topic. It is challenging, and it will require some effort to learn it and to shape your brain in such a way that you see the model in your mind when you are thinking of the scenario. So, data modeling is complex, challenging, and mind-stretching. In other words, it is totally fun!

This chapter provides you with some basic examples of reports where the correct data model makes the formulas easier to compute. Of course, being examples, they might not fit your business perfectly. Still, we hope they will give you an idea of why data modeling is an important skill to acquire. Being a good data modeler basically means being able to match your specific model with one of the many different patterns that have already been studied and solved by others. Your model is not so different than all the other ones. Yes, it has some peculiarities, but it is very likely that your specific problem has already been solved by somebody else. Learning how to discover the similarities between your data model and the ones described in the examples is difficult, but it's also very satisfying. When you do, the solution appears in front of you, and most of the problems with your calculations suddenly disappear.

For most of our demos, we will use the Contoso database. Contoso is a fictitious company that sells electronics all over the world, through different sales channels. It is likely that your business is different, in which case, you will need to match the reports and insights we grab from Contoso to your specific business.

Because this is the first chapter, we will start by covering basic terminology and concepts. We will explain what a data model is and why relationships are an important part of a data model. We also give a first introduction to the concepts of normalization, denormalization, and star schemas. This process of introducing concepts by examples will continue through the whole book, but here, during the first steps, it is just more evident.

Fasten your seatbelt! It's time to get started learning all the secrets of data modeling.

Working with a single table

If you use Excel and PivotTables to discover insights about your data, chances are you load data from some source, typically a database, using a query. Then, you create a PivotTable on top of this dataset and start exploring. Of course, by doing that, you face the usual limitations of Excel—the most relevant being that the dataset cannot exceed 1,000,000 rows. Otherwise, it will not fit into a worksheet. To be honest, the first time we learned about this limitation, we did not even consider it a limitation at all. Why on Earth would somebody load more than 1,000,000 rows in Excel and not use a database instead? The reason, you might guess, is that Excel does not require you to understand data modeling, whereas a database does.

Anyway, this first limitation—if you want to use Excel—can be a very big one. In Contoso, the database we use for demos, the table containing the sales is made of 12,000,000 rows. Thus, there is no way to simply load all these rows in Excel to start the analysis. This problem has an easy solution: Instead of retrieving all the rows, you can perform some grouping to reduce their number. If, for example, you are interested in the analysis of sales by category and subcategory, you can choose not to load the sales of each product, and you can group data by category and subcategory, significantly reducing the number of rows.

For example, the 12,000,000-row sales table—when grouped by manufacturer, brand, category, and subcategory, while retaining the sales for each day—produces a result of 63,984 rows, which are easy to manage in an Excel workbook. Of course, building the right query to perform this grouping is typically a task for an IT department or for a good query editor, unless you already learned SQL as part of your training. If not, then you must ask your IT department to produce such a query. Then, when they come back with the code, you can start to analyze your numbers. In Figure 1-1, you can see the first few rows of the table when imported into Excel.

When the table is loaded in Excel, you finally feel at home, and you can easily create a PivotTable to perform an analysis on the data. For example, in Figure 1-2, you can see the sales divided by manufacturer for a given category, using a standard PivotTable and a slicer.

FullDateLabel	Manufacturer	BrandName	ProductSubcategoryName	ProductCategoryName	SalesQuantity	SalesAmount	TotalCost
2007-03-31	Adventure Works	Adventure Works	Coffee Machines	Home Appliances	55	14332.268	7651.84
2008-10-22	Contoso, Ltd	Contoso	Cell phones Accessories	Cell phones	2040	23504.88	12648.94
2009-01-31	Adventure Works	Adventure Works	Televisions	TV and Video	194	51593.106	28146.4
2009-01-21	Fabrikam, Inc.	Fabrikam	Camcorders	Cameras and camcorders	282	163007.2	76709.45
2007-12-31	Adventure Works	Adventure Works	Laptops	Computers	29	14008.43	7944.32
2007-06-22	Contoso, Ltd	Contoso	Cell phones Accessories	Cell phones	680	6107.24	3420.44
2007-06-22	Proseware, Inc.	Proseware	Projectors & Screens	Computers	86	71417.6	30786.94
2007-08-23	Adventure Works	Adventure Works	Laptops	Computers	43	22672.2	9954.6
2009-03-30	The Phone Company	The Phone Company	Touch Screen Phones	Cell phones	198	48500.37	24164.56
2008-03-24	Contoso, Ltd	Contoso	Home & Office Phones	Cell phones	306	7353.594	3914.64
2007-09-30	Fabrikam, Inc.	Fabrikam	Microwaves	Home Appliances	44	4805.604	2824.24
2007-11-13	Adventure Works	Adventure Works	Desktops	Computers	153	47357.97	28256.02
2008-12-06	Contoso, Ltd	Contoso	Projectors & Screens	Computers	32	10790.4	6477.2
2007-11-14	Contoso, Ltd	Contoso	Digital SLR Cameras	Cameras and camcorders	146	55397.5	25876
2009-12-30	Adventure Works	Adventure Works	Desktops	Computers	32	15107.75	7952.97
2009-03-13	Wide World Importers	Wide World Importers	Recording Pen	Audio	42	7990.92	3607.26
2009-08-11	Wide World Importers	Wide World Importers	Recording Pen	Audio	9	1466.1	749.16
2009-09-28	Contoso, Ltd	Contoso	Microwaves	Home Appliances	78	9955.268	5189.27
2008-02-18	A. Datum Corporation	A. Datum	Digital Cameras	Cameras and camcorders	345	70989.93	32872.58
2007-08-15	Litware, Inc.	Litware	Washers & Dryers	Home Appliances	69	112603.8	56472.35

FIGURE 1-1   Data from sales, when grouped, produces a small and easy-to-analyze table.

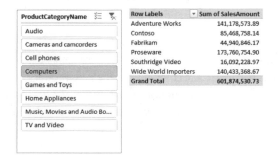

Row Labels	Sum of SalesAmount
Adventure Works	141,178,573.89
Contoso	85,468,758.14
Fabrikam	44,940,846.17
Proseware	173,760,754.90
Southridge Video	16,092,228.97
Wide World Importers	140,433,368.67
Grand Total	**601,874,530.73**

ProductCategoryName

- Audio
- Cameras and camcorders
- Cell phones
- Computers
- Games and Toys
- Home Appliances
- Music, Movies and Audio Bo…
- TV and Video

FIGURE 1-2   You can easily create a PivotTable on top of an Excel table.

Believe it or not, at this point, you've already built a data model. Yes, it contains only a single table, but it is a data model. Thus, you can start exploring its analytical power and maybe find some way to improve it. This data model has a strong limitation because it has fewer rows than the source table.

As a beginner, you might think that the limit of 1,000,000 rows in an Excel table affects only the number of rows that you can retrieve to perform the analysis. While this holds true, it is important to note that the limit on the size directly translates into a limit on the data model. Therefore, there is also a limit on the analytical capabilities of your reports. In fact, to reduce the number of rows, you had to perform a grouping of data at the source level, retrieving only the sales grouped by some columns. In this example, you had to group by category, subcategory, and some other columns.

Doing this, you implicitly limited yourself in your analytical power. For example, if you want to perform an analysis slicing by color, then the table is no longer a good source because you don't have the product color among the columns. Adding one column to the query is not a big issue. The problem is that the more columns you add, the larger the table becomes—not only in width (the number of columns), but also in length (the number of rows). In fact, a single line holding the sales for a given category—Audio, for example—will become a set of multiple rows, all containing Audio for the category, but with different values for the different colors.

On the extreme side, if you do not want to decide in advance which columns you will use to slice the data, you will end up having to load the full 12,000,000 rows—meaning an Excel table is no longer an option. This is what we mean when we say that Excel's modeling capabilities are limited. Not being able to load many rows implicitly translates into not being able to perform advanced analysis on large volumes of data.

This is where Power Pivot comes into play. Using Power Pivot, you no longer face the limitation of 1,000,000 rows. Indeed, there is virtually no limit on the number of rows you can load in a Power Pivot table. Thus, by using Power Pivot, you can load the whole sales table in the model and perform a deeper analysis of your data.

> **Note**   Power Pivot has been available in Excel since Excel 2010 as an external add-in, and it has been included as part of the product since Excel 2013. Starting in Excel 2016, Microsoft began using a new name to describe a Power Pivot model: Excel Data Model. However, the term Power Pivot is still used, too.

Because you have all the sales information in a single table, you can perform a more detailed analysis of your data. For example, in Figure 1-3, you can see a PivotTable coming from the data model (that is, Power Pivot), with all the columns loaded. Now, you can slice by category, color, and year, because all this information is in the same place. Having more columns available in your table increases its analytical power.

ProductCategoryName			
Audio			
Cameras and camcorders			
Cell phones			
Computers			
Games and Toys			
Home Appliances			
Music, Movies and Audio Bo...			
TV and Video			

Sum of SalesAmount	Column Labels			
Row Labels	2007	2008	2009	Grand Total
Black	$59,783,936.63	$63,073,257.64	$70,489,997.35	$193,347,191.62
Blue	$5,128,405.12	$6,516,691.17	$7,715,161.42	$19,360,257.71
Brown	$6,301,722.60	$7,183,128.75	$4,904,738.33	$18,389,589.68
Gold		$39,185.40	$122,755.63	$161,941.03
Green	$1,747,237.19	$1,566,822.01	$2,159,190.14	$5,473,249.35
Grey	$6,318,419.68	$5,924,762.67	$6,410,704.05	$18,653,886.41
Orange		$12,800.63	$84,766.80	$97,567.43
Pink	$20,078.44	$43,870.83	$228,526.86	$292,476.13
Red	$6,926,045.96	$7,872,382.02	$11,495,613.50	$26,294,041.47
Silver	$43,375,399.72	$39,082,679.67	$36,471,502.90	$118,929,582.29
White	$64,963,894.39	$64,142,854.42	$70,639,615.97	$199,746,364.78
Yellow	$260,512.33	$330,165.82	$537,704.67	$1,128,382.82
Grand Total	$194,825,652.07	$195,788,601.04	$211,260,277.62	$601,874,530.73

FIGURE 1-3   If all the columns are available, you can build more interesting PivotTables on top of your data.

This simple example is already useful to learn the first lesson about data modeling: *Size matters because it relates to granularity.* But what is *granularity*? Granularity is one of the most important concepts you will learn in this book, so we are introducing the concept as early as we can. There will be time to go deeper in the rest of the book. For now, let us start with a simple description of granularity. In the first dataset, you grouped information at the category and subcategory levels, losing some detail in favor of a smaller size. A more technical way to express this is to say that you chose the granularity of the information at the category and subcategory level. You can think of granularity as the level of detail in your tables. The higher the granularity, the more detailed your information. Having more details means being able to perform more detailed (granular) analyses. In this last dataset, the one loaded in Power Pivot, the granularity is at the product level (actually, it is even finer than that—it is at the level of the individual sale of the product), whereas in the previous model, it was at the category and subcategory level. Your ability to slice and dice depends on the number of columns in the table—thus, on its granularity. You have already learned that increasing the number of columns increases the number of rows.

Choosing the correct granularity level is always challenging. If you have data at the wrong granularity, formulas are nearly impossible to write. This is because either you have lost the information (as in the previous example, where you did not have the color information) or it is scattered around the table, where it is organized in the wrong way. In fact, it is not correct to say that a higher granularity is always a good option. You must have data at the *right* granularity, where *right* means the best level of granularity to meet your needs, whatever they are.

You have already seen an example of lost information. But what do we mean by scattered information? This is a little bit harder to see. Imagine, for example, that you want to compute the average yearly income of customers who buy a selection of your products. The information is there because, in the sales table, you have all the information about your customers readily available. This is shown in Figure 1-4, which contains a selection of the columns of the table we are working on. (You must open the Power Pivot window to see the table content.)

ProductCategoryName	ProductSubcategoryName	ProductName	SalesAmount	FirstName	LastName	YearlyIncome
Cameras and camcorders	Digital SLR Cameras	A. Datum SLR Camera X137 Grey	$627.00	Katrina	Xie	€ 20,000.00
Cameras and camcorders	Digital SLR Cameras	A. Datum SLR Camera X137 Grey	$627.00	Seth	Rodriguez	€ 80,000.00
Cameras and camcorders	Digital SLR Cameras	A. Datum SLR Camera X137 Grey	$627.00	Evelyn	Arun	€ 10,000.00
Cameras and camcorders	Digital SLR Cameras	A. Datum SLR Camera X137 Grey	$627.00	Christy	Beck	€ 40,000.00
Cameras and camcorders	Digital SLR Cameras	A. Datum SLR Camera X137 Grey	$627.00	Alejandro	Nara	€ 40,000.00
Cameras and camcorders	Digital SLR Cameras	A. Datum SLR Camera X137 Grey	$627.00	Leah	Lu	€ 30,000.00
Cameras and camcorders	Digital SLR Cameras	A. Datum SLR Camera X137 Grey	$627.00	Robyn	Torres	€ 20,000.00
Cameras and camcorders	Digital SLR Cameras	A. Datum SLR Camera X137 Grey	$627.00	Jimmy	Moreno	€ 30,000.00
Cameras and camcorders	Digital SLR Cameras	A. Datum SLR Camera X137 Grey	$627.00	Rafael	Cai	€ 20,000.00
Cameras and camcorders	Digital SLR Cameras	A. Datum SLR Camera X137 Grey	$627.00	Jenny	Ferrier	€ 110,000.00
Cameras and camcorders	Digital SLR Cameras	A. Datum SLR Camera X137 Grey	$627.00	Levi	Arun	€ 70,000.00
Cameras and camcorders	Digital SLR Cameras	A. Datum SLR Camera X137 Grey	$627.00	Randall	Torres	€ 40,000.00

FIGURE 1-4 The product and customer information is stored in the same table.

On every row of the Sales table, there is an additional column reporting the yearly income of the customer who bought that product. A simple trial to compute the average yearly income of customers would involve authoring a DAX measure like the following:

```
AverageYearlyIncome := AVERAGE ( Sales[YearlyIncome] )
```

The measure works just fine, and you can use it in a PivotTable like the one in Figure 1-5, which shows the average yearly income of the customers buying home appliances of different brands.

ProductCategoryName		
Audio		
Cameras and camcorders		
Cell phones		
Computers		
Games and Toys		
Home Appliances		
Music, Movies and Audio Bo...		
TV and Video		

Row Labels	AverageYearlyIncome
Adventure Works	$9,614,894.80
Contoso	$8,307,093.90
Fabrikam	$9,461,956.24
Litware	$9,170,201.49
Northwind Traders	$2,230,398.67
Proseware	$9,586,214.41
Wide World Importers	$9,765,456.65
Grand Total	$8,957,859.39

FIGURE 1-5 The figure shows an analysis of the average yearly income of customers buying home appliances.

The report looks fine, but, unfortunately, the computed number is incorrect: It is highly exaggerated. In fact, what you are computing is the average over the sales table, which has a granularity at the individual sale level. In other words, the sales table contains a row for each sale, which means there are potentially multiple rows for the same customer. So if a customer buys three products on three different dates, it will be counted three times in the average, producing an inaccurate result.

You might argue that, in this way, you are computing a weighted average, but this is not totally true. In fact, if you want to compute a weighted average, you must define the weight—and you would not choose the weight to be the number of buy events. You are more likely to use the number of products as the weight, or the total amount spent, or some other meaningful value. Moreover, in this example, we just wanted to compute a basic average, and the measure is not computing it accurately.

Even if it is a bit harder to notice, we are also facing a problem of an incorrect granularity. In this case, the information is available, but instead of being linked to an individual customer, it is scattered all around the sales table, making it hard to write the calculation. To obtain a correct average, you must fix the granularity at the customer level by either reloading the table or relying on a more complex DAX formula.

If you want to rely on DAX, you would use the following formulation for the average, but it is a little challenging to comprehend:

```
CorrectAverage :=
AVERAGEX (
    SUMMARIZE (
        Sales,
        Sales[CustomerKey],
        Sales[YearlyIncome]
    ),
    Sales[YearlyIncome]
)
```

This formula is not easy to understand because you must first aggregate the sales at the customer level (of granularity) and then perform an AVERAGE operation on the resulting table where each customer appears only once. In the example, we are using SUMMARIZE to perform the pre-aggregation at the customer level in a temporary table, and then we average the YearlyIncome of that temporary table. As you can see in Figure 1-6, the correct number is very different from the incorrect number we previously calculated.

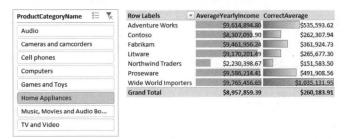

ProductCategoryName		Row Labels	AverageYearlyIncome	CorrectAverage
Audio		Adventure Works	$9,614,894.80	$535,593.62
Cameras and camcorders		Contoso	$8,307,093.90	$262,307.94
Cell phones		Fabrikam	$9,461,956.24	$361,924.73
Computers		Litware	$9,170,201.49	$265,677.30
Games and Toys		Northwind Traders	$2,230,398.67	$151,583.50
Home Appliances		Proseware	$9,586,214.41	$491,908.56
Music, Movies and Audio Bo...		Wide World Importers	$9,765,456.65	$1,035,131.95
TV and Video		Grand Total	$8,957,859.39	$260,183.91

FIGURE 1-6 The correct average side-by-side data (including the incorrect average) show how far we were from the accurate insight.

It is worth spending some time to acquire a good understanding of this simple fact: The yearly income is a piece of information that has a meaning at the customer granularity. At the individual sale level, that number—although correct—is not in the right place. Or, stated differently, you cannot use a value that has a meaning at the customer level with the same meaning at the individual sale level. In fact, to gather the right result, we had to reduce the granularity, although in a temporary table.

There are a couple of important lessons to learn from this example:

- The correct formula is much more complex than a simple AVERAGE. You needed to perform a temporary aggregation of values to correct the granularity of the table because the data is scattered around the table instead of being in an organized placement.

- It is very likely that you would not notice these errors if you were not familiar with your data. Looking at the report in Figure 1-6, you might easily spot that the yearly income looks too high to be true—as if none of your customers earns less than $2,000,000 a year! But for more complex calculations, identifying the error can be much more complex and might result in a report showing inaccurate numbers.

You must increase the granularity to produce reports at the desired detail, but increasing it too much makes it harder to compute some numbers. How do you choose the correct granularity? Well, this is a difficult question; we will save the answer for later. We hope to be able to transfer to you the knowledge to detect the correct granularity of data in your models, but keep in mind that choosing the correct granularity is a hard skill to develop, even for seasoned data modelers. For now, it is enough to start learning what granularity is and how important it is to define the correct granularity for each table in your model.

In reality, the model on which we are working right now suffers from a bigger issue, which is somewhat related to granularity. In fact, the biggest issue with this model is that it has a single table that contains all the information. If your model has a single table, as in this example, then you must choose the granularity of the table, taking into account all the possible measures and analyses that you might want to perform. No matter how hard you work, the granularity will never be perfect for all your measures. In the next sections, we will introduce the method of using multiple tables, which gives you better options for multiple granularities.

Introducing the data model

You learned in the previous section that a single-table model presents issues in defining the correct granularity. Excel users often employ single-table models because this was the only option available to build PivotTables before the release of the 2013 version of Excel. In Excel 2013, Microsoft introduced the Excel Data Model, to let you load many tables and link them through relationships, giving users the capability to create powerful data models.

What is a data model? A *data model* is just a set of tables linked by relationships. A single-table model is already a data model, although not a very interesting one. As soon as you have multiple tables, the presence of relationships makes the model much more powerful and interesting to analyze.

Building a data model becomes natural as soon as you load more than one table. Moreover, you typically load data from databases handled by professionals who created the data model for you. This means your data model will likely mimic the one that already exists in the source database. In this respect, your work is somewhat simplified.

Unfortunately, as you learn in this book, it is very unlikely that the source data model is perfectly structured for the kind of analysis you want to perform. By showing examples of increasing complexity, our goal is to teach you how to start from any data source to build your own model. To simplify your learning experience, we will gradually cover these techniques in the rest of the book. For now, we will start with the basics.

To introduce the concept of a data model, load the Product and Sales tables from the Contoso database into the Excel data model. When the tables are loaded, you'll get the diagram view shown in Figure 1-7, where you can see the two tables along with their columns.

> **Note** The relationship diagram is available in Power Pivot. To access it, click the **Power Pivot** tab in the Excel ribbon and click **Manage**. Then, in the Home tab of the Power Pivot window, click **Diagram View** in the View group.

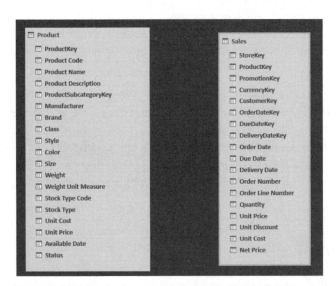

FIGURE 1-7 Using the data model, you can load multiple tables.

Two disconnected tables, as in this example, are not yet a true data model. They are only two tables. To transform this into a more meaningful model, you must create a relationship between the two tables. In this example, both the Sales table and the Product table have a ProductKey column. In Product, this is a *primary key*, meaning it has a different value in each row and can be used to uniquely identify a product. In the Sales table, it serves a different purpose: to identify the product sold.

Info The primary key of a table is a column that has a different value for every row. Thus, once you know the value of the column, you can uniquely identify its position in the table—that is, its row. You might have multiple columns that have a unique value; all of them are keys. The primary key is nothing special. From a technical point of view, it is just the column that you consider as the one that uniquely identifies a row. In a customer table, for example, the primary key is the customer code, even if it might be the case that the name is also a unique column.

When you have a unique identifier in a table, and a column in another table that references it, you can create a relationship between the two tables. Both facts must hold true for the relationship to be valid. If you have a model where the desired key for the relationship is not a unique identifier in one of the two tables, you must massage the model with one of the many techniques you learn in this book. For now, let us use this example to state some facts about a relationship:

- **The Sales table is called the *source table*** The relationship starts from Sales. This is because, to retrieve the product, you always start from Sales. You gather the product key value in the Sales and search for it in the Product table. At that point, you know the product, along with all its attributes.

- **The Product table is known as the *target* of the relationship** This is because you start from Sales and you reach Product. Thus, Product is the target of your search.

- **A relationship starts from the source and it reaches the target** In other words, a relationship has a direction. This is why it is often represented as an arrow starting from the source and indicating the target. Different products use different graphical representations for a relationship.

- **The source table is also called the *many side* of the relationship** This name comes from the fact that, for any given product, there are likely to be many sales, whereas for a given sale, there is only one product. For this same reason, the target table is known as the *one side* of the relationship. This book uses *one side* and *many side* terminology.

- **The ProductKey column exists in both the Sales and Product tables** ProductKey is a key in Product, but it is not a key in Sales. For this reason, it is called a primary key when used in Product, whereas it is called a foreign key when used in Sales. A *foreign key* is a column that points to a primary key in another table.

All these terms are very commonly used in the world of data modeling, and this book is no exception. Now that we've introduced them here, we will use them often throughout the book. But don't worry. We will repeat the definitions a few times in the first few chapters until you become acquainted with them.

Using both Excel and Power BI, you can create a relationship between two tables by dragging the foreign key (that is, ProductKey in Sales) and dropping it on the primary key (that is, ProductKey in Product). If you do so, you will quickly discover that both Excel and Power BI do not use arrows to show relationships. In fact, in the diagram view, a relationship is drawn identifying the *one* and the *many* side with a number (one) and an asterisk (many). Figure 1-8 illustrates this in Power Pivot's diagram view. Note that there is also an arrow in the middle, but it does not represent the direction of the relationship. Rather, it is the direction of filter propagation and serves a totally different purpose, which we will discuss later in this book.

> **Note** If your Power Pivot tab disappears, it is likely because Excel ran into an issue and disabled the add-in. To re-enable the Power Pivot add-in, click the **File** tab and click **Options** in the left pane. In the left pane of the Excel Options window, click **Add-Ins**. Then, open the **Manage** list box at the bottom of the page, select **COM Add-Ins**, and click **Go**. In the COM Add-Ins window, select **Microsoft Power Pivot for Excel**. Alternatively, if it is already selected, then deselect it. Then click **OK**. If you deselected Power Pivot, return to the COM Add-Ins window and re-select the add-in. The Power Pivot tab should return to your ribbon.

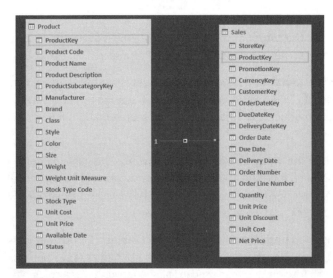

FIGURE 1-8 A relationship is represented as a line, in this case connecting the Product and Sales tables, with an indication of the side (1 for one side, * for many side).

When the relationship is in place, you can sum the values from the Sales table, slicing them by columns in the Product table. In fact, as shown in Figure 1-9, you can use Color (that is, a column from the Product table—refer to Figure 1-8) to slice the sum of Quantity (that is, a column in the Sales table).

You have seen your first example of a data model with two tables. As we said, a data model is simply a set of tables (Sales and Product, in this example) that are linked by relationships. Before moving on with more examples, let us spend a little more time discussing granularity—this time, in the case where there are multiple tables.

Row Labels	Sum of Quantity
Azure	60
Black	4307
Blue	985
Brown	453
Gold	155
Green	374
Grey	1551
Orange	179
Pink	600
Purple	10
Red	896
Silver	3604
Silver Grey	143
Transparent	141
White	3746
Yellow	294
Grand Total	**17498**

FIGURE 1-9 Once a relationship is in place, you can slice the values from one table by using columns in another one.

In the first section of this chapter, you learned how important—and complex—it is to define the correct granularity for a single table. If you make the wrong choice, calculations suddenly become much harder to author. What about granularity in the new data model, which now contains two tables? In this case, the problem is somewhat different, and to some extent, easier to solve, even if—at the same time—it's a bit more complex to understand.

Because there are two tables, now you have two different granularities. Sales has a granularity at the individual sale level, whereas Product has a granularity at the product level. In fact, granularity is a concept that is applied to a table, not to the model as a whole. When you have many tables, you must adjust the granularity level for each table in the model. Even if this looks to be more complex than the scenario where you have a single table, it naturally leads to models that are simpler to manage and where granularity is no longer an issue.

In fact, now that you have two tables, it is very natural to define the granularity of Sales at the individual sale level and the granularity of Product to its correct one, at the product level. Recall the first example in this chapter. You had a single table containing sales at the granularity of the product category and subcategory. This was because the product category and product subcategory were stored in the Sales table. In other words, *you had to make a decision about granularity, mainly because you stored information in the wrong place*. Once each piece of information finds its right place, granularity becomes much less of a problem.

In fact, the product category is an attribute of a product, not of an individual sale. It is—in some sense—an attribute of a sale, but only because a sale is pertinent to a product. Once you store the product key in the Sales table, you rely on the relationship to retrieve all the attributes of the product, including the product category, the color, and all the other product information. Thus, because you do not need to store the product category in Sales, the problem of granularity becomes much less of an issue. Of course, the same happens for all the attributes of Product—for example the color, the unit price, the product name, and, generally, all the columns in the Product table.

Info In a correctly designed model, granularity is set at the correct level for each table, leading to a simpler and, at the same time, more powerful structure. This is the power of relationships—a power that you can use once you start thinking in terms of multiple tables and get rid of the single-table approach you probably inherited from Excel.

If you look carefully at the Product table, you will notice that the product category and subcategory are missing. Instead, there is a ProductSubcategoryKey column, whose name suggests that it is a reference (that is, a foreign key) to the key in another table (where it is a primary key) that contains the product subcategories. In fact, in the database, there are two tables containing a product category and product subcategory. Once you load both of them into the model and build the right relationships, the structure mirrors the one shown in Figure 1-10, in Power Pivot's diagram view.

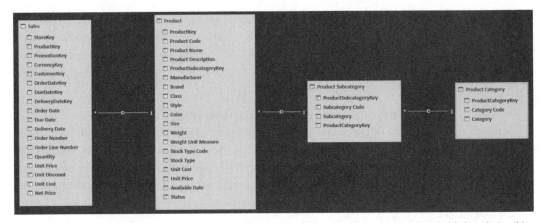

FIGURE 1-10 Product categories and subcategories are stored in different tables, which are reachable by relationships.

As you can see, information about a product is stored in three different tables: Product, Product Subcategory, and Product Category. This creates a chain of relationships, starting from Product, reaching Product Subcategory, and finally Product Category.

What is the reason for this design technique? At first sight, it looks like a complex mode to store a simple piece of information. However, this technique has many advantages, even if they are not very evident at first glance. By storing the product category in a separate table, you have a data model where the category name, although referenced from many products, is stored in a single row of the Product Category table. This is a good method of storing information for two reasons. First, it reduces the size on disk of the model by avoiding repetitions of the same name. Second, if at some point you must update the category name, you only need to do it once on the single row that stores it. All the products will automatically use the new name through the relationship.

There is a name for this design technique: *normalization*. An attribute such as the product category is said to be normalized when it is stored in a separate table and replaced with a key that points to that table. This is a very well-known technique and is widely used by database designers when they create a data model. The opposite technique—that is, storing attributes in the table to which they belong—is called *denormalization*. When a model is denormalized, the same attribute appears multiple times, and if you need to update it, you will have to update all the rows containing it. The color of a product, for instance, is denormalized, because the string "Red" appears in all the red products.

At this point, you might wonder why the designer of the Contoso database decided to store categories and subcategories in different tables (in other words, to normalize them), but to store the color, manufacturer, and brand in the Product table (in other words, to denormalize them). Well, in this specific case, the answer is an easy one: Contoso is a demo database, and its structure is intended to illustrate different design techniques. In the real world—that is, with your organization's databases—you will probably find a data structure that is either highly normalized or highly denormalized because the choice depends on the usage of the database. Nevertheless, be prepared to find some attributes that are normalized and some other that are denormalized. It is perfectly normal because when it comes to data modeling, there are a lot of different options. It might be the case that, over time, the designer has been driven to take different decisions.

Highly normalized structures are typical of online transactional processing (OLTP) systems. OLTP systems are databases that are designed to handle your everyday jobs. That includes operations like preparing invoices, placing orders, shipping goods, and solving claims. These databases are very normalized because they are designed to use the least amount of space (which typically means they run faster) with a lot of insert and update operations. In fact, during the everyday work of a company, you typically update information—for example, about a customer—want it to be automatically updated on all the data that reference this customer. This happens in a smooth way if the customer information is correctly normalized. Suddenly, all the orders from the customer will refer to the new, updated information. If the customer information were denormalized, updating the address of a customer would result in hundreds of update statements executed by the server, causing poor performance.

OLTP systems often consist of hundreds of tables because nearly every attribute is stored in a separate table. In products, for example, you will probably find one table for the manufacturer, one for the brand, one for the color, and so on. Thus, a simple entity like the product might be stored in 10 or 20 different tables, all linked through relationships. This is what a database designer would proudly call a "well designed data model," and, even if it might look strange, she would be right in being proud of it. Normalization, for OLTP databases, is nearly always a valuable technique.

The point is that when you analyze data, you perform no insert and no update. You are interested only in reading information. When you only read, normalization is almost never a good technique. As an example, suppose you create a PivotTable on the previous data model. Your field list will look similar to what you see in Figure 1-11.

FIGURE 1-11 The field list on a normalized model has too many tables available and might become messy.

The product is stored in three tables; thus, you see three tables in the field list (in the PivotTable Fields pane). Worse, the Product Category and Product Subcategory tables contain only a single column each. Thus, even if normalization is good for OLTP systems, it is typically a bad choice for an analytical system. When you slice and dice numbers in a report, you are not interested in a technical representation of a product; you want to see the category and subcategory as columns in the Product table, which creates a more natural way of browsing your data.

> **Note** In this example, we deliberately hid some useless columns like the primary keys of the table, which is always a good technique. Otherwise you would see multiple columns, which make the model even harder to browse. You can easily imagine what the field list would look like with tens of tables for the product; it would take a considerable amount time to find the right columns to use in the report.

Ultimately, when building a data model to do reporting, you must reach a reasonable level of de-normalization no matter how the original data is stored. As you've seen, if you denormalize too much, you face the problem of granularity. Later in this book, you will see that over-denormalizing a model has other negative consequences, too. What is, then, the correct level of denormalization?

There is no defined rule on how to obtain the perfect level of denormalization. Nevertheless, intuitively, you denormalize up to the point where a table is a self-contained structure that completely describes the entity it stores. Using the example discussed in this section, you should move the Product Category and Product Subcategory columns in the Product table because they are attributes of a prod-uct, and you do not want them to reside in separate tables. But you do not denormalize the product in the Sales table because products and sales are two different pieces of information. A sale is pertinent to a product, but there is no way a sale can be completely identified with a product.

At this point, you might think of the model with a single table as being over-denormalized. That is perfectly true. In fact, we had to worry about product attribute granularity in the Sales table, which is wrong. If the model is designed the right way, with the right level of denormalization, then granularity comes out in a very natural way. On the other hand, if the model is over-denormalized, then you must worry about granularity, and you start facing issues.

Introducing star schemas

So far, we have looked at very simple data models that contained products and sales. In the real world, few models are so simple. In a typical company like Contoso, there are several informational assets: products, stores, employees, customers, and time. These assets interact with each other, and they generate events. For example, a product is sold by an employee, who is working in a store, to a particular customer, and on a given date.

Obviously, different businesses manage different assets, and their interactions generate different events. However, if you think in a generic way, there is almost always a clear separation between assets and events. This structure repeats itself in any business, even if the assets are very different. For example, in a medical environment, assets might include patients, diseases, and medications, whereas an event is a patient being diagnosed with a specific disease and obtaining a medication to resolve it. In a claim system, assets might include customers, claims, and time, while events might be the different statuses of a claim in the process of being resolved. Take some time to think about your specific business. Most likely, you will be able to clearly separate between your assets and events.

This separation between assets and events leads to a data-modeling technique known as a *star schema*. In a star schema, you divide your entities (tables) into two categories:

- **Dimensions** A *dimension* is an informational asset, like a product, a customer, an employee, or a patient. Dimensions have attributes. For example, a product has attributes like its color, its category and subcategory, its manufacturer, and its cost. A patient has attributes such as a name, address, and date of birth.

- **Facts** A *fact* is an event involving some dimensions. In Contoso, a fact is the sale of a product. A sale involves a product, a customer, a date, and other dimensions. Facts have metrics, which are numbers that you can aggregate to obtain insights from your business. A metric can be the quantity sold, the sales amount, the discount rate, and so on.

Once you mentally divide your tables into these two categories, it becomes clear that facts are related to dimensions. For one individual product, there are many sales. In other words, there is a relationship involving the Sales and Product tables, where Sales is on the *many* side and Product is on the *one* side. If you design this schema, putting all dimensions around a single fact table, you obtain the typical figure of a star schema, as shown in Figure 1-12 in Power Pivot's diagram view.

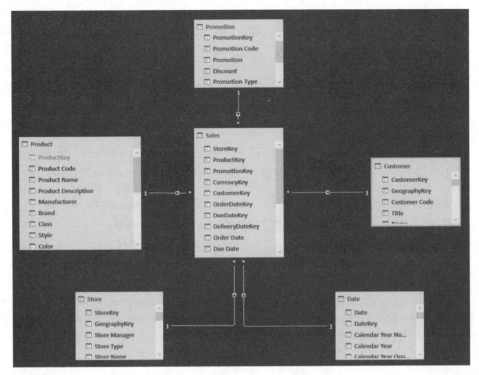

FIGURE 1-12 A star schema becomes visible when you put the fact table in the center and all the dimensions around it.

Star schemas are easy to read, understand, and use. You use dimensions to slice and dice the data, whereas you use fact tables to aggregate numbers. Moreover, they produce a small number of entries in the PivotTable field list.

Note Star schemas have become very popular in the data warehouse industry. Today, they are considered the standard way of representing analytical models.

Because of their nature, dimensions tend to be small tables, with fewer than 1,000,000 rows—generally in the order of magnitude of a few hundred or thousand. Fact tables, on the other hand, are much larger. They are expected to store tens—if not hundreds of millions—of rows. Apart from this, the structure of star schemas is so popular that most database systems have specific optimizations that are more effective when working with star schemas.

Tip Before reading further, spend some time trying to figure out how your own business model might be represented as a star schema. You don't need to build the perfect star schema right now, but it is useful to try this exercise, as it is likely to help you focus on a better way to build fact tables and dimensions.

It is important to get used to star schemas. They provide a convenient way to represent your data. In addition, in the business intelligence (BI) world, terms related to star schemas are used very often, and this book is no exception. We frequently write about fact tables and dimensions to differentiate between large tables and smaller ones. For example, in the next chapter, we will cover the handling of header/detail tables, where the problem is more generically that of creating relationships between different fact tables. At that point, we will take for granted that you have a basic understanding of the difference between a fact table and a dimension.

Some important details about star schemas are worth mentioning. One is that fact tables are related to dimensions, but dimensions should not have relationships among them. To illustrate why this rule is important and what happens if you don't follow it, suppose we add a new dimension, Geography, that contains details about geographical places, like the city, state, and country/region of a place. Both the Store and Customer dimensions can be related to Geography. You might think about building a model like the one in Figure 1-13, shown in Power Pivot's diagram view.

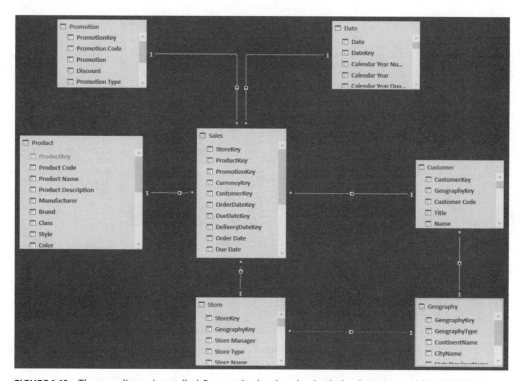

FIGURE 1-13 The new dimension, called Geography, is related to both the Customer and Store dimensions.

This model violates the rule that dimensions cannot have relationships between them. In fact, the three tables, Customer, Store, and Geography, are all dimensions, yet they are related. Why is this a bad model? Because it introduces *ambiguity*.

Imagine you slice by city, and you want to compute the amount sold. The system might follow the relationship between Geography and Customer, returning the amount sold, sliced by the city of the customer. Or, it might follow the relationship between Geography and Store, returning the amount sold in the city where the store is. As a third option, it might follow both relationships, returning the sales amount sold to customers of the given city in stores of the given city. The data model is ambiguous, and there is no easy way to understand what the number will be. Not only this is a technical problem, it is also a logical one. In fact, a user looking at the data model would be confused and unable to understand the numbers. Because of this ambiguity, neither Excel nor Power BI let you build such a model. In further chapters, we will discuss ambiguity to a greater extent. For now, it is important only to note that Excel (the tool we used to build this example) deactivated the relationship between Store and Geography to make sure that the model is not ambiguous.

You, as a data modeler, must avoid ambiguity at all costs. How would you resolve ambiguity in this scenario? The answer is very simple. You must denormalize the relevant columns of the Geography table, both in Store and in Customer, removing the Geography table from the model. For example, you could include the ContinentName columns in both Store and in Customer to obtain the model shown in Figure 1-14 in Power Pivot's diagram view.

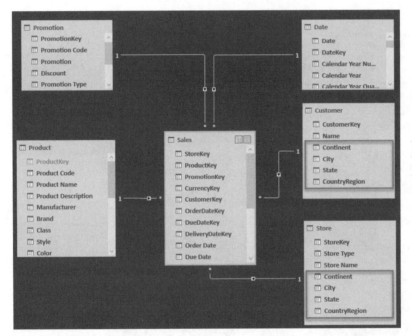

The columns from Geography are denormalized in Customer and Store, and the Geography table is no longer part of the model.

FIGURE 1-14 When you denormalize the columns from Geography, the star schema shape returns.

With the correct denormalization, you remove the ambiguity. Now, any user will be able to slice by columns in Geography using the Customer or Store table. In this case, Geography is a dimension but, to be able to use a proper star schema, we had to denormalize it.

Before leaving this topic, it is useful to introduce another term that we will use often: snowflake. A *snowflake* is a variation of a star schema where a dimension is not linked directly to the fact table. Rather, it is linked through another dimension. You have already seen examples of a snowflake; one is in Figure 1-15, shown in Power Pivot's diagram view.

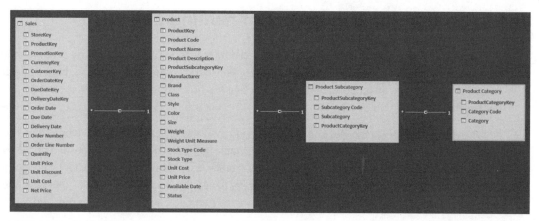

FIGURE 1-15 Product Category, Subcategory, and Product form a chain of relationships and are snowflaked.

Do snowflakes violate the rule of dimensions being linked together? In some sense, they do, because the relationship between Product Subcategory and Product is a relationship between two dimensions. The difference between this example and the previous one is that this relationship is the only one between Product Subcategory and the other dimensions linked to the fact table or to Product. Thus, you can think of Product Subcategory as a dimension that groups different products together, but it does not group together any other dimension or fact. The same, obviously, is true for Product Category. Thus, even if snowflakes violate the aforementioned rule, they do not introduce any kind of ambiguity, and a data model with snowflakes is absolutely fine.

Note You can avoid snowflakes by denormalizing the columns from the farthest tables into the one nearer to the fact table. However, sometimes snowflakes are a good way of representing your data and—apart from a small performance degradation—there is nothing wrong with them.

As you will see throughout this book, star schemas are nearly always the best way to represent your data. Yes, there are some scenarios in which star schemas are not the *perfect* way to go. Still, whenever you work with a data model, representing it with a star schema is the right thing to do. It might not be perfect, but it will be near-to-perfect enough to be a good solution.

Note As you learn more about data modeling, you might encounter a situation in which you think it is best to deviate from star schemas. Don't. There are several reasons why star schemas are nearly always your best option. Unfortunately, most of these reasons can be appreciated only after you have had some experience in data modeling. If you don't have a lot of experience, just trust the tens of thousands of BI professionals all around the planet who know that star schemas are nearly always the best option—no matter what.

Understanding the importance of naming objects

When you build your data model, you typically load data from a SQL Server database or some other data source. Most likely, the developer of the data source decided the naming convention. There are tons of these naming conventions, up to the point that it is not wrong to say that everybody has his or her own personal naming convention.

When building data warehouses, some database designers prefer to use Dim as a prefix for dimensions and Fact for fact tables. Thus, it is very common to see table names such as DimCustomer and FactSales. Others like to differentiate between views and physical tables, using prefixes like Tbl for tables and Vw for views. Still others think names are ambiguous and prefer to use numbers instead, like Tbl_190_Sales. We could go on and on, but you get the point: There are many standards, and each one has pros and cons.

> **Note** We could argue whether these standards make any sense in the database, but this would go outside of the scope of this book. We will stick to discussing how to handle standards in the data model that you browse with Power BI or Excel.

You do not need to follow any technical standard; only follow common sense and ease of use. For example, it would be frustrating to browse a data model where tables have silly names, like VwDimCstmr or Tbl_190_FactShpmt. These names are strange and non-intuitive. Still, we encounter these types of names in data models quite a lot. And we are talking about table names only. When it comes to column names, the lack of creativity gets even more extreme. Our only word of advice here is to get rid of all these names and use readable names that clearly identify the dimension or the fact table.

We have built many analytical systems over the years. Over time, we have developed a very simple set of rules for table and column naming:

- **Table names for dimensions should consist of only the business asset name, in singular or plural form**   Thus, customers are stored in a table called Customer or Customers. Products are stored in a table called Product or Products. (In our opinion, singular is preferable because it works slightly better with natural language queries in Power BI.)

- **If the business asset contains multiple words, use casing to separate the words**   Thus, product categories are stored in ProductCategory, and the country of shipment might be CountryShip or CountryShipment. Alternatively, you can use spaces instead of casing—for example, using table names like Product Category. This is fine, but it does make the writing of DAX code a bit harder. It is more a matter of personal choice than anything else.

- **Table names for facts should consist of the business name for the fact, which is always plural**   Thus, sales are stored in a table named Sales, and purchases, as you might imagine, are stored in a table named Purchases. By using plural instead of singular, when you look at your model, you will naturally think of one customer (the Customer table) with many sales (the Sales table), stating and enforcing the nature of the one-to-many relationship whenever you look at the tables.

- **Avoid names that are too long**   Names like CountryOfShipmentOfGoodsWhenSoldByReseller are confusing. Nobody wants to read such a long name. Instead, find good abbreviations by eliminating the useless words.

- **Avoid names that are too short**   We know you are used to speaking with acronyms. But while acronyms might be useful when speaking, they are unclear when used in reports. For example, you might use the acronym *CSR* for *country of shipment for resellers*, but that will be hard to remember for anybody who does not work with you all day long. Remember: Reports are meant to be shared with a vast number of users, many of whom do not understand your acronyms.

- **The key to a dimension is the dimension name followed by *Key***   Thus, the primary key of Customer is CustomerKey. The same goes for foreign keys. You will know something is a foreign key because it is stored in a table with a different name. Thus, CustomerKey in Sales is a foreign key that points to the Customer table, whereas in Customer it is the primary key.

This set of rules is very short. Anything else is up to you. You can decide the names of all the remaining columns by following the same common sense. A well-named data model is easy to share with anybody. In addition, you are much more likely to find errors or issues in the data model if you follow these standard naming techniques.

Tip   When you are in doubt about a name, ask yourself, "Will somebody else be able to understand this name?" Don't think you are the only user of your reports. Sooner or later, you will want to share a report with somebody else, who might have a completely different background than yours. If that person will be able to understand your names, then you are on the right track. If not, then it is time to re-think the names in your model.

Conclusions

In this chapter, you learned the basics of data modeling, namely:

- A single table is already a data model, although in its simplest form.

- With a single table, you must define the granularity of your data. Choosing the right granularity makes calculations much easier to author.

- The difference between working with a single table and multiple ones is that when you have multiple tables, they are joined by relationships.

- In a relationship, there is a *one* side and a *many* side, indicating how many rows you are likely to find if you follow the relationship. Because one product has many sales, the Product table will be the *one* side, and the Sales table will be the *many* side.

- If a table is the target of a relationship, it needs to have a primary key, which is a column with unique values that can be used to identify a single row. If a key is not available, then the relationship cannot be defined.

- A normalized model is a data model where the data is stored in a compact way, avoiding repetitions of the same value in different rows. This structure typically increases the number of tables.

- A denormalized model has a lot of repetitions (for example, the name *Red* is repeated multiple times, once for each red product), but has fewer tables.

- Normalized models are used for OLTP, whereas denormalized models are used in analytical data models.

- A typical analytical model differentiates between informational assets (dimensions) and events (facts). By classifying each entity in the model as either a fact or a dimension, the model is built in the form of a star schema. Star schemas are the most widely used architecture for analytical models, and for a good reason: They work fine nearly always.

CHAPTER 2

Using header/detail tables

Now that you have a basic understanding of the concepts of data modeling, we can start discussing the first of many scenarios, which is the use of header/detail tables. This scenario happens very frequently. By themselves, header/detail tables are not a complex model to use. Nevertheless, this scenario hides some complexities whenever you want to mix reports that aggregate numbers at the two different levels.

Examples of header/detail models include invoices with their lines or orders with their lines. Bills of materials are also typically modeled as header/detail tables. Another example would be if you need to model teams of people. In this case, the two different levels would be the team and the people.

Header/detail tables are not to be confused with standard hierarchies of dimensions. Think, for example, about the natural hierarchy of a dimension that is created when you have products, subcategories, and categories. Although there are three levels of data, this is not a header/detail pattern. The header/detail structure is generated by some sort of hierarchical structure on top of your events—that is, on top of your fact tables. Both an order and its lines are facts, even if they are at different granularities, whereas products, categories, and subcategories are all dimensions. To state it in a more formal way, header/detail tables appear whenever you have some sort of relationship between two fact tables.

Introducing header/detail

As an example, we created a header/detail scenario for the Contoso database. You can see its data model in Figure 2-1.

Based on the previous chapter, you might recognize this model as a slightly modified star schema. In fact, if you look at SalesHeader or SalesDetail individually, with their respective related tables, they *are* star schemas. However, when you combine them, the star shape is lost because of the relationship linking SalesHeader and SalesDetail. This relationship breaks the star schema rules because both the header and detail tables are fact tables. At the same time, the header table acts as a dimension for the detail.

At this point, you might argue that if we consider SalesHeader a dimension instead of a fact table, then we have a snowflake schema. Moreover, if we denormalize all columns from Date, Customer, and Store in SalesHeader, we can re-create a perfect star schema. However, there are two points that prevent us from performing this operation. First, SalesHeader contains a TotalDiscount metric. Most likely, you will aggregate values of TotalDiscount by customer. The presence of a metric is an indicator that the table is more likely to be a fact table than a dimension. The second, and much more important, consideration is that it would be a modeling error to mix Customer, Date, and Store in the same dimension by denormalizing their attributes in SalesOrderHeader. This is because these three dimensions make perfect sense as business assets of Contoso, whereas if you mix all their attributes into a single dimension to rebuild a star schema, the model would become much more complex to browse.

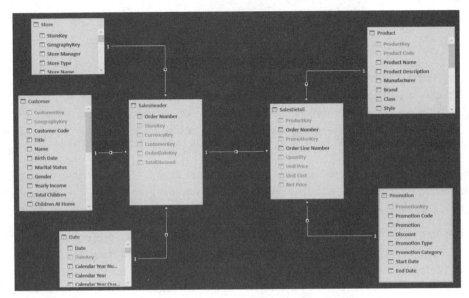

FIGURE 2-1 SalesHeader and SalesDetail comprise a header/detail scenario.

As you will learn later in this chapter, for such a schema, the correct solution is not to mix the dimensions linked to the header into a single, new dimension, even if it looks like a nice idea. Instead, the best choice is to flatten the header into the detail table, increasing the granularity. There will be more on this later in the chapter.

Aggregating values from the header

Apart from aesthetic issues (it is not a perfect star schema), with header/detail models, you need to worry about performance and, most importantly, how to perform the calculations at the right granularity. Let us analyze the scenario in more detail.

You can compute any measure at the detail level (such as the sum of quantity and sum of sales amount), and everything works fine. The problems start as soon as you try to aggregate values from the header table. You might create a measure that computes the discount value, stored in the header table, with the following code:

```
DiscountValue := SUM ( SalesHeader[TotalDiscount] )
```

The discount is stored in the header because it is computed over the whole order at the time of the sale. In other words, the discount is granted over the entire order instead of being applied to each line. For this reason, it is saved in the header table. The DiscountValue measure works correctly as long as you slice it with any attribute of a dimension that is directly linked to SalesHeader. In fact, the PivotTable shown in Figure 2-2 works just fine. It slices the discount by continent (the column in Store, linked to SalesHeader) and year (the column in Date, again linked to SalesHeader).

DiscountValue	Column Labels			
Row Labels	CY 2007	CY 2008	CY 2009	Grand Total
Asia	$56,282.74	$52,457.75	$42,562.23	$151,302.72
Europe	$52,153.03	$25,881.80	$32,700.45	$110,735.27
North America	$50,070.90	$42,118.73	$41,404.66	$133,594.29
Grand Total	$158,506.66	$120,458.29	$116,667.34	$395,632.29

FIGURE 2-2 You can slice discount by year and continent, producing this PivotTable.

However, as soon as you use one of the attributes of any dimension that is not directly related to SalesHeader, the measure stops working. If, for example, you slice by the color of a product, then the result is what is shown in Figure 2-3. The filter on the year works fine, exactly as it did in the previous PivotTable. However, the filter on the color repeats the same value for each row. In some sense, the number reported is correct, because the discount is saved in the header table, which is not related to any product. Product is related to the detail table, and a discount saved in the header is not expected to be filtered by product.

DiscountValue	Column Labels			
Row Labels	CY 2007	CY 2008	CY 2009	Grand Total
Azure	$158,506.66	$120,458.29	$116,667.34	$395,632.29
Black	$158,506.66	$120,458.29	$116,667.34	$395,632.29
Blue	$158,506.66	$120,458.29	$116,667.34	$395,632.29
Brown	$158,506.66	$120,458.29	$116,667.34	$395,632.29
Gold	$158,506.66	$120,458.29	$116,667.34	$395,632.29
Green	$158,506.66	$120,458.29	$116,667.34	$395,632.29
Grey	$158,506.66	$120,458.29	$116,667.34	$395,632.29
Orange	$158,506.66	$120,458.29	$116,667.34	$395,632.29
Pink	$158,506.66	$120,458.29	$116,667.34	$395,632.29
Purple	$158,506.66	$120,458.29	$116,667.34	$395,632.29
Red	$158,506.66	$120,458.29	$116,667.34	$395,632.29
Silver	$158,506.66	$120,458.29	$116,667.34	$395,632.29
Silver Grey	$158,506.66	$120,458.29	$116,667.34	$395,632.29
Transparent	$158,506.66	$120,458.29	$116,667.34	$395,632.29
White	$158,506.66	$120,458.29	$116,667.34	$395,632.29
Yellow	$158,506.66	$120,458.29	$116,667.34	$395,632.29
Grand Total	$158,506.66	$120,458.29	$116,667.34	$395,632.29

FIGURE 2-3 If you slice the discount by a product color, the same number is repeated on each row.

A very similar issue would occur for any other value stored in the header table. For example, think about the freight cost. The cost of the shipment of an order is not related to the individual products in the order. Instead, the cost is a global cost for the shipment, and again, it is not related to the detail table.

In some scenarios, this behavior is correct. Users know that some measures cannot simply be sliced by all the dimensions, as it would compute inaccurate values. Nevertheless, in this specific case, we want to compute the average discount percentage for each product and then deduct this information from the header table. This is a bit more complicated than one might imagine. This is due to the data model.

If you are using Power BI or Analysis Services Tabular 2016 or later, then you have access to bidirectional filtering, meaning you can instruct the model to propagate the filter on SalesDetail to SalesHeader. In this way, when you filter a product (or a product color), the filter will be active on both SalesHeader and SalesDetail, showing only the orders containing a product of the given color. Figure 2-4 shows the model with bidirectional filtering activated for the relationship between SalesHeader and SalesDetail.

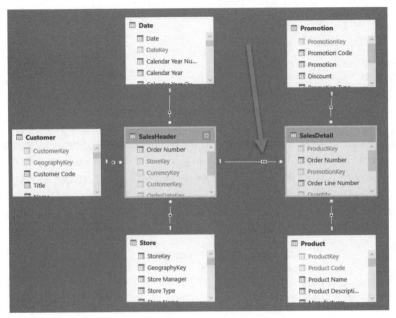

FIGURE 2-4   If bidirectional filtering is available, you can let the filter propagate in both directions of the relationship.

If you work with Excel, then bidirectional filtering is not an option at the data-model level. However, you can obtain the same result by modifying the measure using the bidirectional pattern with the following code. (We'll talk about this in more detail in Chapter 8, "Many-to-many relationships.")

```
DiscountValue :=
CALCULATE (
    SUM ( SalesHeader[TotalDiscount] ),
    CROSSFILTER ( SalesDetail[Order Number], SalesHeader[Order Number], BOTH )
)
```

It appears that a small change in the data model (enabling bidirectional filtering on the relationship) or in the formula (using the bidirectional pattern) solves the issue. Unfortunately, however, neither of these measures compute a meaningful value. To be precise, they compute a meaningful value, but it has a meaning that is totally different from what you would expect.

Both techniques move the filter from SalesDetail to SalesHeader, but they then aggregate the total discount for all the orders that contain the selected products. The issue is evident if you create a report that slices by brand (which is an attribute of Product, indirectly related to SalesHeader) and by year (which is an attribute of Date, directly related to SalesHeader). Figure 2-5 shows an example of this, in which the sum of the highlighted cells is much greater than the grand total.

The issue is that, for each brand, you are summing the total discount of the orders that contain at least one product of that brand. When an order contains products of different brands, its discount is counted once for each of the brands. Thus, the individual numbers do not sum at the grand total. At the grand total, you get the correct sum of discounts, whereas for each brand, you obtain a number that is greater than what is expected.

DiscountValue	Column Labels			
Row Labels	CY 2007	CY 2008	CY 2009	Grand Total
A. Datum	$23,396.50	$6,625.26	$6,818.09	$36,839.84
Adventure Works	$31,014.00	$11,358.74	$10,899.31	$53,272.05
Contoso	$51,975.46	$24,946.38	$28,580.97	$105,502.81
Fabrikam	$14,426.09	$22,265.30	$17,478.13	$54,169.52
Litware	$13,876.12	$17,539.56	$14,796.98	$46,212.66
Northwind Traders	$21,013.75	$3,754.67	$5,361.97	$30,130.39
Proseware	$12,812.25	$9,740.69	$15,318.93	$37,871.87
Southridge Video	$23,171.83	$4,380.71	$4,788.64	$32,341.19
Tailspin Toys	$1,029.51	$707.81	$1,775.78	$3,513.10
The Phone Company	$4,027.90	$7,067.17	$6,330.28	$17,425.35
Wide World Importers	$7,125.39	$19,366.80	$14,494.74	$40,986.93
Grand Total	$158,506.66	$120,458.29	$116,667.34	$395,632.29

FIGURE 2-5 In this PivotTable, the sum of the highlighted cells is $458,265.70, which is greater than the grand total.

> **Info** This is an example of a wrong calculation that is not so easy to spot. Before we proceed, let us explain exactly what is happening. Imagine you have two orders: one with apples and oranges, and one with apples and peaches. When you slice by product using bidirectional filtering, the filter will make both orders visible on the row with apples, so the total discount will be the sum of the two orders. When you slice by oranges or peaches, only one order will be visible. Thus, if the two orders have a discount of 10 and 20, respectively, you will see three lines: apples 30, oranges 10, and peaches 20. For the grand total, you will see 30, which is the total of the two orders.

It is important to note that by itself, the formula is not wrong. In the beginning, before you are used to recognizing issues in the data model, you tend to expect DAX to compute a correct number, and if the number is wrong, you might think there is an error in the formula. This is often the case, but not always. In scenarios like this one, the problem is not in the code, but in the model. The issue here is that DAX computes exactly what you are asking for, but what you are asking for is not what you want.

Changing the data model by simply updating the relationship is not the right way to go. We need to find a different path to the solution. Because the discount is stored in the header table as a total value, you can only aggregate that value, and this is the real source of the error. What you are missing is a column that contains the discount for the individual line of the order so that when you slice by one of the attributes of a product, it returns a correct value. This problem is again about granularity. If you want to be able to slice by product, you need the discount to be at the order-detail granularity. Right now, the discount is at the order header granularity, which is wrong for the calculation you are trying to build.

At the risk of being pedantic, let us highlight an important point: You do not need the discount value at the product granularity, but at the SalesDetail granularity. The two granularities might be different—for example, in case you have two rows in the detail table that belong to the same order and have the same product ID. How can you obtain such a result? It is easier than you might think, once you recognize the problem. In fact, you can compute a column in SalesHeader that stores the discount as a percentage instead of an absolute value. To perform this, you need to divide the total discount by the total of the order. Because the total of the order is not stored in the SalesHeader table in our model, you can compute it on the fly by iterating over the related detail table. You can see this in the following formula for a calculated column in SalesHeader:

```
SalesHeader[DiscountPct] =
DIVIDE (
    SalesHeader[TotalDiscount],
    SUMX (
        RELATEDTABLE ( SalesDetail ),
        SalesDetail[Unit Price] * SalesDetail[Quantity]
    )
)
```

Figure 2-6 shows the result, with the SalesHeader table with the new column formatted as a percentage to make its meaning easy to understand.

Order Number	StoreKey	CurrencyKey	CustomerKey	OrderDateKey	TotalDiscount	DiscountPct
20080604724008	307	1	13009	20080604	€ 0.54	10.00%
20080510CS561	307	1	19098	20080510	€ 13.99	10.00%
20070605820430	307	1	9431	20070605	€ 181.80	10.00%
20070510215734	307	1	4735	20070510	€ 32.90	10.00%
20080115 6CS531	307	1	19092	20080115	€ 311.99	15.00%
20070401 3CS473	307	1	19082	20070401	€ 698.60	20.00%
20071115726159	307	1	15160	20071115	€ 1.33	15.00%
200905028CS712	307	1	19122	20090502	€ 97.80	10.00%
20070422714011	307	1	3012	20070422	€ 5.59	20.00%
200902218CS699	307	1	19116	20090221	€ 335.98	20.00%
20070213824162	307	1	13163	20070213	€ 307.36	20.00%
200902076CS697	307	1	19115	20090207	€ 12.20	20.00%
20071227722905	307	1	11906	20071227	€ 13.91	15.00%
20080414822856	307	1	11857	20080414	€ 363.78	20.00%

FIGURE 2-6 The DiscountPct column computes the discount percentage of the order.

Once you have this column, you know that each of the individual lines of the same order has the same discount percentage. Thus, you can compute the discount amount at the individual line level by iterating over each row of the SalesDetail table. You can then compute the discount of that line by multiplying the header discount percentage by the current sales amount. For example, the following code replaces the previous version of the DiscountValue measure:

```
[DiscountValueCorrect] =
SUMX (
    SalesDetail,
    RELATED ( SalesHeader[DiscountPct] ) * SalesDetail[Unit Price] * SalesDetail[Quantity]
)
```

It is also worth noting that this formula no longer needs the relationship between SalesHeader and SalesDetail to be bidirectional. In the demo file, we left it bidirectional because we wanted to show both values together. In fact, in Figure 2-7, you can see the two measures side by side in a PivotTable. You will also see that DiscountValueCorrect reports a slightly lower number, which sums correctly at the grand-total level.

Row Labels	DiscountValue	DiscountValueCorrect
A. Datum	$36,839.84	$26,489.32
Adventure Works	$53,272.05	$47,608.89
Contoso	$105,502.81	$89,994.41
Fabrikam	$54,169.52	$49,618.90
Litware	$46,212.66	$43,991.90
Northwind Traders	$30,130.39	$29,794.45
Proseware	$37,871.87	$34,436.21
Southridge Video	$32,341.19	$17,100.27
Tailspin Toys	$3,513.10	$3,513.10
The Phone Company	$17,425.35	$17,287.23
Wide World Importers	$40,986.93	$35,797.62
Grand Total	$395,632.29	$395,632.29

FIGURE 2-7 Having the two measures side by side shows the difference between them. Moreover, the correct value produces a sum that is identical to the grand total, as expected.

Another option, with a simpler calculation, is to create a calculated column in SalesDetail that contains the following expression, which is the discount value for the individual row that is precomputed in SalesDetail:

```
SalesDetail[LineDiscount] =
    RELATED ( SalesHeader[DiscountPct] ) *
    SalesDetail[Unit Price] *
    SalesDetail[Quantity]
```

In this case, you can easily compute the discount value by summing the LineDiscount column, which already contains the correct discount allocated at the individual row level.

This approach is useful because it shows more clearly what we did. We changed the data model by denormalizing the discount from the SalesHeader table into the SalesDetail table. Figure 2-8 (which presents the diagram view) shows the two fact tables after we added the LineDiscount calculated column. SalesHeader no longer contains any value that is directly aggregated in a measure. The only metrics in the SalesHeader table are TotalDiscount and DiscountPct, which are used to compute LineDiscount in the SalesDetail table. These two columns should be hidden because they are not useful for analysis unless you want to use DiscountPct to slice your data. In that case, it makes sense to leave it visible.

Let us now draw some conclusions about this model. Think about this carefully. Now that the metric that was present in SalesHeader is denormalized in SalesDetail, you can think of SalesHeader as being a dimension. Because it is a dimension that has relationships with other dimensions, we have essentially transformed the model into a snowflake, which is a model where dimensions are linked to the fact table through other dimensions. Snowflakes are not the perfect choice for performance and analysis, but they work just fine and are valid from a modeling point of view. In this case, a snowflake makes perfect sense because the different dimensions involved in the relationships are, one by one, operational assets of the business. Thus, even if it is not very evident in this example, we solved the problem by changing the data model to make it simpler.

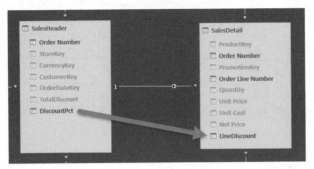

FIGURE 2-8 The DiscountPct and TotalDiscount columns are used to compute LineDiscount.

Before leaving this example, let us summarize what we have learned:

- In header/detail models, the header table acts as both a dimension and a fact table at the same time. It is a dimension to slice the detail, and it is a fact table when you need to summarize values at the header granularity.

- If you summarize values from the header, any filters from dimensions linked to the detail are not applied unless you activate bidirectional filtering or you use the many-to-many pattern.

- Both bidirectional filtering and the bidirectional DAX pattern summarize the values at the header granularity, leading to totals that do not sum. This might or might not be an issue. In this example, it was an issue and we had to fix it.

- To fix the problem of additivity, you can move the total values stored in the header table by allocating them as percentages to the detail table. Once the data is allocated to the detail table, it can be easily summed and sliced by any dimension. In other words, you denormalize the value at the correct granularity to make the model easier to use.

A seasoned data modeler would have spotted the problem before building the measure. How? Because the model contained a table that was neither a fact table nor a dimension, as we saw at the beginning. Whenever you cannot easily tell whether a table is used to slice or to aggregate, then you know that the danger of complex calculations is around the corner.

Flattening header/detail

In the previous example, we denormalized a single value (the discount) from the header to the detail by first computing it as a percentage on the header and then moving the value from the header to the detail. This operation can be moved forward for all the other columns in the header table, like StoreKey, PromotionKey, CustomerKey, and so on. This extreme denormalization is called *flattening* because you move from a model with many tables (two, in our case) to one with a single table containing all the information.

The process of flattening a model is typically executed before the data is loaded into the model, via SQL queries or M code, using the query editor in Excel or Power BI Desktop. If you are loading data from a data warehouse, then it is very likely that this process of flattening already happened before the data was moved to the data warehouse. However, we think it is useful to see the differences between querying and using a flat model against a structured one.

> **Warning** In the example we used for this section, we did something weird. The original model was already flattened. On top of this, for educational purposes, we built a structured model with a header/detail. Later, we used M code in Power BI Desktop to rebuild the original flat structure. We did it to demonstrate the process of flattening. Of course, in the real world, we would have loaded the flat model straight in, avoiding this complex procedure.

The original model is the one previously shown in Figure 2-1. Figure 2-9 shows the flattened model, which is basically a pure star schema with all the columns from SalesHeader denormalized in Sales.

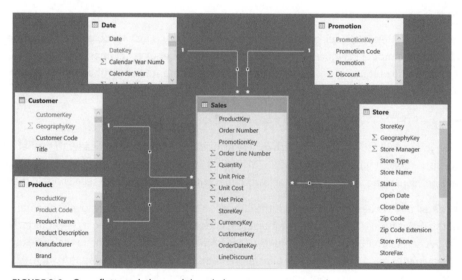

FIGURE 2-9 Once flattened, the model again becomes a pure star schema.

The following steps are carried out in the query that loads the Sales table:

1. We joined SalesHeader and SalesDetail together based on Order Number, and we added the related columns of Sales Header to Sales.

2. We created a new hidden query that computes, out of Sales Detail, the total order, and we joined this query with Sales to retrieve the total order.

3. We added a column that computes the line discount the same way we did it in the previous example. This time, however, we used M code instead of DAX.

When these three steps are complete, you end up with a perfect star schema that offers all the advantages of a star schema. Flattening foreign keys to dimensions, like CustomerKey and OrderDateKey, is straightforward because you simply make a copy of the value. However, flattening metrics like the discount typically requires some kind of reallocation, as we did in this example by allocating the discount as the same percentage on all the lines. (In other words, it is allocated using the line amount as the allocation's weight.)

The only drawback of this architecture is that whenever you need to compute values based on columns that were originally stored in the header, you need to pay attention. Let us elaborate on this. If you wanted to count the number of orders in the original model, you could easily create a measure like the following one:

```
NumOfOrders := COUNTROWS ( SalesHeader )
```

This measure is very simple. It basically counts how many rows are visible, in the current filter context, in the SalesHeader table. It worked because, for SalesHeader, there is a perfect identity between the orders and rows in the table. For each order, there is a single line in the table. Thus, counting the rows results in a count of the orders.

When using the flattened model, on the other hand, this identity is lost. If you count the number of rows in Sales in the model in Figure 2-9, you compute the number of order lines, which is typically much greater than the number of orders. In the flat model, to compute the number of orders, you need to compute a distinct count of the Order Number column, as shown in the following code:

```
NumOfOrders := DISTINCTCOUNT ( Sales[Order Number] )
```

Obviously, you should use the same pattern for any attribute moved from the header to the flat table. Because the distinct count function is very fast in DAX, this is not a typical issue for medium-sized models. (It might be a problem if you have very large tables, but that is not the typical size of self-service BI models.)

Another detail that we already discussed is the allocation of values. When we moved the total discount of the order from the header to the individual lines, we allocated it using a percentage. This operation is needed to enable you to aggregate values from the lines and still obtain the same grand total, which you might need to do later. The allocation method can be different depending on your specific needs. For example, you might want to allocate the freight cost based on the weight of the item being sold instead of equally allocating it to all the order lines. If this is the case, then you will need to modify your queries in such a way that allocation happens in the right way.

On the topic of flattened models, here is a final note about performance. Most analytical engines (including SQL Server Analysis Services, hence Power BI and Power Pivot) are highly optimized for star schemas with small dimensions and large fact tables. In the original, normalized model, we used the sales header as a dimension to slice the sales detail. In doing this, however, we used a potentially large table (sales order header) as a dimension. As a rule of thumb, dimensions should contain fewer than 100,000 rows. If they grow larger, you might start to notice some performance degradation. Flattening sales headers into their details is a good option to reduce the size of dimensions. Thus, from the performance point of view, flattening is nearly always a good option.

Conclusions

This chapter started looking at different options to build a data model. As you have learned, the same piece of information can be stored in multiple ways by using tables and relationships. The information stored in the model is identical. The only difference is the number of tables and the kind of relationships that link them. Nevertheless, choosing the wrong model makes the calculation much more complex, which means the numbers will not aggregate in the expected way.

Another useful lesson from this chapter is that granularity matters. The discount as an absolute value could not be aggregated when slicing by dimensions linked to the line order. Once transformed into a percentage, it became possible to compute the line discount, which aggregates nicely over any dimension.

CHAPTER 3

Using multiple fact tables

In the previous chapter, you learned how to handle a scenario where there are two fact tables related to each other: header and detail tables. You saw how the best option to obtain a simple data model is modifying it to make it more like a star schema, which makes calculations much easier to perform.

This chapter moves one step further to cover a scenario where you have multiple fact tables that are not related to each other. This is a very common occurrence. Think, for example, of sales and purchases. Both sales and purchases are facts involving some common assets (products, for instance) and some unrelated ones (such as customers for sales and suppliers for purchases).

In general, using multiple fact tables is not an issue if the model is correctly designed and everything works fine. The scenario becomes more challenging when the fact tables are not correctly related to intermediate dimensions, as shown in the first examples, or when you need to create cross-filters between the fact tables. The latter is a technique you will learn in this chapter.

Using denormalized fact tables

The first example we look at is that of having two fact tables that, because of an excessive level of denormalization, are impossible to relate to each other. As you will learn, the solution is very simple: You re-create a star schema out of the unrelated tables to restore proper functionality of the model.

For this demo, we start with a very simple data model that contains only two tables: Sales and Purchases. They have nearly the same structure, and they are completely *denormalized*, meaning that all information is stored in the tables. They have no relationships with dimensions. This model is shown in Figure 3-1.

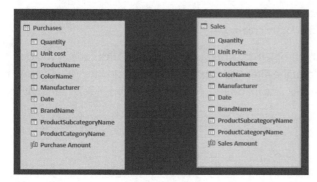

FIGURE 3-1 The Sales and Purchases tables, when completely denormalized, do not have any relationship.

This is a common scenario when you want to merge two queries that you have already used for different purposes. Each of these two tables, by themselves, are perfectly good candidates to perform analysis with an Excel PivotTable. The problem arises when you want to merge the two tables into a single model and perform an analysis by using numbers gathered from the two tables together.

Let us consider an example. Suppose you define two measures, Purchase Amount and Sales Amount, with the following DAX code:

```
Purchase Amount := SUMX ( Purchases, Purchases[Quantity] * Purchases[Unit Cost] )
Sales Amount    := SUMX ( Sales, Sales[Quantity] * Sales[Unit Price] )
```

You are interested in looking at the sales and purchase amount in a single report and you want to perform a computation on these two measures. Unfortunately, this is not as simple as it might seem. For example, if you put the manufacturer from Purchases on the rows of a PivotTable and both measures in the values, you obtain the result shown in Figure 3-2. There, the value of Sales Amount is clearly wrong, repeating itself for all the rows.

Row Labels	Purchase Amount	Sales Amount
A. Datum Corporation	2,533,963.42	30,202,685.54
Adventure Works	6,048,167.59	30,202,685.54
Contoso, Ltd	12,314,395.68	30,202,685.54
Fabrikam, Inc.	10,003,071.13	30,202,685.54
Litware, Inc.	6,377,548.93	30,202,685.54
Northwind Traders	1,713,836.80	30,202,685.54
Proseware, Inc.	5,305,305.29	30,202,685.54
Southridge Video	2,199,989.35	30,202,685.54
Tailspin Toys	646,571.47	30,202,685.54
The Phone Company	3,045,608.33	30,202,685.54
Wide World Importers	4,151,139.81	30,202,685.54
Grand Total	54,339,597.80	30,202,685.54

FIGURE 3-2 The Sales Amount and Purchase Amount measures in the same PivotTable produce the wrong results.

What is happening is that the filter created by the Manufacturer column in the Purchases table is active on that table only. It cannot reach the Sales table because there are no relationships between the two tables. Moreover, you cannot create a relationship between the two tables because there is no column suitable for building such a relationship. As you might remember, to create a relationship, the column used needs to be the primary key in the target table. In this case, the product name is not a key in either of the two tables because it has many repetitions in both. To be a key, the column must be unique.

You can easily check this by trying to create the relationship. When you do, you will receive an error message stating that the relationship cannot be created.

As is often the case, you can solve this problem by writing some complex DAX code. If you decide to use columns from Purchases to perform the filter, you can rewrite Sales Amount in such a way that it detects the filters coming from Purchases. The following code is for a version of Sales Amount that senses the filter on the manufacturer:

```
Sales Amount Filtered :=
CALCULATE (
    [Sales Amount],
    INTERSECT ( VALUES ( Sales[BrandName] ), VALUES ( Purchases[BrandName] ) )
)
```

Using the INTERSECT function, this measure computes the set of Sales[BrandName] that exists in the current selection of Purchases[BrandName]. As a result, any filter on Purchases[BrandName] will be moved to a filter on Sales[BrandName] to effectively filter the Sales table. Figure 3-3 shows the measure in action.

BrandName	Purchase Amount	Sales Amount	Sales Amount Filtered
A. Datum	2.533.963,42	30.202.685,54	1.966.583,30
Adventure Works	6.048.167,59	30.202.685,54	4.022.462,56
Contoso	12.314.395,68	30.202.685,54	6.722.804,20
Fabrikam	10.003.071,13	30.202.685,54	5.040.864,58
Litware	6.377.548,93	30.202.685,54	3.425.045,95
Northwind Traders	1.713.836,80	30.202.685,54	1.205.185,61
Proseware	5.305.305,29	30.202.685,54	2.656.623,00
Southridge Video	2.199.989,35	30.202.685,54	1.463.471,36
Tailspin Toys	646.571,47	30.202.685,54	333.143,41
The Phone Company	3.045.608,33	30.202.685,54	1.293.603,00
Wide World Importers	4.151.139,81	30.202.685,54	2.072.898,57
Total	54.339.597,80	30.202.685,54	30.202.685,54

FIGURE 3-3 Sales Amount Filtered uses the filter from the Purchases table to filter the Sales table.

Even though it works, this measure is not an optimal solution for the following reasons:

- The current version works with a filter on the brand name, but if you must use different columns, you need to add them all as separate INTERSECT statements inside the CALCULATE statement. This makes the formula complex.

- The performance is not optimal because DAX generally works better with relationships than with filters created with CALCULATE.

- If you have many measures that aggregate values from Sales, all of them need to follow the same complex pattern. This negatively affects the maintainability of the solution.

Just to give you an idea of how complex the formula would become if you added all the product columns to the filter, consider the following code, in which we expanded the previous pattern to all the relevant columns:

```
Sales Amount Filtered :=
CALCULATE (
    [Sales Amount],
    INTERSECT ( VALUES ( Sales[BrandName] ), VALUES ( Purchases[BrandName] ) ),
    INTERSECT ( VALUES ( Sales[ColorName] ), VALUES ( Purchases[ColorName] ) ),
    INTERSECT ( VALUES ( Sales[Manufacturer] ), VALUES ( Purchases[Manufacturer] ) ),
    INTERSECT (
        VALUES ( Sales[ProductCategoryName] ),
        VALUES ( Purchases[ProductCategoryName] )
    ),
    INTERSECT (
        VALUES ( Sales[ProductSubcategoryName] ),
        VALUES ( Purchases[ProductSubcategoryName] )
    )
)
```

This code is error-prone and needs a lot of effort to maintain it over time. If, for example, you increase the granularity of the tables by adding a column, then you will need to iterate over all the measures and fix them, adding the new INTERSECT for the newly introduced column. A better option involves updating the data model.

To write simpler code, you must modify the data model and transform it into a star schema. Everything would be much easier with a data structure like the one in Figure 3-4, where we added a Product dimension that is capable of filtering both the Sales and Purchases tables. Even if it does not look like it, this model is a perfect star schema, with two fact tables and a single dimension.

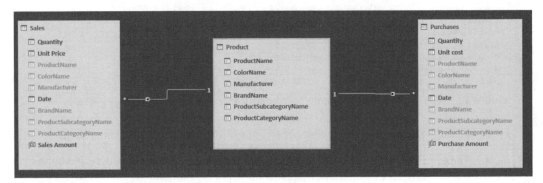

FIGURE 3-4 With a Product dimension, the data model becomes much easier to use.

Note We hid the columns that have been normalized in the Product table. This makes it impossible for users to use one of those columns in a report, as they would not be able to filter both tables.

To build such a data model, you typically face the following two problems:

- You need a source for the Product table, and often you do not have access to the original tables.

- The Product table needs a key to make it the target of a relationship.

The first problem is very simple to solve. If you have access to the original Product table, you can create the dimension from there by loading the data into the model. If, on the other hand, you cannot load the original Product table from the database, then you can create a technical one by using a Power Query transformation that loads both Sales and Purchases, performs a union of the two tables, and finally removes duplicates. The following is the M code that does the trick:

```
let
    SimplifiedPurchases = Table.RemoveColumns(
        Purchases,
        {"Quantity", "Unit cost", "Date"}
    ),
```

```
    SimplifiedSales = Table.RemoveColumns(
        Sales,
        {"Quantity", "Unit Price", "Date"}
    ),
    ProductColumns = Table.Combine ( { SimplifiedPurchases, SimplifiedSales } ),
    Result = Table.Distinct (ProductColumns )
in
    Result
```

As you can see, the M code first prepares two local tables, SimplifiedPurchases and SimplifiedSales, which contain only the relevant columns from Product and remove the unwanted ones. Then it combines the two tables by adding the rows of SimplifiedSales to SimplifiedPurchases. Finally, it retrieves only the distinct values, resulting in a table with unique products.

> **Note** You can obtain the very same result with the query editor in either Excel or Power BI Desktop. You create two queries that remove the quantity and unit price from the original sources, and then you merge them into a single query by using the union operator. The details of how to perform this operation are beyond the scope of this book, however. We are focused on data modeling more than on user-interface details.

To create the technical dimension, you must combine the two queries with Sales and Purchases. It is possible that a given product exists in only one of these two tables. If you then retrieve the distinct values from only one of the two queries, the result will be a partial dimension, which might produce incorrect results when used in the model.

After you load the Product dimension in the model, you still must create relationships. In this case, you have the option of using the product name as the column to create the relationship because the product name is unique. In different scenarios, such as when you don't have a suitable primary key for the intermediate dimension, you might be in trouble. If your original tables do not contain product names, then you cannot create the relationship with the product. For example, if you have the product category and product subcategory, but no product name, then you must create dimensions at the degree of granularity that is available. You would need a dimension for the product category and another dimension for the product subcategory, which you obtain by replicating the same technique shown before—only this time it is for different tables.

As is often the case, these kinds of transformations are better done before the data is loaded into the model. If you are loading data from a SQL Server database, for example, you can easily build SQL queries that perform all these operations for you, obtaining a simpler analytical model.

Before leaving this topic, it is worth noting that the same result can be obtained in Power BI by using calculated tables. Calculated tables are not available in Excel at the time of this writing, but they are available in Power BI and in SQL Server Analysis Services 2016. The following code creates a calculated table that contains the product dimension, and it is even simpler than the M code:

```
Products =
DISTINCT (
    UNION (
        ALL (
            Sales[ProductName],
            Sales[ColorName],
            Sales[Manufacturer],
            Sales[BrandName],
            Sales[ProductCategoryName],
            Sales[ProductSubcategoryName]
        ),
        ALL (
            Purchases[ProductName],
            Purchases[ColorName],
            Purchases[Manufacturer],
            Purchases[BrandName],
            Purchases[ProductCategoryName],
            Purchases[ProductSubcategoryName]
        )
    )
)
```

This calculated table performs two ALL operations on product columns from Sales and Purchases, reducing the number of columns and computing the distinct combinations of the required data. Then it uses UNION to merge them together. Finally, it uses DISTINCT to remove further duplicates, which are likely to appear because of the UNION function.

> **Note** The choice between using M or DAX code is entirely up to you and your personal taste. There are no relevant differences between the two solutions.

Once again, the correct solution to the model is to restore a star schema. This simple concept bears frequent repetition: Star schemas are good, but everything else might be bad. If you are facing a modeling problem, before doing anything else, ask yourself if you can rebuild your model to move toward a star schema. By doing this, you will likely go in the right direction.

Filtering across dimensions

In the previous example, you learned the basics of multiple dimension handling. There, you had two over-denormalized dimensions and, to make the model a better one, you had to revert to a simpler star schema. In this next example, we analyze a different scenario, again using Sales and Purchases.

You want to analyze the purchases of only the products sold during a given period—or, more generally, the products that satisfy a given selection. You learned in the previous section that if you have two fact tables, the best way to model the scenario is to relate them to dimensions. That would give you the ability to use a single dimension to filter both. Thus, the starting scenario is the one shown in Figure 3-5.

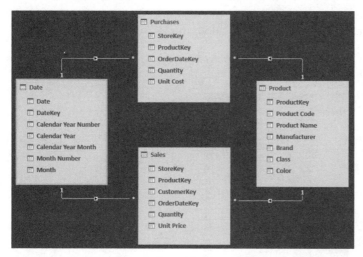

FIGURE 3-5 In this model, two fact tables are related to two dimensions.

Using this model and two basic measures, you can easily build a report like the one shown in Figure 3-6, where you can see both the sales and purchases divided by brand and year.

Row Labels	Column Labels					
	CY 2007		CY 2008		CY 2009	
	SalesAmount	PurchaseAmount	SalesAmount	PurchaseAmount	SalesAmount	PurchaseAmount
A. Datum	172,402.30	377,595.04	49,041.20	198,535.71	63,833.30	155,342.88
Adventure Works	314,134.24	497,009.03	104,682.71	712,240.38	91,447.12	667,970.20
Contoso	386,632.02	1,305,738.32	203,720.91	1,261,663.37	286,950.54	1,037,721.10
Fabrikam	162,562.59	1,187,357.20	246,991.46	946,301.02	240,629.62	875,143.39
Litware	96,785.49	566,904.05	229,148.47	826,981.12	212,760.01	619,481.69
Northwind Traders	143,663.45	240,835.80	24,634.61	151,027.82	37,071.35	93,302.03
Proseware	121,561.23	618,920.68	97,117.49	523,853.01	143,423.69	560,833.66
Southridge Video	109,442.64	216,844.05	44,369.98	205,290.92	70,698.45	190,134.32
Tailspin Toys	9,773.60	48,775.54	8,725.16	58,749.03	19,065.02	99,833.60
The Phone Company	41,899.00	412,052.18	65,457.00	271,149.68	70,472.00	238,469.42
Wide World Importers	58,866.05	371,410.01	169,104.35	493,992.51	122,850.85	475,717.76
Grand Total	**1,617,722.61**	**5,843,441.90**	**1,242,993.34**	**5,649,784.57**	**1,359,201.95**	**5,013,950.05**

FIGURE 3-6 In this simple star schema, sales and purchases divided by year and brand are computed easily.

A more difficult calculation is to show the number of purchases for only the products that are being sold. In other words, you want to use Sales as a filter to further refine the products so that any other filter imposed on sales (the date, for example) restricts the list of products for which you are computing purchases. There are different approaches to handling this scenario. We will show you some of them and discuss the advantages and disadvantages of each solution.

If you have bidirectional filtering available in your tool (at the time of this writing, bidirectional filtering is available in Power BI and SQL Server Analysis Services, but not in Excel), you might be tempted to change the data model that enables bidirectional filtering on Sales versus Product so that you see only the products sold. Unfortunately, to perform this operation, you must disable the relationship between Product and Purchases, as shown in Figure 3-7. Otherwise, you would end up with an ambiguous model, and the engine would refuse to make all the relationships bidirectional.

Info The DAX engine refuses to create any ambiguous model. You will learn more about ambiguous models in the next section.

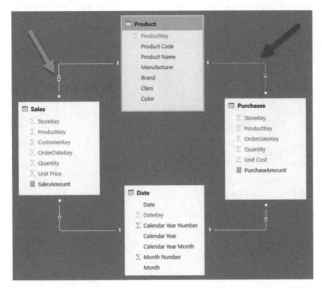

FIGURE 3-7 To enable bidirectional filtering between the Sales and Product tables, you must disable the relationship between Product and Purchases.

If you follow the filtering options of this data model, you will quickly discover that it does not solve the problem. If you place a filter on the Date table, for example, the filter will propagate to Sales, then to Product (because bidirectional filtering is enabled), but it will stop there, without having the option of filtering Purchases. If you enable bidirectional filtering on Date, too, then the data model will not show the purchases of products sold. Instead, it will show the purchases of any product made on the dates where any of the selected products were sold, becoming even less intuitive. Bidirectional filtering is a powerful feature, but it is not an option in this case because you want finer control over the way the filtering happens.

The key to solve this scenario is to understand the flow of filtering. Let us start from the Date table and revert to the original model shown in Figure 3-5. When you filter a given year in Date, the filter is automatically propagated to both Sales and Purchases. However, because of the direction of the relationship, it does not reach Product. What you want to achieve is to calculate the products that are present in Sales and use this list of products as a further filter to Purchases. The correct formula for the measure is as follows:

```
PurchaseOfSoldProducts :=
CALCULATE (
    [PurchaseAmount],
    CROSSFILTER ( Sales[ProductKey], Product[ProductKey], BOTH )
)
```

In this code, you use the CROSSFILTER function to activate the bidirectional filter between Products and Sales for only the duration of the calculation. In this way, by using standard filtering processes, Sales will filter Product, which then filters Purchases. (For more information on the CROSSFILTER function, see Appendix A, "Data modeling 101.")

To solve this scenario, we only leveraged DAX code. We did not change the data model. Why is this relevant to data modeling? Because in this case, changing the data model was not the right option, and we wanted to highlight this. Updating the data model is generally the right way to go, but sometimes, such as in this example, you must author DAX code to solve a specific scenario. It helps to acquire the skills needed to understand when to use what. Besides, the data model in this case already consists of two star schemas, so it is very hard to build a better one.

Understanding model ambiguity

The previous section showed that setting a bidirectional filter on a relationship will not work because the model becomes ambiguous. In this section, we want to dive more into the concept of ambiguous models to better understand them and—more importantly—why they are forbidden in Tabular.

An *ambiguous model* is a model where there are multiple paths joining any two tables through relationships. The simplest form of ambiguity appears when you try to build multiple relationships between two tables. If you try to build a model where the same two tables are linked through multiple relationships, only one of them (by default, the first one you create) will be kept active. The other ones will be marked as inactive. Figure 3-8 shows an example of such a model. Of the three relationships shown, only one is solid (active), whereas the remaining ones are dotted (inactive).

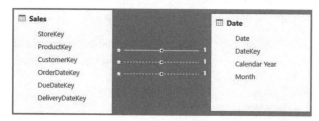

FIGURE 3-8 You cannot keep multiple active relationships between two tables.

Why is this limitation present? The reason is straightforward: The DAX language offers multiple functionalities that work on relationships. For example, in Sales, you can reference any column of the Date table by using the RELATED function, as in the following code:

```
Sales[Year] = RELATED ( 'Date'[Calendar Year] )
```

RELATED works without you having to specify which relationship to follow. The DAX language automatically follows the only active relationship and then returns the expected year. In this case, it would be the year of the sale, because the active relationship is the one based on OrderDateKey. If you could define multiple active relationships, then you would have to specify which one of the many active relationships to use for each implementation of RELATED. A similar behavior happens with the automatic filter context propagation whenever you define a filter context by using, for example, CALCULATE.

The following example computes the sales in 2009:

```
Sales2009 := CALCULATE ( [Sales Amount], 'Date'[Calendar Year] = "CY 2009" )
```

Again, you do not specify the relationship to follow. It is implicit in the model that the active relationship is the one using OrderDateKey. (In the next chapter, you will learn how to handle multiple relationships with the Date table in an efficient way. The goal of this section is simply to help you understand why an ambiguous model is forbidden in Tabular.)

You can activate a given relationship for a specific calculation. For example, if you are interested in the sales delivered in 2009, you can compute this value by taking advantage of the USERELATIONSHIP function, as in the following code:

```
Shipped2009 :=
CALCULATE (
    [Sales Amount],
    'Date'[Calendar Year] = "CY 2009",
    USERELATIONSHIP ( 'Date'[DateKey], Sales[DeliveryDateKey] )
)
```

As a general rule, keeping inactive relationships in your model is useful only when you make very limited use of them or if you need the relationship for some special calculation. A user has no way to activate a specific relationship while navigating the model with the user interface. It is the task of the data modeler, not the user, to worry about technical details like the keys used in a relationship. In advanced models, where billions of rows are present in the fact table or the calculations are very complex, the data modeler might decide to keep inactive relationships in the model to speed up certain calculations. However, such optimization techniques will not be necessary at the introductory level at which we are covering data modeling, and inactive relationships will be nearly useless.

Now, let us go back to ambiguous models. As we said, a model might be ambiguous for multiple reasons, even if all those reasons are connected to the presence of multiple paths between tables. Another example of an ambiguous model is the one depicted in Figure 3-9.

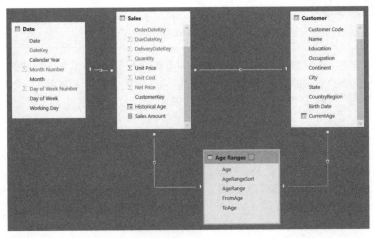

FIGURE 3-9 This model is ambiguous, too, although the reason is less evident.

In this model, there are two different age columns. One is Historical Age, which is stored in the fact table. The other is CurrentAge, which is stored in the Customer dimension. Both of these columns are used as foreign keys in the Age Ranges table, but only one of the relationships is permitted to remain active. The other relationship is deactivated. In this case, ambiguity is a bit less evident, but it is there. Imagine you built a PivotTable and sliced it by age range. Would you expect to slice it by the historical age (how old each customer was at the moment of sale) or the current age (how old each customer is today)? If both relationships were kept active, this would be ambiguous. Again, the engine refuses to let you build such a model. It forces you to solve ambiguity by either choosing which relationship to maintain as active or duplicating the table. That way, when you filter either a Current Age Ranges or a Historical Age Ranges table, you specify a unique path to filter data. The resulting model, once the Age Ranges table has been duplicated, is shown in Figure 3-10.

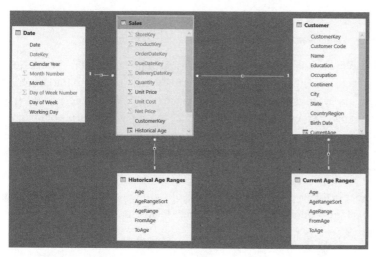

FIGURE 3-10   In the model, there are now two Age Ranges tables.

Using orders and invoices

The next example is a very practical one that you are likely to encounter in your daily work. Suppose you receive orders from your customers and, once a month, you send out an invoice that includes multiple orders. Each invoice contains some orders, but the relationship between the invoices and the orders is not clearly stated in the model. So, we will need to work a bit to re-create it.

You start with a data model like the one shown in Figure 3-11.

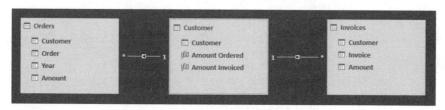

FIGURE 3-11   The data model of orders and invoices is a simple star schema.

This time, the starting data model is a star schema with two fact tables and a dimension in the middle. In the Customer dimension, we have already defined the following two measures:

```
Amount Ordered := SUM ( Orders[Amount] )
Amount Invoiced:= SUM ( Invoices[Amount] )
```

With the two measures in place, you can easily build a report that shows the amount ordered and the amount invoiced for each customer. This makes it easy to spot how much you need to invoice each customer for, like in the example shown in Figure 3-12.

Row Labels ▾	Amount Ordered	Amount Invoiced
John	2,000.00	1,800.00
Melanie	3,000.00	2,000.00
Paul	4,000.00	3,600.00
Grand Total	9,000.00	7,400.00

FIGURE 3-12 The amount ordered and invoiced per customer is an easy report to build.

If you are interested only in the top-level numbers, like in this pivot table, everything works just fine. Unfortunately, you will face problems as soon as you want to dig a bit more into the details. For example, how do you determine which orders have not yet been invoiced? Before proceeding, spend some time looking at the data model shown in Figure 3-11 and try to spot where the problem is. When you're finished, continue reading. Because this example hides some complexity, we will need to do some trial and error to identify the issue. Thus, we will show you several wrong solutions to highlight the reason why they are wrong.

If you put the order number in the PivotTable, the result will be hard to read and understand, as shown in Figure 3-13, where all the orders are listed under John, Melanie, and Paul.

Row Labels ▾	Amount Ordered	Amount Invoiced
⊟ John	2,000.00	1,800.00
1	100.00	1,800.00
2		1,800.00
3		1,800.00
4	400.00	1,800.00
5		1,800.00
6		1,800.00
7	500.00	1,800.00
8		1,800.00
9		1,800.00
10	100.00	1,800.00
11		1,800.00
12		1,800.00
13	400.00	1,800.00
14		1,800.00
15		1,800.00
16	500.00	1,800.00
17		1,800.00
18		1,800.00
⊟ Melanie	3,000.00	2,000.00
1		2,000.00
2		2,000.00
3	500.00	2,000.00

FIGURE 3-13 When you drill down to the order level, the Amount Invoiced column returns the wrong results.

This scenario is very similar to the one at the beginning of this chapter, which had two completely denormalized fact tables. The filter on the order number is not effective against the invoices because an invoice does not have an order number. Therefore, the value shown by Amount Invoiced uses the filter only on the customer, showing the total invoiced per customer on all the rows.

At this point, it is worth repeating one important concept: The number reported by the PivotTable is correct. It is the correct number given the information present in the model. If you carefully think about it, there is no way the engine can split the amount invoiced among the different orders because the information about which order was invoiced is missing from the model. Thus, the solution to this scenario requires us to build a proper data model. It needs to contain not only the information about the total invoiced, but also the details about which orders have been invoiced and which invoice contains what orders. As usual, before moving further, it is worth spending some time trying to figure out how you would solve this case.

There are multiple solutions to this scenario, depending on the complexity of the data model. Before going into more details, let us take a look at the data shown in Figure 3-14.

Customer
John
Paul
Melanie

Order	Customer	Year	Amount
1	John	2015	100
2	Paul	2015	250
3	Melanie	2015	500
4	John	2015	400
5	Paul	2015	1000
6	Melanie	2015	500
7	John	2015	500
8	Paul	2015	750
9	Melanie	2015	500
10	John	2016	100
11	Paul	2016	250
12	Melanie	2016	500
13	John	2016	400
14	Paul	2016	1000
15	Melanie	2016	500
16	John	2016	500
17	Paul	2016	750
18	Melanie	2016	500

Invoice	Customer	Amount
1	John	1000
2	Paul	2000
3	Melanie	1500
4	John	800
5	Paul	1600
6	Melanie	500

FIGURE 3-14 The figure shows the actual data used in this model.

As you can see, the Invoices and Orders tables both have a Customer column, which contains customer names. Customer is on the *one* side of two many-to-one relationships that start from Orders and Invoices. What we need to add to the model is a new relationship between Orders and Invoices that states which order is invoiced with what invoice. There are two possible scenarios:

- **Each order is related to an individual invoice** You face this scenario when an order is always fully invoiced. Thus, an invoice can contain multiple orders, but one order always has a single invoice. You can read, in this description, a one-to-many relationship between the invoices and orders.

- **Each order can be invoiced in multiple invoices** If an order can be partially invoiced, then the same order might belong to multiple invoices. If this is the case, then one order can belong to multiple invoices, and, at the same time, one invoice can contain multiple orders. In such a case, you are facing a many-to-many relationship between orders and invoices, and the scenario is a bit more complex.

The first scenario is very simple to solve. In fact, you only need to add the invoice number to the Orders table by using one additional column. The resulting model is shown in Figure 3-15.

Customer
John
Paul
Melanie

Order	Customer	Year	Amount	Invoice
1	John	2015	100	1
2	Paul	2015	250	2
3	Melanie	2015	500	3
4	John	2015	400	1
5	Paul	2015	1000	2
6	Melanie	2015	500	3
7	John	2015	500	1
8	Paul	2015	750	2
9	Melanie	2015	500	3
10	John	2016	100	4
11	Paul	2016	250	5
12	Melanie	2016	500	6
13	John	2016	400	4
14	Paul	2016	1000	5
15	Melanie	2016	500	6
16	John	2016	500	4
17	Paul	2016	750	5
18	Melanie	2016	500	6

Invoice	Customer	Amount
1	John	1000
2	Paul	2000
3	Melanie	1500
4	John	800
5	Paul	1600
6	Melanie	500

FIGURE 3-15 The highlighted column contains the invoice number for each given order.

Even if it looks like a simple modification to the model, it is not so easy to handle. In fact, when you load the new model and try to build the relationship, you will experience a bad surprise: The relationship can be created, but it is left inactive, as shown in Figure 3-16.

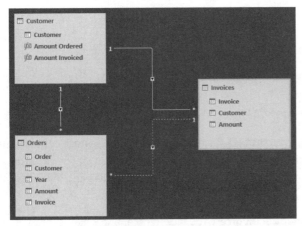

FIGURE 3-16 The relationship between the Orders and Invoices tables is created as an inactive relationship.

Where is the ambiguity in the model? If the relationship between Orders and Invoices would remain active, then you would have two paths from Orders to Customer: one straight, using the relationship between Orders and Customer, and an indirect one going from Orders to Invoices and then, finally, to Customer. Even if, in this case, the two relationships would end up pointing to the same customer, this is not known to the model and only depends on the data. Nothing in the model prevents you from incorrectly relating an order with an invoice that points to a customer who is different from the one in the invoice. Thus, the model, as it is, does not work.

The way to fix this is much simpler than expected. In fact, if you look carefully at the model, there is a one-to-many relationship between Customer and Invoices, and another one-to-many relationship between Invoices and Orders. The customer of an order can be safely retrieved using Invoices as a middle table. Thus, you can remove the relationship between Customer and Orders and rely on the other two, obtaining the model shown in Figure 3-17.

FIGURE 3-17 When the relationship between Orders and Customer is removed, the model is much simpler.

Does the model in Figure 3-17 look familiar? This is the very same pattern of the header/detail data model that we discussed in Chapter 2, "Using header/detail tables." You now have two fact tables: one containing the invoices and the other one containing the orders. Orders acts as the detail table, whereas Invoices acts as the header table.

Being a header/detail pattern, this model inherits all the pros and cons of that model. To some extent, the problem of the relationship is solved, but the problem of amounts is not. If you browse the model with a PivotTable, the result is the same as the one shown in Figure 3-13, with all the order numbers listed for all the customers. The reason for this is that, whatever order you choose, the total invoiced per customer is always the same. Even if the chain of relationships is set in the correct way, the data model is still incorrect.

In reality, the situation is a bit subtler than this. When you browse by customer name and order number, what data do you want to report? Review the following data measurements:

- **The total invoiced for that customer** This is the number reported by the system right now, and it looks wrong.

- **The total number of invoices that include the given order of the given customer** In such a case, you want to report the total invoiced if the order was present in the invoice, and make the result blank otherwise.

- **The amount of the order, if invoiced** In this case, you report the full amount of the order if it has been invoiced or a zero otherwise. You might report values higher than the actual invoices because you report the full order, not only the invoiced part.

> **Note** The list might end here, but we are forgetting an important part. What if an order was included in an invoice but not completely invoiced? There might be several reasons for this, and the calculations are even more complex. We will focus on that scenario later. For now, let's solve these first three calculations.

Calculating the total invoiced for the customer

The first calculation is the one that exists right now. Because the amount invoiced does not depend on the order, you simply sum the invoice amounts and produce a result. The major drawback of this solution is that the filter on the order number is not effective against the invoices, so you will always report the amount invoiced to the customer, regardless of the order number.

Calculating the number of invoices that include the given order of the given customer

To compute the second calculation, you must explicitly force the filter on the orders to work on the invoices. This can be performed by using the bidirectional pattern, as in the following code:

```
Amount Invoiced Filtered by Orders :=
CALCULATE (
    [Amount Invoiced],
    CROSSFILTER ( Orders[Invoice], Invoices[Invoice], BOTH )
)
```

The result of this calculation is that [Amount Invoiced] is computed for only the invoices that are present in the current selection of orders. You can see the resulting PivotTable in Figure 3-18.

Customer	Order	Invoice	Amount Ordered	Amount Invoiced Filtered by Orders
John	1	1	100.00	1,000.00
	4	1	400.00	1,000.00
	7	1	500.00	1,000.00
	10	4	100.00	800.00
	13	4	400.00	800.00
	16	4	500.00	800.00
John Total			2,000.00	1,800.00
Melanie	3	3	500.00	1,500.00
	6	3	500.00	1,500.00
	9	3	500.00	1,500.00
	12	6	500.00	500.00
	15	6	500.00	500.00
	18	6	500.00	500.00
Melanie Total			3,000.00	2,000.00
Paul	2	2	250.00	2,000.00
	5	2	1,000.00	2,000.00
	8	2	750.00	2,000.00
	11	5	250.00	1,600.00
	14	5	1,000.00	1,600.00
	17	5	750.00	1,600.00
Paul Total			4,000.00	3,600.00

FIGURE 3-18 Moving the filter from orders to invoices changes the result.

Calculating the amount of the order, if invoiced

The last measure, as expected, is non-additive. In fact, because it reports the total invoiced for each order, it will typically show a much higher value than the order amount. You might recall this behavior from the previous chapter. Because we are aggregating a value from the header table, when we browse using a filter on the detail, the resulting calculation is non-additive.

To make the measure additive, you should check for each order to determine whether it has been invoiced. If so, then the amount invoiced is the amount of the order. Otherwise it is zero. This can be easily done with a calculated column or with a slightly more complex measure, like the following:

```
Amount Invoiced Filtered by Orders :=
CALCULATE (
    SUMX (
        Orders,
        IF ( NOT ( ISBLANK ( Orders[Invoice] ) ), Orders[Amount] )
    ),
    CROSSFILTER ( Orders[Invoice], Invoices[Invoice], BOTH )
)
```

This measure works well if an order is always fully invoiced, but otherwise it computes a wrong number because it returns the amount invoiced. An example is shown in Figure 3-19, which reports the same value for the total invoiced and the total ordered, even if we know that the two numbers should be different. This is because we are computing the amount invoiced from the orders instead of from the invoices.

Customer	Order	Invoice	Amount Ordered	Amount Invoiced Filtered by Orders
John	1	1	100.00	100.00
	4	1	400.00	400.00
	7	1	500.00	500.00
	10	4	100.00	100.00
	13	4	400.00	400.00
	16	4	500.00	500.00
John Total			2,000.00	2,000.00
Melanie	3	3	500.00	500.00
	6	3	500.00	500.00
	9	3	500.00	500.00
	12	6	500.00	500.00
	15	6	500.00	500.00
	18	6	500.00	500.00
Melanie Total			3,000.00	3,000.00
Paul	2	2	250.00	250.00
	5	2	1,000.00	1,000.00
	8	2	750.00	750.00
	11	5	250.00	250.00
	14	5	1,000.00	1,000.00
	17	5	750.00	750.00
Paul Total			4,000.00	4,000.00

FIGURE 3-19 If an order is not fully invoiced, the last measure shows an incorrect result.

There is no easy way to compute the partial amount of the order invoiced because that information is not there, in the model. In the case of partial invoicing, if you only store for each order the invoice that contains it, you are missing the important value of the amount invoiced. To provide a correct result, you should store this value, too, and use the amount invoiced instead of the amount of the order in the previous formula.

In addressing this point, we go one step further and build a complete model to solve the scenario. We will build a model that enables you to invoice an order with different invoices and to state, for each pair of invoices and orders, the amount invoiced. The model needs to be a bit more complex. It will involve an additional table that stores the invoice number, the order number, and the amount of the order invoiced. The model is shown in in Figure 3-20.

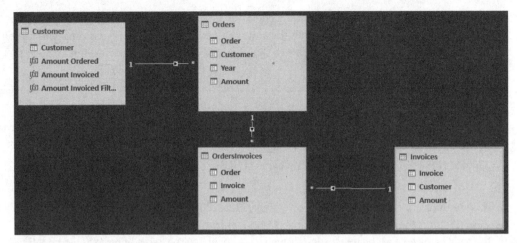

FIGURE 3-20 This structure models one order with multiple invoices, and one invoice with multiple orders, with the amount invoiced for each order.

The model involves a many-to-many relationship between orders and invoices. A single order can be invoiced with multiple invoices, and, at the same time, a single invoice can contain multiple orders. The amount invoiced for each order is stored in the OrdersInvoices table, so each order can be partially invoiced in different documents.

We will cover in more detail many-to-many handling in Chapter 8, "Many-to-many relationships." But it is useful, even at this point, to show a correct model to handle invoices and orders. Here, we are deliberately violating the star schema rules to correctly build the model. In fact, the OrdersInvoices table is neither a fact table nor a dimension. It is similar to a fact table because it contains the Amount metric, and it is related to the Invoices dimension. However, it is related to Orders, which is, at the same time, a fact table and a dimension. Technically, the OrdersInvoices table is called a *bridge table*, because it acts as a bridge between orders and invoices.

Now that the amount invoiced is stored in the bridge table, the formula to compute the amount invoiced for the order selection is a slight variation from the previous one, as you can see in the following code:

```
Amount Invoiced :=
CALCULATE (
    SUM ( OrdersInvoices[Amount] ),
    CROSSFILTER ( OrdersInvoices[Invoice], Invoices[Invoice], BOTH )
)
```

You sum the Amount column in the bridge table and the CROSSFILTER function activates bidirectional filtering between the bridge table and Invoices. The result of using this formula is much more interesting because you can now easily spot the amount ordered and invoiced for every order, and you can obtain reports like the one shown in Figure 3-21.

Customer ▼	Order ▼	Amount Ordered	Amount Invoiced
⊟ John	1	100.00	100.00
	4	400.00	400.00
	7	500.00	500.00
	10	100.00	100.00
	13	400.00	400.00
	16	500.00	300.00
John Total		**2,000.00**	**1,800.00**
⊟ Melanie	3	500.00	500.00
	6	500.00	500.00
	9	500.00	500.00
	12	500.00	250.00
	15	500.00	100.00
	18	500.00	150.00
Melanie Total		**3,000.00**	**2,000.00**
⊟ Paul	2	250.00	250.00
	5	1,000.00	1,000.00
	8	750.00	750.00
	11	250.00	250.00
	14	1,000.00	750.00
	17	750.00	600.00
Paul Total		**4,000.00**	**3,600.00**

FIGURE 3-21 Using the bridge table, you can produce a report showing the amount ordered and invoiced.

Conclusions

In this chapter, you learned how to handle different scenarios with multiple fact tables that are, in turn, related through dimensions or through bridge tables. The most important topics you learned in this chapter are as follows:

- If you denormalize too much, you reach a point at which your tables are over-denormalized. In such a scenario, filtering different fact tables becomes impossible. To correct this, you must build a proper set of dimensions to be able to slice values from the different fact tables.

- Although you can leverage DAX to handle over-denormalized scenarios, the DAX code quickly becomes too complex to handle. A change in the data model makes the code much easier.

- Complex relationships between dimensions and fact tables can create ambiguous models, which cannot be handled by the DAX engine. Ambiguous models must be solved at the data-model level by duplicating some tables and/or denormalizing their columns.

- Complex models like orders and invoices involve multiple fact tables. To model them the right way, you must build a bridge table so that the information is related to the correct entity.

CHAPTER 4

Working with date and time

In business models, you typically compute year-to-date (YTD), year-over-year comparisons, and percentage of growth. In scientific models, you might need to compute forecasts based on previous data or check the accuracy of numbers over time. Nearly all these models contain some calculations related to time, which is why we have dedicated a full chapter to these kinds of calculations.

In more technical terms, we say time is a dimension, meaning you typically use a Calendar table to slice your data by year, month, or day. Time is not just a dimension, however. It is a very special dimension that you need to create in the right way and for which there are some special considerations.

This chapter shows several scenarios and provides a data model for each one. Some examples are very simple, whereas others require very complex DAX code to be solved. Our goal is to show you examples of data models and to give you a better idea of how to correctly model date and time.

Creating a date dimension

Time is a dimension. A simple column in your fact table containing the date of the event is not enough. If, for example, you need to use the model shown in Figure 4-1 to create a report, you will quickly discover that the date alone is not enough to produce useful reports.

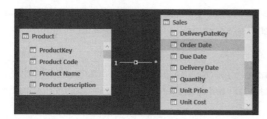

FIGURE 4-1 The Sales table contains the Order Date column with the date of the order.

By using the date in Sales, you can slice values by individual dates. However, if you need to aggregate them by year or by month, then you need additional columns. You can easily address the issue by creating a set of calculated columns directly in the fact table (although this is not an optimal solution because it prevents you from using time-intelligence functions). For example, you can use the following simple formulas to create a set of three columns—Year, Month Name, and Month Number:

```
Sales[Year] = YEAR ( Sales[Order Date] )
Sales[Month] = FORMAT ( Sales[Order Date], "mmmm" )
Sales[MonthNumber] = MONTH ( Sales[Order Date] )
```

Obviously, the month numbers are useful for sorting the month names in the correct way. When you include them, you can use the Sort by Column feature that is available in both Power BI Desktop and the Excel data model. As shown in Figure 4-2, these columns work perfectly fine to create reports that slice values, like the sales amount, by time.

Row Labels	Sales Amount
⊟ 2007	1,459,215.95
January	101,097.12
February	108,553.20
March	119,707.83
April	121,085.74
May	123,413.41
June	121,707.44
July	139,381.00
August	87,384.31
September	155,275.94
October	99,872.65
November	122,522.86
December	159,214.45
⊞ 2008	1,122,535.05
⊞ 2009	1,242,534.61
Grand Total	3,824,285.61

FIGURE 4-2 The report shows sales sliced by date, by using calculated columns in the fact table.

However, there are a couple of issues with this model. For example, if you need to slice purchases by date, you end up repeating the same setup of the calculated columns for the Purchases table. Because the columns belong to the fact tables, you cannot use the years in Sales to slice Purchases. As you might recall from Chapter 3, "Using multiple fact tables," you need a dimension to correctly slice two fact tables at once. Moreover, you typically have many columns in a date dimension—for example, columns for fiscal years and months, holiday information, and working days. Storing all these columns in a single, easily manageable table is a great plus.

There is another more important reason to use dimensions. Using columns in the fact table makes the coding of time-intelligence calculations much more complex, whereas using a date dimension makes all these formulas much easier to write.

Let us elaborate on this concept with an example. Suppose you want to compute the YTD value of Sales Amount. If you can rely only on columns in the fact table, the formula becomes quite complicated, as in the following:

```
Sales YTD :=
VAR CurrentYear = MAX ( Sales[Year] )
VAR CurrentDate = MAX ( Sales[Order Date] )
RETURN
CALCULATE (
    [Sales Amount],
    Sales[Order Date] <= CurrentDate,
    Sales[Year] = CurrentYear,
    ALL ( Sales[Month] ),
    ALL ( Sales[MonthNumber] )
)
```

Specifically, the code needs to do the following:

1. Apply a filter on the date by filtering only the ones before the last visible date.

2. Keep a filter on the year, taking care to show only the last visible one in case there are multiple in the filter context.

3. Remove any filter from the month (in Sales).

4. Remove any filter from the month number (again, in Sales).

> **Note** If you are not familiar with DAX, gaining a deep understanding of why this formula works is a great mental exercise to become more familiar with the way filter context and variables work together.

This code works just fine, as shown in Figure 4-3. However, it is unnecessarily complex. The biggest problem with the formula is that you cannot leverage the built-in DAX functions that are designed to help you author time-intelligence calculations. In fact, those functions rely on the presence of a specific table dedicated to dates.

Row Labels	Sales Amount	Sales YTD
⊟ 2007	1,459,215.95	1,459,215.95
January	101,097.12	101,097.12
February	108,553.20	209,650.32
March	119,707.83	329,358.16
April	121,085.74	450,443.90
May	123,413.41	573,857.31
June	121,707.44	695,564.75
July	139,381.00	834,945.75
August	87,384.31	922,330.06
September	155,275.94	1,077,606.00
October	99,872.65	1,177,478.64
November	122,522.86	1,300,001.50
December	159,214.45	1,459,215.95
⊞ 2008	1,122,535.05	1,122,535.05
⊞ 2009	1,242,534.61	1,242,534.61
Grand Total	3,824,285.61	1,242,534.61

FIGURE 4-3 Sales YTD reports the correct values, but its code is too complicated.

If you update the data model by adding a date dimension, like the one in Figure 4-4, the formula becomes much easier to author.

FIGURE 4-4 Adding a date dimension to the model makes the code much easier to write.

At this point, you can use the predefined time-intelligence functions to author Sales YTD in the following way:

```
Sales YTD :=
CALCULATE (
    [Sales Amount],
    DATESYTD ( 'Date'[Date] )
)
```

Note   This is true not just for YTD calculations. All time-intelligence metrics are much easier to write when you use a date dimension.

By using a date dimension, you achieve the following:

- You simplify the writing of measures.

- You obtain a central place to define all columns related to the time that you will need to build reports.

- You improve the performance of the queries.

- You create a model that is simpler to navigate.

These are the advantages, but what about the disadvantages? In this case, there are none. Always using a time dimension, yields only advantages. Get used to creating a calendar dimension every time you build a data model, and don't fall into the trap of choosing the easy way of using calculated columns. If you do, you will regret that decision sooner rather than later.

Understanding automatic time dimensions

In Excel 2016 and in Power BI Desktop, Microsoft has built an automated system to work with time intelligence—although the two tools use different mechanisms. We discuss both in this section.

Note   As you will learn in this section, we discourage you from using either of these systems because they do not provide the necessary flexibility and ease of use that you need in your models.

Automatic time grouping in Excel

When you use a PivotTable on an Excel data model, adding a date column to the PivotTable prompts Excel to automatically generate a set of columns in the PivotTable to automate date calculations. For example, you might start with the model shown in Figure 4-5, where the Sales table contains only one date column, the Order Date column.

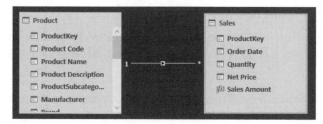

FIGURE 4-5 The Sales table contains a date column, which is Order Date, and no columns with the year and/or month.

If you create a PivotTable with Sales Amount in the values area and Order Date in the columns, you will notice a small delay. Then, surprisingly, instead of seeing the Order Date, you will see the PivotTable shown in Figure 4-6.

Row Labels	Sales Amount
⊟2007	1,459,215.95
⊞Qtr1	329,358.16
⊞Qtr2	366,206.60
⊞Qtr3	382,041.25
⊞Qtr4	381,609.95
⊞2008	1,122,535.05
⊞2009	1,242,534.61
Grand Total	3,824,285.61

FIGURE 4-6 The PivotTable slices the date by year and quarter, even if you did not have those columns in the model.

To make this PivotTable slice by year, Excel automatically added some columns to the Sales table, which you can see if you reopen the data model. The result is shown in Figure 4-7, which highlights the new columns added by Excel.

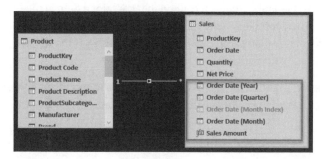

FIGURE 4-7 The Sales table contains new columns, which were automatically created by Excel.

Notice that Excel did exactly what we suggested you avoid: It created a set of columns to perform the slicing directly in the table that contains the date column. If you perform the same operation on another fact table, you will obtain a new set of columns, and the two cannot be used to cross-filter the tables. Moreover, because the columns are created in the fact table, on large datasets, this takes time and space in the Excel file. You can find more information about this feature at *https://blogs.office.com/2015/10/13/ time-grouping-enhancements-in-excel-2016/*. This article also contains a link to a procedure that involves editing the registry to turn off this feature. Unless you work with very simple models, we recommend you follow the procedure to disable automatic time grouping and learn the correct way to handle it by hand, which we explain in this chapter.

Automatic time grouping in Power BI Desktop

Power BI Desktop tries to make time-intelligence calculations easier by automating some of the steps. Unfortunately, even if it automates the steps slightly better than Excel, Power BI Desktop is not the best solution for time intelligence.

If you use the same data model as in Figure 4-7 in Power BI Desktop and you build a matrix with the Order Date column, you obtain the visualization shown in Figure 4-8.

Year ▼	Quarter	Month	Day	Sales Amount
2009	Qtr 1	January	1	2.198,95
			2	1.325,89
			3	1.775,52
			4	2.167,90
			5	511,70
			6	907,89
			7	332,37
			8	4.605,52
			9	4.442,14
			10	82,70
			11	60,44

FIGURE 4-8   The matrix shows Year, Quarter, and Month columns, even though these columns are not part of the model.

Like Excel, Power BI Desktop automatically generates a calendar hierarchy. However, it uses a different technique. In fact, if you look at the Sales table, you will not find any new calculated columns. Instead, Power BI Desktop generates a hidden table for each column that contains a date in the model and builds the necessary relationship. When you slice by the date, it uses the hierarchy created in the hidden table. Thus, it is somewhat smarter than Excel. However, this approach has the following limitations:

- The automatically generated table is hidden and there is no way for you to modify its content. For example, there is no way to change the column names or the way data is sorted, or to handle fiscal calendars.

- Power BI Desktop generates one table per column. Thus, if you have multiple fact tables, they will be linked to different Date tables, and you cannot slice multiple tables using a single calendar.

Over time, we have gotten used to disabling automatic calendar generation in Power BI Desktop. (To do so, click the **File** tab, click **Options and Settings** to open the Options dialog box, choose the **Data Load** page, and deselect the **Auto Date/Time** check box.) And we are always prepared to configure a custom Calendar table over which we have full control that can filter all the fact tables we add to the model. We suggest you do the same.

Using multiple date dimensions

One fact table might contain multiple dates. This happens very frequently. In the Contoso database, for example, each order has three different dates: order date, due date, and delivery date. Moreover, different fact tables might contain dates. Thus, the number of dates in a data model is frequently high. What is the right way to create a model when there are multiple dates? The answer is very simple: Apart from some very exceptional scenarios, there should be a single date dimension in the whole model. This section is dedicated to understanding the reason for using a single date dimension.

As mentioned, there are three dates in Sales that can be used to relate Sales with Date. You might try to create multiple relationships between the two tables that are based on the three pairs of columns. Unfortunately, the result is that the first relationship you create will be activated, whereas the next two will be created but kept inactive, as shown in Figure 4-9.

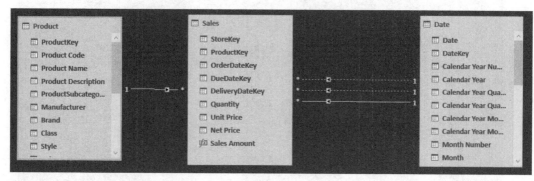

FIGURE 4-9 Of the three relationships between Sales and Date, only one is active (a solid line). The other relationships are inactive (dotted lines).

You can temporarily activate inactive relationships by using the USERELATIONSHIP function, but this is a technique we will use later for some formulas. When you project this data model in a PivotTable or a report, inactive relationships are not used by any of your formulas. A user has no way to instruct Excel, for example, to activate a specific relationship in a single PivotTable.

Note Relationships cannot be made active because the engine cannot create data models that contain ambiguity. Ambiguity occurs whenever there are multiple ways to start from one table (Sales, in this example) and reach another table (Date, in this example). Imagine you want to create a calculated column in Sales that contains RELATED (Date[Calendar Year]). In such a scenario, DAX would not know which of the three relationships to use. For this reason, only one can be active, and it determines the behavior of RELATED, RELATEDTABLE, and the automatic filter context propagation.

Because using inactive relationships does not seem to be the way to go, you should modify the data model by duplicating the dimension. In our example, you can load the Date table three times: once for the order date, once for the due date, and once for the delivery date. You should obtain a non-ambiguous model like the one shown in Figure 4-10.

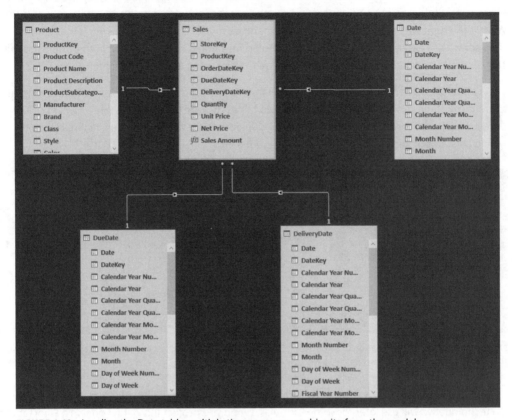

FIGURE 4-10 Loading the Date table multiple times removes ambiguity from the model.

Using this model, it is now possible to create reports that show, for example, the amount sold in one year but delivered in a different one, as shown in Figure 4-11.

Sales Amount	Column Labels				
Row Labels	2007	2008	2009	2010	Grand Total
2007	1,412,267.47	46,948.48			1,459,215.95
2008		1,092,620.19	29,914.86		1,122,535.05
2009			1,193,051.71	49,482.90	1,242,534.61
Grand Total	1,412,267.47	1,139,568.67	1,222,966.57	49,482.90	3,824,285.61

FIGURE 4-11 The report shows the amount sold in one year and shipped in a different one.

At first glance, the PivotTable in Figure 4-11 is hard to read. It is very difficult to quickly grasp whether the delivery year is in rows or in columns. You can deduce that the delivery year is in columns by analyzing the numbers because delivery always happens after the placement of the order. Nevertheless, this is not evident as it should be in a good report.

It is enough to change the content of the year column using the prefix *OY* for the order year and *DY* for the delivery year. This modifies the query of the Calendar table and it makes the report much easier to understand, as shown in Figure 4-12.

Sales Amount	Column Labels				
Row Labels	DY 2007	DY 2008	DY 2009	DY 2010	Grand Total
OY 2007	1,412,267.47	46,948.48			1,459,215.95
OY 2008		1,092,620.19	29,914.86		1,122,535.05
OY 2009			1,193,051.71	49,482.90	1,242,534.61
Grand Total	1,412,267.47	1,139,568.67	1,222,966.57	49,482.90	3,824,285.61

FIGURE 4-12 Changing the prefix of the order and delivery years makes the report much easier to understand.

So far, it looks like you can easily handle multiple dates by duplicating the date dimension as many times as needed, taking care to rename columns and add prefixes to the column values to make the report easy to read. To some extent, this is correct. Nevertheless, it is important to learn what might happen as soon as you have multiple fact tables. If you add another fact table to the data model, like Purchases, the scenario becomes much more complex, as shown in Figure 4-13.

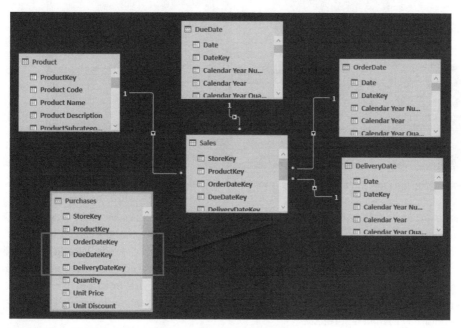

FIGURE 4-13 The Purchases table has three additional dates.

The simple addition of the Purchases table to the model generates three additional dates because purchases also have an order, delivery, and due date. The scenario now requires more skill to correctly design it. In fact, you can add three additional date dimensions to the model, reaching six dates in a single model. Users will be confused by the presence of all these dates. Therefore, although the model is very powerful, it is not easy to use, and it is very likely to lead to a poor user experience. Besides that, can you imagine what happens if, at some point, you need to add further fact tables? This explosion of date dimensions is not good at all.

Another option would be to use the three dimensions that are already present in the model to slice the purchases and sales. Thus, Order Date filters the order dates of both Sales and Purchases. The same thing happens for the other two dimensions, too. The data model becomes the one shown in Figure 4-14.

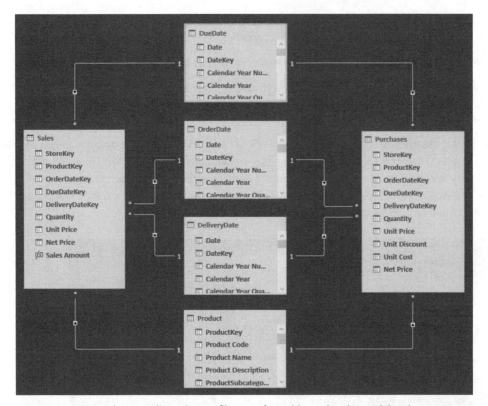

FIGURE 4-14 Using the same dimensions to filter two fact tables makes the model easier to use.

The model in Figure 4-14 is much easier to use, but it is still too complex. Moreover, it is worth noting that we were very lucky with the dimension we added. Purchases had the same three dates as Sales, which is not very common in the real world. It is much more likely that you will add fact tables with dates that have nothing to share with the previous facts. In such cases, you must decide whether to create additional date dimensions, making the model harder to browse, or to join the new fact table to one of the existing dates, which might create problems in terms of the user experience because the names are not likely to match perfectly.

The problem can be solved in a much easier way if you resist the urge to create multiple date dimensions in your model. In fact, if you stick with a single date dimension, the model will be much easier to browse and understand, as shown in Figure 4-15.

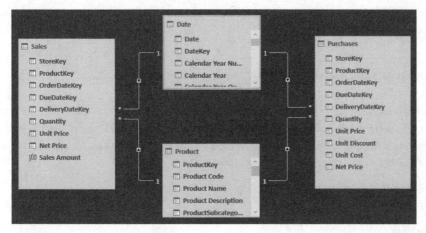

FIGURE 4-15 In this simpler model, there is a single date dimension that is linked to OrderDate in both fact tables.

Using a single date dimension makes the model extremely easy to use. In fact, you intuitively know that Date will slice both Sales and Purchases using their main date column, which is the date of the order. At first sight, this model looks less powerful than the previous ones, and to some extent, this is true. Nevertheless, before concluding that this model is in fact less powerful, it is worth spending some time analyzing what the differences are in analytical power between a model with many dates and one with a single date.

Offering many Date tables to the user makes it possible to produce reports by using multiple dates at once. You saw in a previous example that this might be useful to compute the amount sold versus the amount shipped. Nevertheless, the real question is whether you need multiple dates to show this piece of information. The answer is no. You can easily address this issue by creating specific measures that compute the needed values without having to change the data model.

If, for example, you want to compare the amount sold versus the amount shipped, you can keep an inactive relationship between Sales and Date, based on the DeliveryDateKey, and then activate it for some very specific measure. In our case, you would add one inactive relationship between Sales and Date, obtaining the model shown in Figure 4-16.

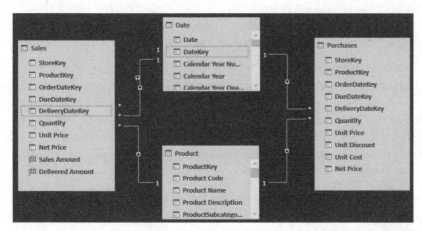

FIGURE 4-16 The relationship between DeliveryDateKey and DateKey is in the model, but it is disabled.

Once the relationship is in place, you can write the Delivered Amount measure in the following way:

```
Delivered Amount :=
CALCULATE (
    [Sales Amount],
    USERELATIONSHIP ( Sales[DeliveryDateKey], 'Date'[DateKey] )
)
```

This measure enables the inactive relationship between Sales and Date for only the duration of the calculation. Thus, you can use the Date table to slice your data, and you still get information that is related to the delivery date, as shown in the report in Figure 4-17. By choosing an appropriate name for the measure, you will not incur any ambiguity when using it.

Row Labels	Sales Amount	Delivered Amount
CY 2007	1,459,215.95	1,410,787.80
CY 2008	1,122,535.05	1,145,421.73
CY 2009	1,242,534.61	1,221,566.90
CY 2010		46,509.18
Grand Total	3,824,285.61	3,824,285.61

FIGURE 4-17 Delivered Amount uses the relationship based on a delivery date, but its logic is hidden in the measure.

Thus, the simple rule is to create a single date dimension for the whole model. Obviously, this is not a strict rule. There are scenarios where having multiple date dimensions makes perfect sense. But there must be a powerful need to justify the pain of handling multiple Date tables.

In our experience, most data models do not really require multiple Date tables. One is enough. If you need some calculations made using different dates, then you can create measures to compute them, leveraging inactive relationships. Most of the time, adding many date dimensions comes from some lack in the analysis of the requirements of the model. Thus, before adding another date dimension, always ask yourself whether you *really* need it, or if you can compute the same values using DAX code. If the latter is true, then go for more DAX code and fewer date dimensions. You will never regret that.

Handling date and time

Date is almost always a needed dimension in any model. Time, on the other hand, appears much less frequently. With that said, there are scenarios where both the date and the time are important dimensions, and in those cases, you need to carefully understand how to handle them.

The first important point to note is that a Date table cannot contain time information. In fact, to mark a table as a Date table (which you must do if you intend to use any time-intelligence functions on a table), you need to follow the requirements imposed by the DAX language. Among those requirements is that the column used to hold the datetime value should be at the day granularity, without time information. You will not get an error from the engine if you use a Date table that also contains time information. However, the engine will not be able to correctly compute time-intelligence functions if the same date appears multiple times.

So what can you do if you need to handle time too? The easiest and most efficient solution is to create one dimension for the date and a separate dimension for the time. You can easily create a time dimension by using a simple piece of M code in Power Query, like the following:

```
Let
    StartTime = #datetime(1900,1,1,0,0,0),
    Increment = #duration(0,0,1,0),
    Times = List.DateTimes(StartTime, 24*60, Increment),
    TimesAsTable = Table.FromList(Times,Splitter.SplitByNothing()),
    RenameTime = Table.RenameColumns(TimesAsTable,{{"Column1", "Time"}}),
    ChangedDataType = Table.TransformColumnTypes(RenameTime,{{"Time", type time}}),
    AddHour = Table.AddColumn(
        ChangedDataType,
        "Hour",
        each Text.PadStart(Text.From(Time.Hour([Time])), 2, "0" )
    ),
    AddMinute = Table.AddColumn(
        AddHour,
        "Minute",
        each Text.PadStart(Text.From(Time.Minute([Time])), 2, "0" )
    ),
    AddHourMinute = Table.AddColumn(
        AddMinute,
        "HourMinute", each [Hour] & ":" & [Minute]
    ),
    AddIndex = Table.AddColumn(
        AddHourMinute,
        "TimeIndex",
        each Time.Hour([Time]) * 60 + Time.Minute([Time])
    ),
    Result = AddIndex
in
    Result
```

The script generates a table like the one shown in Figure 4-18. The table contains a TimeIndex column (with the numbers from 0 to 1439), which you can use to link the fact table, and a few columns to slice your data. If your table contains a different column for the time, you can easily modify the previous script to generate a time as the primary key.

Time	Hour	Minute	TimeIndex	HourMinute
00.00.00	00	00	0	00:00
00.01.00	00	01	1	00:01
00.02.00	00	02	2	00:02
00.03.00	00	03	3	00:03
00.04.00	00	04	4	00:04
00.05.00	00	05	5	00:05
00.06.00	00	06	6	00:06
00.07.00	00	07	7	00:07
00.08.00	00	08	8	00:08
00.09.00	00	09	9	00:09
00.10.00	00	10	10	00:10
00.11.00	00	11	11	00:11
00.12.00	00	12	12	00:12
00.13.00	00	13	13	00:13
00.14.00	00	14	14	00:14
00.15.00	00	15	15	00:15

FIGURE 4-18 This is a simple time table that is generated with Power Query.

The time index is computed by multiplying the hours by 60 and adding the minutes, so it can be easily included as a key in your fact table. This calculation should be done in the data source that feeds the table.

Using a separate time table lets you slice data by hours, minutes, or different columns that you might add to the time table. Frequent options are periods of the day (morning, afternoon, or night) or time ranges—for example hourly ranges, like the ones we used in the report in Figure 4-19.

Sales Amount	Column Labels			
Row Labels	CY 2007	CY 2008	CY 2009	Grand Total
From 06:00 to 07:00	79,518.54	47,981.26	67,825.28	195,325.08
From 07:00 to 08:00	27,692.12	39,036.69	37,788.93	104,517.75
From 08:00 to 09:00	54,368.20	52,602.75	56,441.84	163,412.79
From 09:00 to 10:00	69,017.22	55,524.44	55,657.92	180,199.58
From 10:00 to 11:00	63,355.05	49,343.90	44,823.41	157,522.37
From 11:00 to 12:00	51,625.55	49,563.19	42,184.88	143,373.62
From 12:00 to 13:00	52,189.03	29,557.34	45,533.05	127,279.42
From 13:00 to 14:00	47,517.66	35,557.72	46,450.37	129,525.75
From 14:00 to 15:00	74,327.75	52,080.15	45,249.45	171,657.35
From 15:00 to 16:00	48,098.40	46,725.44	37,985.21	132,809.04
From 16:00 to 17:00	43,919.20	36,328.50	53,859.38	134,107.08
From 17:00 to 18:00	62,586.62	47,388.08	47,082.21	157,056.92
From 18:00 to 19:00	64,856.62	40,480.32	74,347.68	179,684.62
From 19:00 to 20:00	68,391.58	32,012.46	52,723.16	153,127.20
Grand Total	807,463.55	614,182.24	707,952.78	2,129,598.57

FIGURE 4-19   The time dimension is useful to generate reports that show sales divided by hour, for example.

There are scenarios, however, where you do not need to stratify numbers by time ranges. For example, you might want to compute values based on the difference in hours between two events. Another scenario is if you need to compute the number of events that happened between two timestamps, with a granularity below the day. For example, you might want to know how many customers entered your shop between 8:00 a.m. on January 1st and 1:00 p.m. on January 7th. These scenarios are a bit more advanced, and they are covered in Chapter 7, "Analyzing date and time intervals."

Time-intelligence calculations

If your data model is prepared in the correct way, time-intelligence calculations are easy to author. To compute time intelligence, you need to apply a filter on the Calendar table that shows the rows for the period of interest. There is a rich set of functions that you can use to obtain these filters. For example, a simple YTD can be written as follows:

```
Sales YTD :=
CALCULATE (
    [Sales Amount],
    DATESYTD ( 'Date'[Date] )
)
```

DATESYTD returns the set of dates starting from the 1st of January of the currently selected period and reaching the last date included in the context. Other useful functions are SAMEPERIODLASTYEAR, PARALLELPERIOD, and LASTDAY. You can combine these functions to obtain more complex aggregations.

For example, if you need to compute YTD of the previous year, you can use the following formula:

```
Sales PYTD :=
CALCULATE (
    [Sales Amount],
    DATESYTD ( SAMEPERIODLASTYEAR ( 'Date'[Date] ) )
)
```

Another very useful time-intelligence function is DATESINPERIOD, which returns the set of dates in a given period. It can be useful for computing moving averages, like in the following example, where DATESINPERIOD returns the last 12 months, using the last date in the filter context as a reference point:

```
Sales Avg12M :=
CALCULATE (
    [Sales Amount] / COUNTROWS ( VALUES ( 'Date'[Month] ) ),
    DATESINPERIOD (
        'Date'[Date],
        MAX ( 'Date'[Date] ),
        -12,
        MONTH
    )
)
```

You can see the result of this average in Figure 4-20.

Row Labels	Sales Amount	Sales Avg12M
⊞2007	1,459,215.95	121,601.33
⊞2008	1,122,535.05	93,544.59
⊟2009	1,242,534.61	103,544.55
January	71,828.15	94,146.79
February	59,980.01	94,048.68
March	71,327.93	94,596.90
April	103,551.11	93,559.09
May	160,137.28	96,306.46
June	93,484.82	96,631.05
July	145,604.22	101,094.13
August	98,972.35	97,565.15
September	90,457.03	95,765.51
October	91,665.16	98,482.67
November	133,481.80	100,581.92
December	122,044.75	103,544.55
Grand Total	3,824,285.61	

FIGURE 4-20 The measure computes the average over 12 months.

Handling fiscal calendars

Another very good reason you should create your own Calendar table is that it makes it very easy to work with a fiscal calendar. Alternatively, in more extreme situations, you can work with more complex calendars, like weekly or seasonal calendars.

When handling a fiscal calendar, you do not need to add additional columns to your fact table. Instead, you simply add a set of columns to your Date table so that you will be able to slice by using both the standard and the fiscal calendar. As an example, imagine you need to handle a fiscal calendar that sets the first month of the year as July. Thus, the calendar goes from July 1st to June 30th. In such a scenario, you need to modify the calendar so that it shows fiscal months, and you will need to modify some calculations to make them work with fiscal calendars.

First, you need to add a suitable set of columns to hold the fiscal months (if they are not yet there already). Some people prefer to see July as the name of the first fiscal month, whereas other people prefer to avoid month names and use numbers instead. Thus, by using numbers, they browse the month as Fiscal Month 01 instead of July. For this example, we use the standard names for months.

No matter which naming technique you prefer, for proper sorting, you will need an additional column to hold the fiscal month name. In standard calendars, you have a Month Name column, which is sorted by Month Number, so that January is put in the first place and December in the last place. In contrast, when using the fiscal calendar, you want to put July as the first month and June as the last one. Because you cannot sort the same column using different sorters, you will need to replicate the month name in a new column, Fiscal Month, and create a new sort column that sorts the fiscal month the way you want.

After these steps are done, you can browse the model using columns in your Calendar table, and you can have the months sorted the right way. Nevertheless, some calculations will not work as expected. For example, look at the Sales YTD calculation in the PivotTable shown in Figure 4-21.

Row Labels	Sales Amount	Sales YTD
⊟ FY 2007	695,564.75	695,564.75
January	101,097.12	101,097.12
February	108,553.20	209,650.32
March	119,707.83	329,358.16
April	121,085.74	450,443.90
May	123,413.41	573,857.31
June	121,707.44	695,564.75
⊟ FY 2008	1,286,923.00	523,271.80
July	139,381.00	834,945.75
August	87,384.31	922,330.06
September	155,275.94	1,077,606.00
October	99,872.65	1,177,478.64
November	122,522.86	1,300,001.50
December	159,214.45	1,459,215.95
January	64,601.67	64,601.67
February	61,157.39	125,759.06
March	64,749.27	190,508.33
April	116,004.84	306,513.17
May	127,168.83	433,682.00
June	89,589.80	523,271.80
⊞ FY 2009	1,159,572.55	560,309.30
⊞ FY 2010	682,225.31	
Grand Total	3,824,285.61	

FIGURE 4-21 The YTD calculation does not work correctly with the fiscal calendar.

If you look carefully at the PivotTable, you can see that the value of YTD is reset in January 2008 instead of July. This is because the standard time-intelligence functions are designed to work with standard calendars, and because of that, they do not work with custom calendars. Some functions have an additional parameter that can instruct them on how to work with fiscal calendars. DATESYTD, the function used to compute YTD, is among them. To compute YTD with a fiscal calendar, you can add a second parameter to DATESYTD that specifies the day and month at which the calendar ends, like in the following code:

```
Sales YTD Fiscal :=
CALCULATE (
    [Sales Amount],
    DATESYTD ( 'Date'[Date],  "06/30" )
)
```

Figure 4-22 shows the PivotTable with the standard YTD and the fiscal YTD, side-by-side.

Row Labels	Sales Amount	Sales YTD	Sales YTD Fiscal
FY 2007	**695,564.75**	**695,564.75**	**695,564.75**
January	101,097.12	101,097.12	101,097.12
February	108,553.20	209,650.32	209,650.32
March	119,707.83	329,358.16	329,358.16
April	121,085.74	450,443.90	450,443.90
May	123,413.41	573,857.31	573,857.31
June	121,707.44	695,564.75	695,564.75
FY 2008	**1,286,923.00**	**523,271.80**	**1,286,923.00**
July	139,381.00	834,945.75	139,381.00
August	87,384.31	922,330.06	226,765.31
September	155,275.94	1,077,606.00	382,041.25
October	99,872.65	1,177,478.64	481,913.89
November	122,522.86	1,300,001.50	604,436.75
December	159,214.45	1,459,215.95	763,651.19
January	64,601.67	64,601.67	828,252.87
February	61,157.39	125,759.06	889,410.25
March	64,749.27	190,508.33	954,159.53
April	116,004.84	306,513.17	1,070,164.36
May	127,168.83	433,682.00	1,197,333.20
June	89,589.80	523,271.80	1,286,923.00
FY 2009	**1,159,572.55**	**560,309.30**	**1,159,572.55**
FY 2010	**682,225.31**		**682,225.31**
Grand Total	**3,824,285.61**		

FIGURE 4-22 Sales YTD Fiscal resets correctly, at the end of July.

Obviously, different calculations might require different approaches, but the standard time-intelligence functions provided in DAX can be easily adapted to fiscal calendars. In the last section of this chapter we will cover weekly calendars, which are another useful variation on calendars. If you have different needs, or if you need to work with even more complex calendars, then you need to follow a more complex approach; we suggest you look at the time-intelligence patterns at http://www.daxpatterns.com/time-patterns/.

The important point for the sake of this book is that you do not need additional tables to handle fiscal calendars in a smooth way. If your Date table is designed and used the right way, then handling different calendars is very simple and can be achieved by simply updating your Calendar table.

If you let Power BI Desktop or Excel handle the creation of time-intelligence columns for you, then you cannot adopt this simple technique. You will be on your own in trying to figure out how to write the correct formulas.

Computing with working days

Not all days are working days. Often, you need to perform calculations that take into account this difference. For example, you might want to compute the difference between two dates expressed in working days, or you might want to compute the number of working days in a given period. In this section, we discuss the options for handling working days from the data-modeling point of view.

The first (and most important) consideration is whether a day is always a working day, or if this information might depend on other factors. For example, if you work with different countries, then it is very likely that a given day could be a working day in one country or region and a holiday in another. Thus, a day might be a working day or not, depending on the country or region. As you will see, you need more complex models for holidays depending on the country or region. It is better to start by looking at the simpler model, which is the one with holidays for a single country or region.

Working days in a single country or region

We will start with a simple data model that includes Date, Product, and Sales tables, although we will focus on Date. Our starting Date table looks like the one shown in Figure 4-23.

Date	DateKey	Calendar Year	Month Number	Month	Day of Week Number	Day of Week
1/1/05	20050101	CY 2005		1 January	7	Saturday
2/1/05	20050102	CY 2005		1 January	1	Sunday
3/1/05	20050103	CY 2005		1 January	2	Monday
4/1/05	20050104	CY 2005		1 January	3	Tuesday
5/1/05	20050105	CY 2005		1 January	4	Wednesday
6/1/05	20050106	CY 2005		1 January	5	Thursday
7/1/05	20050107	CY 2005		1 January	6	Friday
8/1/05	20050108	CY 2005		1 January	7	Saturday
9/1/05	20050109	CY 2005		1 January	1	Sunday
10/1/05	20050110	CY 2005		1 January	2	Monday
11/1/05	20050111	CY 2005		1 January	3	Tuesday
12/1/05	20050112	CY 2005		1 January	4	Wednesday
13/1/05	20050113	CY 2005		1 January	5	Thursday

FIGURE 4-23   The starting point of a working-days analysis is a simple Date table.

The table contains no information about whether a day is a working day or not. For this example, let us presume there are two kinds of non-working days: weekends and holidays. If, in your country, the weekend is on Saturday and Sunday, then you can easily create a calculated column that tells you whether a day is a weekend or not, like in the following code. If the weekend is on different days, then you will need to change the following formula to make it work in your specific scenario:

```
'Date'[IsWorkingDay] =
INT (
    AND (
        'Date'[Day of Week Number] <> 1,
        'Date'[Day of Week Number] <> 7
    )
)
```

We converted the Boolean condition to an integer to make it easier to sum its value and count the number of working days. In fact, the number of working days in a period is easy to obtain with a measure like the following one:

```
NumOfWorkingDays = SUM ( 'Date'[IsWorkingDay] )
```

This measure already computes a good number, as shown in Figure 4-24.

Calendar Year	Month	NumOfWorkingDays
CY 2005	January	21
	February	20
	March	23
	April	21
	May	22
	June	22
	July	21
	August	23
	September	22
	October	21
	November	22
	December	22
	Total	260

FIGURE 4-24 NumOfWorkingDays computes the number of working days for any period selected.

So far, we have accounted for Saturdays and Sundays. There are also holidays to take into account, however. For this example, we gathered the list of US federal holidays in 2009 from *www.timeanddate.com*. We then used the query editor in Power BI Desktop to generate the table shown in Figure 4-25.

Date	Weekday	Holiday name	Holiday type
01/01/2009	Thursday	New Year's Day	Federal Holiday
19/01/2009	Monday	Martin Luther King Day	Federal Holiday
16/02/2009	Monday	Presidents' Day	Federal Holiday
25/05/2009	Monday	Memorial Day	Federal Holiday
03/07/2009	Friday	Independence Day observed	Federal Holiday
04/07/2009	Saturday	Independence Day	Federal Holiday
07/09/2009	Monday	Labor Day	Federal Holiday
12/10/2009	Monday	Columbus Day	Federal Holiday
11/11/2009	Wednesday	Veterans Day	Federal Holiday
26/11/2009	Thursday	Thanksgiving Day	Federal Holiday
25/12/2009	Friday	Christmas Day	Federal Holiday

FIGURE 4-25 The Holidays table shows a list of US federal holidays.

At this point, you have two options, depending on whether the Date column in the Holidays table is a key. If so, you can create a relationship between Date and Holidays to generate a model like the one shown in Figure 4-26.

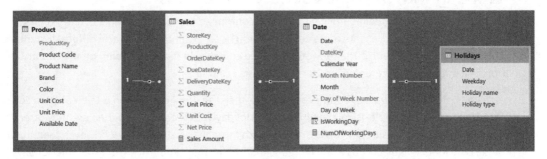

FIGURE 4-26 Holidays can be related to the model easily if Date is a primary key.

After the relationship is set, you can modify the code for the IsWorkingDay calculated column to add a further check. This check notes that a given day is a working day if it is not Saturday or Sunday or it does not appear in the Holidays table. Observe the following code:

```
'Date'[IsWorkingDay] =
INT (
    AND (
        AND (
            'Date'[Day of Week Number] <> 1,
            'Date'[Day of Week Number] <> 7
        ),
        ISBLANK ( RELATED ( Holidays[Date] ) )
    )
)
```

This model is very similar to a star schema. It is a snowflake, and because of the small size of both the Date and the Holidays tables, performance is totally fine.

Sometimes, the Date column in the Holidays table is not a key. For example, if multiple holidays fall on the same day, you will have multiple rows in Holidays with the same date. In such cases, you must modify the relationship as a one-to-many, with Date as the target and Holidays as the source (remember, Date is definitely a primary key in the Date table), and change the code as follows:

```
'Date'[IsWorkingDay] =
INT (
    AND (
        AND (
            'Date'[Day of Week Number] <> 1,
            'Date'[Day of Week Number] <> 7
        ),
        ISEMPTY ( RELATEDTABLE ( Holidays ) )
    )
)
```

The only line changed is the one that checks whether the date appears in the Holidays table. Instead of using the faster RELATED, you use RELATEDTABLE and verify its emptiness. Because we are working with a calculated column, the small degradation in performance is completely acceptable.

Working with multiple countries or regions

As you have learned, modeling holidays when you only need to manage a single country is pretty straightforward. Things become more complex if you need to handle holidays in different countries. This is because you can no longer rely on calculated columns. In fact, depending on the country selection, you might have different values for the IsHoliday column.

If you only have a couple of countries to handle, then the simplest solution is to create two columns for IsHoliday—for example, IsHolidayChina and IsHolidayUnitedStates—and then use the correct column for various measures. If you are dealing with more than two countries, however, then this technique is no longer viable. Let us examine the scenario in its full complexity. Note that the Holidays table has different content from before, as shown in Figure 4-27. Specifically, the Holidays table contains a new column that indicates the country or region where the holiday is defined: CountryRegion. The date is no longer a key because the same date can be a holiday in different countries.

Date	Weekday	Holiday name	Holiday type	CountryRegion
01/01/2009	Thursday	New Year's Day	National holiday	China
01/01/2009	Thursday	New Year's Day	Federal Holiday	United States
01/01/2009	Thursday	New Year's Day	National holiday	Germany
01/05/2009	Friday	Labour Day	National holiday	China
01/05/2009	Friday	May Day	National holiday	Germany
01/06/2009	Monday	Whit Monday	National holiday	Germany
01/10/2009	Thursday	National Day	National holiday	China
02/10/2009	Friday	National Day Golden Week holiday	National holiday	China
03/07/2009	Friday	Independence Day observed	Federal Holiday	United States
03/10/2009	Saturday	National Day Golden Week holiday	National holiday	China
03/10/2009	Saturday	Mid-Autumn Festival	National holiday	China
03/10/2009	Saturday	Day of German Unity	National holiday	Germany
04/07/2009	Saturday	Independence Day	Federal Holiday	United States

FIGURE 4-27 This Holidays table contains holidays in different countries.

The data model is a slight variation of the previous model, as shown in Figure 4-28. The main difference is that the relationship between Date and Holidays is now in the opposite direction.

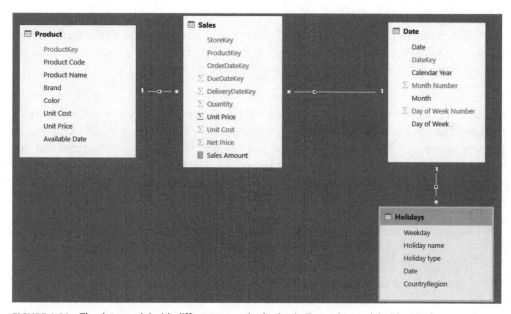

FIGURE 4-28 The data model with different countries looks similar to the model with a single country.

The problem with multiple countries is that you need to better understand the meaning of the numbers to produce. The simple question of "how many working days are in January?" no longer has a clear meaning. In fact, unless you specify a country, the number of working days cannot be computed anymore.

To better understand the issue, consider Figure 4-29. The measure in the report is just a COUNTROWS of the Holidays table, so it computes the number of holidays in each country.

Month	China	Germany	United States	Total
January	4	1	2	**7**
February			1	**1**
April	1	1		**2**
May	2	2	1	**5**
June		1		**1**
July			2	**2**
September			1	**1**
October	4	1	1	**6**
November			2	**2**
December		2	1	**3**
Total	**11**	**8**	**11**	**30**

FIGURE 4-29 The figure shows the number of holidays per country and month.

The numbers are correct for each given country, but at the total-per-month level, they are just a sum of the individual cells; the total does not consider that one day might be a holiday in one country and not a holiday in another. In February, for example, there is a single holiday in the United States, but no holidays in either China or Germany. Thus, what is the total number of holidays in February? The question, posed in this way, makes little sense if you are interested in comparing holidays with working days, for example. In fact, the cumulative total number of holidays for all countries isn't helpful at all. The answer strongly depends on the country you are analyzing.

At this point in the definition of the model, you need to better clarify the meaning of whether a day is a working day or not. Before your computation, you can check whether a single country has been selected in the report by using the IF (HASONEVALUE ()) pattern of DAX.

There is another point to observe before reaching the final formula. You might want to compute the number of working days by subtracting the number of holidays (retrieved from the Holidays table) from the total number of days. In doing so, however, you are not taking into account Saturdays and Sundays. Moreover, if a holiday happens to be on a weekend, then you do not need to take it into account, either. You can solve this problem by using the bidirectional filtering pattern and counting the dates that are neither Saturday nor Sunday and that do not appear in the Holidays table. Thus, the formula would be as follows:

```
NumOfWorkingDays :=
IF (
    OR (
        HASONEVALUE ( Holidays[CountryRegion] ),
        ISEMPTY ( Holidays )
    ),
    CALCULATE (
        COUNTROWS ( 'Date' ),
        AND (
            'Date'[Day of Week Number] <> 1,
            'Date'[Day of Week Number] <> 7
        ),
        EXCEPT ( VALUES ( 'Date'[Date] ), VALUES ( Holidays[Date] ) )
    )
)
```

There are two interesting points in this formula, which are highlighted with a bold font. Following is an explanation of both:

- You need to check that there is only a single value for CountryRegion to protect the measure from showing numbers when multiple countries or regions are selected. At the same time, you need to check if the Holidays table is empty, because for months with no holidays, the CountryRegion column will have zero values and HASONEVALUE will return False.

- As a filter for CALCULATE, you can use the EXCEPT function to retrieve the dates that are not holidays. This set will be put in a logical AND with the set of days that are not in the weekend, producing the final correct result.

Still, the model is not yet perfect. In fact, we are assuming that weekends always happen during Saturday and Sunday, but there are several countries and regions where the weekend falls on different days. If you need to take this into account, then you must make the model slightly more complex. You will need another table that contains the weekdays that are to be considered part of the weekend on a country-by-country basis. Because you have two different tables that need to be filtered by country, you will need to transform the country into a dimension by itself. The complete model is shown in Figure 4-30.

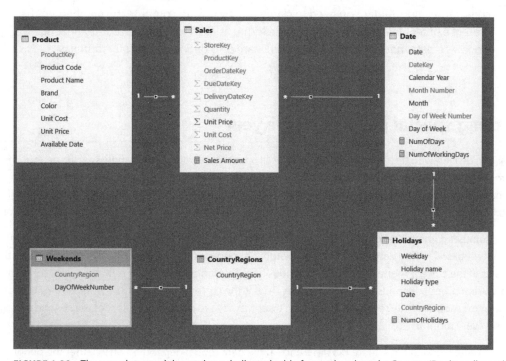

FIGURE 4-30 The complete model contains a dedicated table for weekends and a Country/Regions dimension.

The code is indeed slightly simpler, although it may be a bit harder to read, as shown in the following:

```
NumOfWorkingDays :=
IF (
    HASONEVALUE ( CountryRegions[CountryRegion] ),
    CALCULATE (
        COUNTROWS ( 'Date' ),
        EXCEPT (
            VALUES ( 'Date'[Day of Week Number] ),
            VALUES ( Weekends[Day of Week Number] )
        ),
        EXCEPT ( VALUES ( 'Date'[Date] ), VALUES ( Holidays[Date] ) )
    )
)
```

This latter formula uses the same pattern of the EXCEPT function that is used for holidays and the weekday number. It takes into account the weekday number that needs to be considered as a non-working day in the given country.

> **Note** When the model becomes more complex, you need to author more complex DAX code. More importantly, you need to clarify exactly how to compute the numbers. In the presence of multiple countries, the simple formulas used for a single country no longer work. As a data modeler, you need to work harder to define meaningful formulas.

Handling special periods of the year

When dealing with time intelligence, you typically need to highlight and handle specific periods of the year. For example, if you are analyzing the booking of hotels, the Easter period is relevant, and you might want to compare the performance of Easter in different years. The problem is that Easter falls on different dates every year. Thus, you need to identify a variable period of the year to make comparisons.

Another common requirement is to build reports or dashboards that automatically update their content based on the date of refresh. For example, suppose you want a dashboard that compares the sales of the current month against the previous one. This time the problem is that the very concept of a current month depends on the current day. Today, the current month may be April, but for the same day next month, it will be May, and you don't want to have to update the filters of the dashboard each and every month.

As with working days, there is a difference in the data model depending on whether the periods you want to analyze are overlapping or not.

Using non-overlapping periods

If the periods of time you want to analyze are non-overlapping, then the data model is somewhat easy to build. Similarly to what you did with holidays in the previous sections, you first need a configuration table to store the periods you want to analyze. In our example, we created a table with the Easter and Christmas dates for 2008, 2009, and 2010, because we want them to be a period in time instead of a single date (as was the case for the holidays). The configuration table is shown in Figure 4-31.

Date	DaysBefore	DaysAfter	Description
December 4, 2009	4	3	Easter
March 23, 2008	4	3	Easter
March 27, 2010	4	3	Easter
December 25, 2009	2	1	Christmas
December 25, 2008	2	1	Chirstmas
December 25, 2010	2	1	Christmas

FIGURE 4-31 The figure shows the configuration of special periods in the SpecialPeriods table.

Each Easter period starts some days before the given date and ends a few days after. Even if the SpecialPeriods table contains a date that is also a primary key for the table, it does not make any sense to build a relationship. In fact, the only relevant information in SpecialPeriods is the name of the period we want to analyze, and it is better to denormalize the special period description in a calculated column in Date. To do so, use the following code:

```
'Date'[SpecialPeriod] =
CALCULATE (
    VALUES ( SpecialPeriods[Description] ),
    FILTER (
        SpecialPeriods,
        AND (
            SpecialPeriods[Date] - SpecialPeriods[DaysBefore] <= 'Date'[Date],
            SpecialPeriods[Date] + SpecialPeriods[DaysAfter] > 'Date'[Date]
        )
    )
)
```

The column will store the special period name if the current date falls between the following:

- The date of the special period minus the number of days before it

- The same date plus the number of days after it

You can see the result of this calculated column for Easter 2008 in Figure 4-32.

Once the column is in place, it will filter different periods in different years. This makes it possible to compare the sales of the same special period in different years without worrying about when it occurred. You can see this in Figure 4-33.

Date ↓	DateKey	Calendar Year	Month Number	Month	Day of Week Number	Day of Week	SpecialPeriod
3/11/2008	20080311	CY 2008	3	March	3	Tuesday	
3/12/2008	20080312	CY 2008	3	March	4	Wednesday	
3/13/2008	20080313	CY 2008	3	March	5	Thursday	
3/14/2008	20080314	CY 2008	3	March	6	Friday	
3/15/2008	20080315	CY 2008	3	March	7	Saturday	
3/16/2008	20080316	CY 2008	3	March	1	Sunday	
3/17/2008	20080317	CY 2008	3	March	2	Monday	
3/18/2008	20080318	CY 2008	3	March	3	Tuesday	
3/19/2008	20080319	CY 2008	3	March	4	Wednesday	Easter
3/20/2008	20080320	CY 2008	3	March	5	Thursday	Easter
3/21/2008	20080321	CY 2008	3	March	6	Friday	Easter
3/22/2008	20080322	CY 2008	3	March	7	Saturday	Easter
3/23/2008	20080323	CY 2008	3	March	1	Sunday	Easter
3/24/2008	20080324	CY 2008	3	March	2	Monday	Easter
3/25/2008	20080325	CY 2008	3	March	3	Tuesday	Easter
3/26/2008	20080326	CY 2008	3	March	4	Wednesday	
3/27/2008	20080327	CY 2008	3	March	5	Thursday	

FIGURE 4-32 When a date falls in a special period, it is marked with the period name.

SpecialPeriod	CY 2008	CY 2009	Total
Christmas	6,940.20	30,625.28	**37,565.48**
Easter	18,426.43	32,875.65	**51,302.07**
Total	**25,366.63**	**63,500.93**	**88,867.55**

FIGURE 4-33 This report shows sales for Easter and Christmas in 2008 and 2009.

This technique works fine, and it is very simple to implement, but it comes with a severe limitation: The periods cannot overlap. In fact, if you store overlapping periods in the configuration table, the column will produce an error for all the rows that belong to different periods. Nevertheless, there are many scenarios where this limitation is not an issue. In this case, it is the easiest way to handle special periods. You learn how to handle overlapping periods later in this chapter in the section "Using overlapping periods."

Periods relative to today

In the previous section, you learned how to handle non-overlapping special periods by storing the information in a configuration table. You can adopt a very similar technique to create reports that update their content in a dynamic way. Imagine, for example, that you want to build a dashboard like the one in Figure 4-34, which shows sales of different brands over different time periods along with a gauge that compares the sales of today against the sales of yesterday.

SalesOfToday and SalesOfYesterday

$2.57K

$0,00K $4,93K

Brand	Today	Yesterday	Last 7 days	Last 30 days	Older	Total
A. Datum			241,20	1.800,00	176.431,21	178.472,41
Adventure Works				2.819,82	345.706,27	348.526,09
Contoso	25,11	1.327,50	5.353,07	10.887,87	432.935,37	450.528,93
Fabrikam		3.604,50	10.015,20	568,80	276.107,04	290.295,54
Litware				5.700,87	160.370,70	166.071,57
Northwind Traders				9.822,06	133.477,20	143.299,26
Proseware	2.548,80			7.059,00	164.721,10	174.328,90
Southridge Video			198,78	4.121,90	116.785,81	121.106,49
Tailspin Toys			67,36	1.069,47	14.273,33	15.410,16
The Phone Company				6.012,00	59.671,20	65.683,20
Wide World Importers			2.483,89	20.291,25	128.311,48	151.086,62
Total	2.573,91	4.932,00	18.359,51	70.153,03	2.008.790,71	2.104.809,17

FIGURE 4-34 The report contains a gauge, suitable for a dashboard, that shows the sales of today versus yesterday.

The very concept of *today* depends on when the report was last refreshed. Of course, you do not want to hard-code the date into the formulas. What you want is that every time you refresh the model, it automatically checks what the last available date in the model is and adapts its content accordingly. In such a case, you can use a variation of the previous data model where, this time, the time periods are computed in a dynamic way.

First, you need to prepare a configuration table, like the one shown in Figure 4-35, where you store the descriptions of the periods along with the number of days, relative to today, to consider.

Description	DaysTo	DaysFrom	Code
Today	0	-1	1
Yesterday	1	0	2
Last 7 days	7	1	3
Last 30 days	30	7	4
Older	99999999	30	5

FIGURE 4-35 The RelativePeriods configuration table displays the special periods that are relative to the current day.

Each period has the number of days before today, a description, and a code. The days falling between DatesFrom and DaysTo, relative to today, will be tagged with the description. The code is mainly useful for sorting purposes. Once the table is in place, you need to retrieve the code (for sorting) and the description to tag each date as belonging to the appropriate period. This can be easily accomplished through two calculated columns in Date. The first one computes the code of the relative period and is the following definition:

```
'Date'[RelPeriodCode] =
VAR LastSalesDateKey =
    MAX ( Sales[OrderDateKey] )
VAR LastSaleDate =
    LOOKUPVALUE( 'Date'[Date], 'Date'[DateKey], LastSalesDateKey )
VAR DeltaDays =
    INT ( LastSaleDate - 'Date'[Date] )
VAR ValidPeriod =
    CALCULATETABLE(
        RelativePeriods,
        RelativePeriods[DaysTo] >= DeltaDays,
        RelativePeriods[DaysFrom] < DeltaDays
    )
RETURN
    CALCULATE ( VALUES ( RelativePeriods[Code] ), ValidPeriod )
```

This code performs all its steps through the usage of variables. First, it retrieves the last OrderDateKey from Sales to grab the key of the last available date, which we will consider as today. Once it has the key, it uses LOOKUPVALUE to compute the date associated with the key. DeltaDays represents the difference between today and the current date. All those values are finally used in CALCULATETABLE to compute, in ValidPeriod, the only row of the RelativePeriods table that includes DeltaPeriod between DaysFrom and DaysTo.

The result of this formula is the code of the relative period to which the given date belongs. Once the calculated column with the code is there, you can compute the description of the relative period as follows:

```
'Date'[RelPeriod] =
VAR RelPeriod =
    LOOKUPVALUE(
        RelativePeriods[Description],
        RelativePeriods[Code],
        'Date'[RelPeriodCode]
    )
RETURN
    IF ( ISBLANK ( RelPeriod ), "Future", RelPeriod )
```

The two columns (RelPeriodCode and RelPeriod) are shown in the Date table in Figure 4-36.

Date	DateKey	Calendar Year	Month Number	Month	Day of Week Number	Day of Week	RelPeriodCode	RelPeriod
15/8/08	20080815	CY 2008	8	August	6	Friday		Future
14/8/08	20080814	CY 2008	8	August	5	Thursday		Future
13/8/08	20080813	CY 2008	8	August	4	Wednesday		Future
12/8/08	20080812	CY 2008	8	August	3	Tuesday		Future
11/8/08	20080811	CY 2008	8	August	2	Monday	1	Today
10/8/08	20080810	CY 2008	8	August	1	Sunday	2	Yesterday
9/8/08	20080809	CY 2008	8	August	7	Saturday	3	Last 7 days
8/8/08	20080808	CY 2008	8	August	6	Friday	3	Last 7 days
7/8/08	20080807	CY 2008	8	August	5	Thursday	3	Last 7 days
6/8/08	20080806	CY 2008	8	August	4	Wednesday	3	Last 7 days
5/8/08	20080805	CY 2008	8	August	3	Tuesday	3	Last 7 days
4/8/08	20080804	CY 2008	8	August	2	Monday	3	Last 7 days
3/8/08	20080803	CY 2008	8	August	1	Sunday	4	Last 30 days
2/8/08	20080802	CY 2008	8	August	7	Saturday	4	Last 30 days
1/8/08	20080801	CY 2008	8	August	6	Friday	4	Last 30 days
31/7/08	20080731	CY 2008	7	July	5	Thursday	4	Last 30 days

FIGURE 4-36 The last two columns are computed using the formulas described in the previous paragraphs.

Being calculated columns, they are recomputed at every refresh of the data model. In this way, they change the tags assigned to the dates. You do not need to update the report, as it will always show the last processed day as today, the day before as yesterday, and so on.

Using overlapping periods

The techniques you have seen in the previous sections work fine, but they all have one strong limitation: The time periods cannot overlap. In fact, because you store the attribute that defines the time period in a calculated column, there can only be one value assigned to the column.

There are, however, scenarios where this is not possible. Suppose, for example, that you put some product categories on sale in different periods of the year. It is totally possible that, in the same period, more than one product category is on sale. At the same time, the same category might be on sale during multiple different time periods. Thus, in such a scenario, you cannot store the period of sales in the Products table or in the Date table.

A scenario in which you have many rows (categories) that need to be in relationships with many rows (dates) is known as a *many-to-many model*. Many-to-many models are not easy to manage, but they provide extremely useful analyses and are worth describing. You will find a much more complete discussion on many-to-many models in Chapter 8, "Many-to-many relationships." In this section, we only want to show that when many-to-many relationships are involved, the code tends to be harder to write.

The Discounts configuration table from this example is shown in Figure 4-37.

Description	DateStart	DateEnd	Category
January Sales	1/1/2007	1/31/2007	Computers
January Sales	1/1/2008	1/31/2008	Computers
Start with Audio	1/1/2007	1/15/2007	Audio
Start with Audio	1/1/2008	1/15/2008	Audio
Summer Music	8/1/2007	8/15/2007	Audio
Summer Music	8/1/2008	8/15/2008	Audio
Holidays calls home	7/15/2007	8/15/2007	Cell phones
Holidays calls home	7/15/2007	8/15/2007	Cell phones

FIGURE 4-37 Different sales periods for different categories are stored in the Discounts configuration table.

Looking at the Discounts configuration table, you can see that in the first week of January 2007 and 2008, there are multiple categories on sale (computers and audio). The same applies to the first two weeks of August (audio and cell phones). In such a scenario, you can no longer rely on relationships, and you need to write DAX code that takes the current filter from the sale period and merges it with the already existing filter in Sales. This is accomplished by the following formula:

```
SalesInPeriod :=
SUMX (
    Discounts,
    CALCULATE (
        [Sales Amount],
        INTERSECT (
            VALUES ( 'Date'[Date] ),
            DATESBETWEEN ( 'Date'[Date], Discounts[DateStart], Discounts[DateEnd] )
        ),
        INTERSECT (
            VALUES ( 'Product'[Category] ),
            CALCULATETABLE ( VALUES ( Discounts[Category] ) )
        )
    )
)
```

Using this formula, you can build reports like the one shown in Figure 4-38.

Category	Description	CY 2007	CY 2008	Total
Computers	January Sales	$9,842.11	$20,450.43	**$30,292.54**
	Total	**$9,842.11**	**$20,450.43**	**$30,292.54**
Cell phones	Holidays calls home	$1,556.69		**$1,556.69**
	Total	**$1,556.69**		**$1,556.69**
Audio	Start with Audio	$492.22		**$492.22**
	Summer Music	$35.07		**$35.07**
	Total	**$527.30**		**$527.30**
Total		**$11,926.09**	**$20,450.43**	**$32,376.53**

FIGURE 4-38 When using overlapping periods, you can browse different periods in the same year.

The report in Figure 4-38 shows the sales of different categories over different years, even if the periods overlap. In this case, the model remained fairly simple because we could not rely on changes in the model to make the code easier to write. You will see several examples similar to this one in Chapter 7, but in that chapter we will also create different data models to show how to write simpler (and maybe faster) code. In general, many-to-many relationships are powerful and easy to use, but writing the code to make them work is sometimes (like in this case) difficult.

The reason we wanted to show you this example is not to scare you or to show you a scenario where the model fails in making the code simple to write. It is simply that if you want to produce complex reports, sooner or later, you will need to author complex DAX code.

Working with weekly calendars

As you learned, as long as you work with standard calendars, you can easily compute measures like year-to-date (YTD), month-to-date (MTD), and the same period last year, because DAX offers you a set of predefined functions that perform exactly these types of calculation. This becomes much more complex as soon as you need to work with non-standard calendars, however.

What is a non-standard calendar? It is any kind of calendar that does not follow the canonical division of 12 months, with different days per month. For example, many businesses need to work with weeks instead of months. Unfortunately, weeks do not aggregate in months or years. In fact, a month is made of a variable number of weeks, as is a year. Moreover, there are some common techniques in the handling of weekly based years, but none are a standard that can be formalized in a DAX function. For this reason, DAX does not offer any functionality to handle non-standard calendars. If you need to manage them, you are on your own.

Luckily, even with no predefined function, you can leverage certain modeling techniques to perform time intelligence over non-standard calendars. This section does not cover them all. Our goal here is simply to show you some examples that you will probably need to adapt to your specific needs in the event you want to adopt them. If you are interested in more information about this topic, you will find a more complete treatment here: *http://www.daxpatterns.com/time-patterns/*.

As an example of non-standard calendar, you will learn how to handle weekly based calculations using the ISO 8601 standard. If you are interested in more information about this way of handling weeks, you can find it here: *https://en.wikipedia.org/wiki/ISO_week_date*.

The first step is to build a proper ISO Calendar table. There are many ways to build one. Chances are you already have a well-defined ISO calendar in your database. For this example, we will build an ISO calendar using standard DAX and a lookup table, as this provides a good opportunity to learn more modeling tricks.

The calendar we are using is based on weeks. A week always starts on Monday, and a year always starts when its first week starts. Because of this, it is very likely that a year might start, for example, on the 29th of December of the previous year or on the 2nd of January of the current calendar year.

To handle this, you can add calculated columns to a standard Calendar table to compute the ISO Week number and the ISO Year number. By using the following definitions, you will be able to create a table that contains Calendar Week, ISO Week, and ISO Year columns, as outlined in Figure 4-39:

```
'Date'[Calendar Week] = WEEKNUM ( 'Date'[Date], 2 )

'Date'[ISO Week] = WEEKNUM ('Date'[Date], 21 )

'Date'[ISO Year] =
CONCATENATE (
    "ISO ",
    IF (
        AND ( 'Date'[ISO Week] < 5, 'Date'[Calendar Week] > 50 ),
        YEAR ( 'Date'[Date] ) + 1,
        IF (
            AND ( 'Date'[ISO Week] > 50, 'Date'[Calendar Week] < 5 ),
            YEAR ( 'Date'[Date] ) - 1,
            YEAR ( 'Date'[Date] )
        )
    )
)
```

Date	DateKey	Calendar Year	Month Number	Month	Day of Week Number	Day of Week	ISO Week	Calendar Week	ISO Year
1/1/2005	20050101	CY 2005	1	January	7	Saturday	53	1	ISO 2004
1/2/2005	20050102	CY 2005	1	January	1	Sunday	53	1	ISO 2004
1/3/2005	20050103	CY 2005	1	January	2	Monday	1	2	ISO 2005
1/4/2005	20050104	CY 2005	1	January	3	Tuesday	1	2	ISO 2005
1/5/2005	20050105	CY 2005	1	January	4	Wednesday	1	2	ISO 2005
1/6/2005	20050106	CY 2005	1	January	5	Thursday	1	2	ISO 2005
1/7/2005	20050107	CY 2005	1	January	6	Friday	1	2	ISO 2005
1/8/2005	20050108	CY 2005	1	January	7	Saturday	1	2	ISO 2005
1/9/2005	20050109	CY 2005	1	January	1	Sunday	1	2	ISO 2005
1/10/2005	20050110	CY 2005	1	January	2	Monday	2	3	ISO 2005
1/11/2005	20050111	CY 2005	1	January	3	Tuesday	2	3	ISO 2005
1/12/2005	20050112	CY 2005	1	January	4	Wednesday	2	3	ISO 2005
1/13/2005	20050113	CY 2005	1	January	5	Thursday	2	3	ISO 2005
1/14/2005	20050114	CY 2005	1	January	6	Friday	2	3	ISO 2005
1/15/2005	20050115	CY 2005	1	January	7	Saturday	2	3	ISO 2005
1/16/2005	20050116	CY 2005	1	January	1	Sunday	2	3	ISO 2005

FIGURE 4-39 The ISO year is different from the calendar year because ISO years always start on Monday.

While the week and month can be easily computed with a simple calculated column, the ISO month requires a bit more attention. With the ISO standard, there are different ways to compute the month number. One is to start by dividing the four quarters. Each quarter has three months, and the months are built using one of three groupings: 445, 454, or 544. The digits in these numbers stand for the number of weeks to include in each month. For example, in 445, the first two months in a quarter contain four weeks, whereas the last month contains five weeks. The same concept applies to the other techniques. Instead of searching for a complex mathematical formula that computes the month to which a week belongs in the different standard, it is easier to build a simple lookup table like the one shown in Figure 4-40.

Week	Period445	Period454	Period544
1	1	1	1
2	1	1	1
3	1	1	1
4	1	1	1
5	2	2	1
6	2	2	2
7	2	2	2
8	2	2	2
9	3	2	2
10	3	3	3
11	3	3	3
12	3	3	3
13	3	3	3
14	4	4	4
15	4	4	4
16	4	4	4
17	4	4	4
18	5	5	4

FIGURE 4-40 The Weeks to Months lookup table maps week numbers to months using three columns (one for each technique).

When this Weeks to Months lookup table is in place, you can use the LOOKUPVALUE function with the following code:

```
'Date'[ISO Month] =
CONCATENATE
    "ISO M",
    RIGHT (
        CONCATENATE (
            "00",
            LOOKUPVALUE(
                'Weks To Months'[Period445],
                'Weks To Months'[Week],
                'Date'[ISO Week]
            ),
        2
    )
)
```

The resulting table contains the year and the month, as shown in Figure 4-41.

Date	DateKey	Calendar Year	Month Number	Month	Day of Week Number	Day of Week	ISO Week	Calendar Week	ISO Year	ISO Month
1/1/2005	20050101	CY 2005	1	January		7 Saturday	53	1	ISO 2004	ISO M12
1/2/2005	20050102	CY 2005	1	January		1 Sunday	53	1	ISO 2004	ISO M12
1/3/2005	20050103	CY 2005	1	January		2 Monday	1	2	ISO 2005	ISO M01
1/4/2005	20050104	CY 2005	1	January		3 Tuesday	1	2	ISO 2005	ISO M01
1/5/2005	20050105	CY 2005	1	January		4 Wednesday	1	2	ISO 2005	ISO M01
1/6/2005	20050106	CY 2005	1	January		5 Thursday	1	2	ISO 2005	ISO M01
1/7/2005	20050107	CY 2005	1	January		6 Friday	1	2	ISO 2005	ISO M01
1/8/2005	20050108	CY 2005	1	January		7 Saturday	1	2	ISO 2005	ISO M01
1/9/2005	20050109	CY 2005	1	January		1 Sunday	1	2	ISO 2005	ISO M01
1/10/2005	20050110	CY 2005	1	January		2 Monday	2	3	ISO 2005	ISO M01
1/11/2005	20050111	CY 2005	1	January		3 Tuesday	2	3	ISO 2005	ISO M01
1/12/2005	20050112	CY 2005	1	January		4 Wednesday	2	3	ISO 2005	ISO M01
1/13/2005	20050113	CY 2005	1	January		5 Thursday	2	3	ISO 2005	ISO M01
1/14/2005	20050114	CY 2005	1	January		6 Friday	2	3	ISO 2005	ISO M01

FIGURE 4-41 The ISO month is easily computed using a lookup table.

Now that all the columns are in place, you can easily build a hierarchy and start browsing your model splitting by ISO years, months, and weeks. Nevertheless, on such a calendar, computing values like YTD, MTD, and other time-intelligence calculations will prove to be a bit more challenging. In fact, the canonical DAX functions are designed to work only on standard Gregorian calendars. They are useless if your calendar is non-standard.

This requires you to build the time-intelligence calculations in a different way—that is, without leveraging the predefined functions. For example, to compute ISO YTD, you can use the following measure:

```
Sales ISO YTD :=
IF (
    HASONEVALUE ( 'Date'[ISO Year] ),
    CALCULATE (
        [Sales Amount],
        ALL ('Date' ),
        FILTER ( ALL ( 'Date'[Date] ), 'Date'[Date] <= MAX ( 'Date'[Date] ) ),
        VALUES ( 'Date'[ISO Year] )
    )
)
```

As you can see, the core of the measure is the set of filters you need to apply to the Calendar table to find the correct set of dates that compose the YTD. Figure 4-42 shows the result.

ISO Year	ISO Month	Sales Amount	Sales ISO YTD
ISO 2007	ISO M01	97,104.79	97,104.79
ISO 2007	ISO M02	97,133.79	194,238.58
ISO 2007	ISO M03	144,911.08	339,149.66
ISO 2007	ISO M04	106,741.46	445,891.12
ISO 2007	ISO M05	118,319.01	564,210.13
ISO 2007	ISO M06	131,504.47	695,714.60
ISO 2007	ISO M07	115,924.73	811,639.33
ISO 2007	ISO M08	96,647.19	908,286.52
ISO 2007	ISO M09	169,319.47	1,077,606.00
ISO 2007	ISO M10	91,261.55	1,168,867.54
ISO 2007	ISO M11	117,902.14	1,286,769.69
ISO 2007	ISO M12	169,009.75	1,455,779.43
ISO 2008	ISO M01	67,106.83	67,106.83
ISO 2008	ISO M02	49,376.15	116,482.98

FIGURE 4-42 The ISO YTD measure computes YTD for the ISO calendar, which is a non-standard calendar.

Computing month-to-date (MTD), quarter-to-date (QTD), and measures using a similar pattern is indeed very easy. Things get a bit more complex, however, if you want to compute, for example, calculations like the same period last year. In fact, because you cannot rely on the SAMEPERIODLASTYEAR function, you need to work a bit more on both the data model and the DAX code.

To compute the same period last year, you need to identify the date currently selected in the filter context and then find the same set of dates in the previous year. You cannot use the Date column for this because the ISO date has a completely different structure than the calendar date. Thus, the first step is to add a new column to the Calendar table that contains the ISO day number in the year. This can be accomplished easily with the following calculated column:

```
Date[ISO Day Number] = ( 'Date'[ISO Week] - 1 ) * 7 + WEEKDAY( 'Date'[Date], 2 )
```

You can see the resulting column in Figure 4-43.

Date	↓ DateKey	Calendar Year	Month Number	Month	Day of Week Number	Day of Week	ISO Week	ISO Year	ISO Day Number
1/1/05	20050101	CY 2005		1 January	7	Saturday	53	ISO 2004	370
2/1/05	20050102	CY 2005		1 January	1	Sunday	53	ISO 2004	371
3/1/05	20050103	CY 2005		1 January	2	Monday	1	ISO 2005	1
4/1/05	20050104	CY 2005		1 January	3	Tuesday	1	ISO 2005	2
5/1/05	20050105	CY 2005		1 January	4	Wednesday	1	ISO 2005	3
6/1/05	20050106	CY 2005		1 January	5	Thursday	1	ISO 2005	4
7/1/05	20050107	CY 2005		1 January	6	Friday	1	ISO 2005	5
8/1/05	20050108	CY 2005		1 January	7	Saturday	1	ISO 2005	6
9/1/05	20050109	CY 2005		1 January	1	Sunday	1	ISO 2005	7
10/1/05	20050110	CY 2005		1 January	2	Monday	2	ISO 2005	8

FIGURE 4-43 The ISO Day Number column shows the incremental number of days in the year, according to the ISO standard.

This column is useful because to find the same selected period in the last year, you can now use the following code:

```
Sales SPLY :=
IF (
    HASONEVALUE ( 'Date'[ISO Year Number] ),
    CALCULATE (
        [Sales Amount],
        ALL ( 'Date' ),
        VALUES ( 'Date'[ISO Day Number] ),
        'Date'[ISO Year Number] = VALUES ( 'Date'[ISO Year Number] ) - 1
    )
)
```

As you can see, the formula removes all filters from the Date table and replaces them with two new conditions:

- The ISO Year Number should be the current year reduced by one.

- The ISO Day Numbers need to be the same.

In this way, no matter what selection you have made in the current filter context, it will be moved back by one year, regardless of whether it is a day, a week, or a month.

In Figure 4-44, you can see the Sales SPLY measure working with a report sliced by year and month.

You can author similar calculations, like the previous month and the percentage of growth against the same period in the last year, using a very similar technique. In scenarios like the latter one, adding a simple column to the model makes it extremely easy to compute values. Performing the same calculation without the ISO Day Number column results in a nearly impossible-to-write formula. You can find more information and different dissertations on this topic at *http://www.sqlbi.com/articles/ week-based-time-intelligence-in-dax/*.

ISO Year	ISO Month	Sales Amount	Sales SPLY
ISO 2007	ISO M01	97.104,79	
ISO 2007	ISO M02	97.133,79	
ISO 2007	ISO M03	144.911,08	
ISO 2007	ISO M04	106.741,46	
ISO 2007	ISO M05	118.319,01	
ISO 2007	ISO M06	131.504,47	
ISO 2007	ISO M07	115.924,73	
ISO 2007	ISO M08	96.647,19	
ISO 2007	ISO M09	169.319,47	
ISO 2007	ISO M10	91.261,55	
ISO 2007	ISO M11	117.902,14	
ISO 2007	ISO M12	169.009,75	
ISO 2008	ISO M01	67.106,83	97.104,79
ISO 2008	ISO M02	49.376,15	97.133,79
ISO 2008	ISO M03	72.586,47	144.911,08
ISO 2008	ISO M04	111.633,80	106.741,46
ISO 2008	ISO M05	98.019,09	118.319,01
ISO 2008	ISO M06	125.591,98	131.504,47
ISO 2008	ISO M07	87.074,22	115.924,73
ISO 2008	ISO M08	114.295,00	96.647,19
ISO 2008	ISO M09	137.011,56	169.319,47
ISO 2008	ISO M10	60.111,91	91.261,55
ISO 2008	ISO M11	96.580,97	117.902,14
ISO 2008	ISO M12	101.328,95	169.009,75

FIGURE 4-44 In ISO Year 2008, the Sales SPLY measure reports the sales of the same period in 2007.

Conclusions

Time intelligence is a very broad and interesting topic. It is likely that any BI solution you will ever author will contain some portion devoted to time intelligence. The most important topics covered in this chapter are as follows:

- Most (if not all) time-intelligence calculations require the presence of a Date table in the model.

- The creation of a Calendar table requires attention to details like the sort order of the months.

- If you have multiple dates in the model, this does not mean you need to have multiple Date tables. Using a single Date table in the model makes all the calculations much easier. If you need multiple dates, you will likely need to load the Date table multiple times.

- It is mandatory to separate date and time, both for performance and modeling reasons.

The remaining part of the chapter was devoted to different scenarios related to time, such as working days in one or multiple countries, computing values for special periods of the year by using new columns in the Date table or new tables in the model, and finally handling calculations with ISO calendars.

Due to the vast amount of diversity that exists in time-intelligence calculations, it is likely that none of the examples we have shown fit perfectly with your specific scenario. Nevertheless, you can use these scenarios as inspiration for your own calculations, which will typically require the creation of some specific columns in the Date table and the authoring of DAX code of medium complexity.

CHAPTER 5

Tracking historical attributes

Data changes over time. For some models and reports, it is useful to track both the current and the historical value of some attributes. For example, you might need to track the different addresses of a customer over time. Or, you might have a product that changes some specifications, and you want to perform an analysis of the sales and performance with the different characteristics. Or, you may want to track the total sales at different price points if there is a change in the price of a product or service. All these are very common scenarios, and there are some standard ways of handling them.

Whenever it is necessary to manage the changing nature of a value, it becomes a matter of dealing with historical attributes—or, in more technical language, slowly changing dimensions. Slowly changing dimensions are not a difficult topic, but they come with some hidden complexity.

In this chapter, we analyze several models that show why this is an important aspect to consider when building your reporting system. The models also show how to manage different scenarios.

Introducing slowly changing dimensions

You typically need to track attributes of dimensions. For example, you might need to know a customer's previous addresses so you can analyze his or her purchases in both the old and new locations. Or, you might need to know the previous producer of some part of your products to analyze their quality and reliability. Because these attributes belong to dimensions, and they typically change slowly over time, they are known as *slowly changing dimensions* (*SCDs*).

Before diving into more technical details, let us discuss briefly when and why you need to use an SCD. Imagine that each of your customers has a sales person assigned to him. The easiest way to store this information is to add the sales manager's name as an attribute of the customer. Over time, this relationship between sales manager and customer can change, such as when an existing customer is assigned to a different sales person. For example, a customer (Nicholas) might have had Paul as a sales manager until last year, but then it changed to Louise. If you simply update the sales manager's name in the Customer table, then when you analyze the sales of Louise, it will look like Louise is responsible for all the sales, including those that Paul made in the past. Thus, the figures will not be correct. You need a data model that correctly assigns sales to the manager who oversaw them at the time when the sales happened.

Depending on how you handle variations, SCDs are classified in different categories. Professionals have not yet come to a consensus on a unique taxonomy for the different ways to handle SCDs. Apart from the very basic scenarios, more complex kinds of variations typically require some creativity in their handling, and when somebody finds a new way to handle an SCD, he or she often creates a new name for it. When it comes to naming things, data modelers love to find new names for everything.

In this book, we will try to avoid further confusion on the topic by sticking with the original definition of SCDs:

- **Type 1** In type 1 SCDs, the value stored in a dimension is always the current one. If you discover that something changed during the processing of your model, you simply overwrite the old value with the new one. You store only the last value of any column. Therefore, because you do not actually track any variations, type 1 SCDs are not *really* SCDs.

- **Type 2** Type 2 SCDs are *real* SCDs. With type 2 SCDs, you store the information multiple times, once for each version. If, for example, a customer changes his or her address, then you will store two rows for that customer: one with the old address and one with the new address. The rows in the fact table will point to the right version of the customer. If you slice by customer name, for example, you will see only one row. If, on the other hand, you slice by country, the numbers will be assigned to the country where the customer lived at the time of the event.

Note Type 1 SCDs are extremely simple. They do not track any historical information. For this reason, we will discuss only type 2 SCDs in this chapter and refer to type 2 simply as SCD.

As an example of SCDs, let us consider the scenario with the changing sales manager discussed earlier and see how it is handled in the Contoso database. In Contoso, there are multiple country managers. One manager can handle multiple countries, and the information is stored in a table containing two columns, CountryRegion and Manager, as shown in Figure 5-1.

CountryRegion	Manager
Australia	Louise
Germany	Raoul
United Kingdom	Paul
France	Mark
the Netherlands	Louise
Greece	Raoul
Switzerland	Paul
Ireland	Mark

FIGURE 5-1 The CountryManagers table contains the relationship between a country or region and its manager.

With this table, it is easy to set up the model. You can create a relationship between CountryRegion in the Customer table and CountryRegion in the CountryManagers table. With the relationship in place, you obtain the model shown in Figure 5-2.

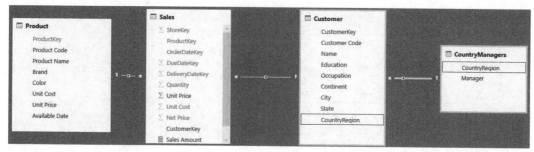

FIGURE 5-2 You can create a relationship between the Customer and CountryManagers tables.

When the model is finished, you can build a report that shows the sales by manager and continent, as shown in Figure 5-3.

Manager	Continent	CY 2007	CY 2008	CY 2009	Total
Louise	Asia	488.792,75	419.828,25	131.572,42	**1.040.193,42**
	Europe		21.331,60	70.311,61	**91.643,21**
	North America	61.577,18	39.782,80	11.658,93	**113.018,92**
	Total	**550.369,94**	**480.942,65**	**213.542,96**	**1.244.855,55**
Mark	Asia			65.381,46	**65.381,46**
	Europe	53.587,61	40.480,90	66.078,71	**160.147,22**
	North America	457.710,49	444.308,45	405.745,64	**1.307.764,58**
	Total	**511.298,10**	**484.789,36**	**537.205,81**	**1.533.293,26**
Paul	Asia			60.640,05	**60.640,05**
	Europe	249.495,88	101.363,69	168.773,28	**519.632,85**
	Total	**249.495,88**	**101.363,69**	**229.413,33**	**580.272,90**
Raoul	Asia			205.557,35	**205.557,35**
	Europe	148.052,02	55.439,35	56.815,17	**260.306,54**
	Total	**148.052,02**	**55.439,35**	**262.372,52**	**465.863,90**
Total		**1.459.215,95**	**1.122.535,05**	**1.242.534,61**	**3.824.285,61**

FIGURE 5-3 This report shows the sales divided by manager and continent.

Although the managers of the countries have changed over time, the model we are using right now is not correctly handling this information. For example, Louise oversaw the United States in 2007, in 2008 it was Paul's responsibility, and in 2009 it became Mark's job. But the report shows the sales in these different years as if they were all generated by Mark because he is the last listed manager of the country.

Suppose the CountryManagers table, instead of relating the manager to the country, were to make this relationship dependent on time, as shown in Figure 5-4.

Each line now stores the start and end year of the relationship. With this new information, you can no longer use the CountryRegion column to create the relationship between customers and managers because CountryRegion is no longer a key in the CountryManagers table. Now the same country or region can appear multiple times, once for each of the managers who was assigned to it.

CountryRegion	Manager	FromYear	ToYear
Australia	Paul	2007	2007
United States	Louise	2007	2008
Canada	Louise	2007	2008
United States	Paul	2008	2009
Australia	Mark	2008	2008
United States	Louise	2009	2010
Canada	Raoul	2009	2010
Australia	Louise	2009	2010
Germany	Raoul	2007	2010
United Kingdom	Paul	2007	2010
France	Mark	2007	2010
the Netherlands	Louise	2007	2010
Greece	Raoul	2007	2010
Switzerland	Paul	2007	2010
Ireland	Mark	2007	2010
Portugal	Louise	2007	2010
Spain	Raoul	2007	2010

FIGURE 5-4 The manager of United States changed over time, as shown in this table.

The scenario suddenly becomes much more complex, but there are multiple ways to manage this. In this chapter, we will show a few of them that help in building an analytical report that can track who the manager was at the time of the sale. Imagine the model has already been created by the IT department managing the data warehouse and submitted to you. If done correctly, the Customer table you receive will contain the following two columns:

- **Historical Manager**   This is the manager of the customer when the event (sale) happened.

- **Current Manager**   This is the current manager of the customer, no matter who was handling the customer at the time of the event.

With this data structure in place, you can create analytical reports like the one shown in Figure 5-5 that report the sales with the historical manager instead of the current one.

Continent	Historical Manager	CY 2007	CY 2008	CY 2009	Total
Asia	Louise			131.572,42	131.572,42
	Mark		419.828,25	65.381,46	485.209,71
	Paul	488.792,75		60.640,05	549.432,80
	Raoul			205.557,35	205.557,35
	Total	488.792,75	419.828,25	463.151,29	1.371.772,29
Europe	Louise		21.331,60	70.311,61	91.643,21
	Mark	53.587,61	40.480,90	66.078,71	160.147,22
	Paul	249.495,88	101.363,69	168.773,28	519.632,85
	Raoul	148.052,02	55.439,35	56.815,17	260.306,54
	Total	451.135,51	218.615,55	361.978,75	1.031.729,82
North America	Louise	519.287,68			519.287,68
	Mark			405.745,64	405.745,64
	Paul		444.308,45		444.308,45
	Raoul		39.782,80	11.658,93	51.441,74
	Total	519.287,68	484.091,26	417.404,57	1.420.783,51
Total		1.459.215,95	1.122.535,05	1.242.534,61	3.824.285,61

FIGURE 5-5 The sales sliced by historical manager correctly assigns North America to Louise in 2007.

Moreover, you can build reports that show both the current and the historical manager at the same time, as shown in Figure 5-6. This report shows the sales in North America (USA and Canada), with the actual manager and the historical one.

Continent	Actual Manager	Historical Manager	CY 2007	CY 2008	CY 2009	Total
☐ Asia	Mark	Louise	457.710,49			457.710,49
☐ Europe		Mark			405.745,64	405.745,64
■ North America		Paul		444.308,45		444.308,45
		Total	**457.710,49**	**444.308,45**	**405.745,64**	**1.307.764,58**
CountryRegion	Raoul	Louise	61.577,18			61.577,18
☐ Canada		Raoul		39.782,80	11.658,93	51.441,74
☐ United States		**Total**	**61.577,18**	**39.782,80**	**11.658,93**	**113.018,92**
	Total		**519.287,68**	**484.091,26**	**417.404,57**	**1.420.783,51**

FIGURE 5-6   Using actual and historical attributes, you can produce very detailed reports.

> **Tip**   Using SCDs in reports is not easy. We suggest you look carefully at the previous figures and get a sense of the data you are reading to better understand the numbers that are assigned to the current and historical attributes.

You can slice sales either by the current manager or by the historical one. As expected, the numbers show different figures. For example, you can easily see a dramatic drop in sales for the country that is currently managed by Raoul. In 2007, when it was in the hands of Louise, North America performed much better.

Slicing by the current manager might be useful to understand the potential of the customers that are managed by a sales person. And you slice by the historical attribute to evaluate the sales person's performances over time. In the report, we show both the historical and the current attribute, enabling you to evaluate how sales performed with the different managers.

Using current and historical attributes, you can generate extremely powerful reports. However, they may be visually difficult to read. To mitigate this, it is important to spend time formatting the values and to carefully choose the columns to include in the report. A careful description of the meaning of the numbers also helps.

In these first introductory pages, we have discussed some of the most important considerations about SCDs:

- Both the current and the historical value are important. You will use both, depending on what kind of insight you want to retrieve by querying the model. A good implementation of an SCD should keep both the historical and the current value for each record.

- While the term is *slowly changing dimensions*, the dimensions themselves do not actually change. Rather, it is one or more of the attributes of the dimensions that change.

Now that you have seen the relevance of handling historical variation and the complexity that comes with using an SCD in a report, it is time to start working on the different kinds of data models you need to build to gracefully handle SCDs.

Using slowly changing dimensions

Having shown you what SCDs are, we will now discuss some considerations with regard to their use. Whenever you use an SCD, some of the calculations become more complex. With standard dimensions, each entity is stored in a row of its table. For example, a customer is always a single line in the customer table. Yet if Customer is instead handled as an SCD, a single customer might be represented with multiple lines in its table if there are multiple versions of him or her. The simple one-to-one relationship of single customer to single row no longer holds. Simple operations, like counting the number of customers, become more complex.

In the example we outlined earlier, we decided to store the country manager as one attribute of the customer. As a result, there will be multiple versions of the same customer, depending on how many different managers that customer had over time. In fact, in the sample database we use for this book, there are 18,869 customers, but the number of rows in the Customer table is 43,882 due to changes in the managers over time. If you define a simple measure to count customers, as in the following code, the result would be incorrect:

```
NumOfCustomers = COUNTROWS ( Customer )
```

You can see this incorrect result in Figure 5-7, which shows the number of customers sliced by the actual manager.

Actual Manager	NumOfCustomers
Louise	10.901
Mark	26.082
Paul	1.937
Raoul	4.962
Total	**43.882**

FIGURE 5-7 Counting the rows does not correctly count the customers, if you are counting from an SCD.

The report is showing the number of *versions* of customers, which is clearly not the actual number of customers. To correctly count the number of customers, you need to perform a distinct count of the customer codes. Use the following code:

```
NumOfCustomers := DISTINCTCOUNT ( Customer[Customer Code] )
```

Using DISTINCTCOUNT, the numbers are now reported in the correct way, as shown in Figure 5-8.

Actual Manager	NumOfCustomers
Louise	3.639
Mark	9.910
Paul	1.937
Raoul	3.383
Total	**18.869**

FIGURE 5-8 With DISTINCTCOUNT, the numbers reflect only the unique customer codes and give the correct amounts.

If you want to slice by one of the attributes of the customer, replacing COUNTROWS with DISTINCTCOUNT is a good solution. The issue becomes more complex if you want to slice by a different attribute that does not belong to the customer dimension. One very common calculation is the number of customers who bought some category of products. If you are using a standard customer dimension, and not a slowly changing one, then you can obtain this number by simply performing a distinct count of the customer key in the fact table. In our example, the code would be as follows:

```
NumOfBuyingCustomers := DISTINCTCOUNT ( Sales[CustomerKey] )
```

If you use this in the model with an SCD, you get a result that appears reasonable but is still incorrect. The result is shown in Figure 5-9.

Brand ▲	NumOfBuyingCustomers
A. Datum	189
Adventure Works	392
Contoso	820
Fabrikam	173
Litware	201
Northwind Traders	151
Proseware	127
Southridge Video	862
Tailspin Toys	594
The Phone Company	76
Wide World Importers	133
Total	**2,395**

FIGURE 5-9 The number of buying customers, computed using DISTINCTCOUNT, appears correct but it is wrong.

By computing the distinct count of the customer keys, you compute the number of distinct versions of the customer, not the real number of customers. If you need to count the correct value, you must count the number of customer codes in Customer by using a bidirectional pattern. You can do this by either marking the relationship between Customer and Sales as bidirectional, or by modifying the code using the following pattern:

```
NumOfBuyingCustomersCorrect :=
CALCULATE (
    DISTINCTCOUNT ( Customers[Customer Code] ),
    Sales
)
```

Figure 5-10 shows the same report as Figure 5-9, but with the new measure. Most of the numbers are identical, and the ones that are different are still somewhat similar. This shows how easy it is to get fooled by the wrong calculation.

Brand	NumOfBuyingCustomers	NumOfBuyingCustomersCorrect
A. Datum	189	189
Adventure Works	392	392
Contoso	820	815
Fabrikam	173	173
Litware	201	199
Northwind Traders	151	151
Proseware	127	125
Southridge Video	862	855
Tailspin Toys	594	594
The Phone Company	76	76
Wide World Importers	133	133
Total	**2.395**	**2.353**

FIGURE 5-10 The two measures side by side show the small difference between the correct and incorrect calculation.

You might have noticed that we used the bidirectional pattern with the Sales table as a filter instead of the way it's been used more frequently in this book, which involves creating a bidirectional relationship between Sales and Customer. If you only use the bidirectional filtering of the relationship between Sales and Customer here, the grand total will not be correct. In fact, if you write the measure using the following code, the grand total (shown in Figure 5-11) will count all the customers, not only the ones who bought something:

```
NumOfBuyingCustomersCorrectCrossFilter :=
CALCULATE (
    DISTINCTCOUNT ( Customer[Customer Code] ),
    CROSSFILTER ( Sales[CustomerKey], Customer[CustomerKey], BOTH )
)
```

Brand	NumOfBuyingCustomers	NumOfBuyingCustomersCorrect
A. Datum	189	189
Adventure Works	392	392
Contoso	820	815
Fabrikam	173	173
Litware	201	199
Northwind Traders	151	151
Proseware	127	125
Southridge Video	862	855
Tailspin Toys	594	594
The Phone Company	76	76
Wide World Importers	133	133
Total	**2.395**	**18.869**

FIGURE 5-11 The grand total shows an incorrect number if you only set bidirectional filtering on.

The reason the grand total is different for the NumOfBuyingCustomersCorrectCrossFilter measure is that the Sales table is not filtered at the grand total. Consequently, the engine has no filter to propagate to Customer. If, instead, you use the full bidirectional pattern with the Sales table as a filter, then the filter is always applied and shows only the customers who appear somewhere in Sales. Because of this, the CROSSFILTER version performs better when no filter needs to be applied and, from a performance point of view, is the preferred one. The difference between the two calculations becomes evident only if there are multiple versions of the customer in the current selection.

By their very nature, SCDs change slowly. Therefore, multiple versions of the same customer are not generally hit by a given selection. Still, this might happen if the selection is large enough. For example, many years of data are likely to contain several versions of the same customer.

It is very useful to learn how to spot these subtle differences between computing the number of customers and the number of versions. Understanding these small details will aid greatly in your data-modeling career and help you identify when a number or total is incorrect.

Loading slowly changing dimensions

This chapter outlines the use of the Power BI Desktop Query Editor to load an SCD. SCDs might not always be present in your original data model, but there may be times when you need to introduce them in a specific model that you are working on. For example, in the demo database we are using in this chapter, the original model does not contain an SCD. However, you will need to load an SCD to track the original and historical sales manager, a piece of information that is not present in the original data warehouse.

To convey the challenges in handling SCDs, we must revive an important topic that we introduced in Chapter 1, "Introduction to data modeling": granularity. The presence of an SCD changes the granularity of both the dimension and the fact table.

Without SCDs, the granularity of the facts in the demo database is only at the customer level. When you introduce an SCD, the granularity increases to each customer *version*. Different versions of the same customer must be linked with different sales, depending on when the sale occurred.

Changing the granularity involves several actions and details to build the correct model. You will also need to change the query of both the dimension and the fact table so their granularity matches. You cannot update the granularity of one table without updating the granularity of the other one, too. Otherwise, the relationship will not work correctly.

Let us start by analyzing the scenario. The database has a Customer table that is not an SCD. It also has a CountryManagers table that contains the sales manager from each country or region with his or her start and end year. The sales manager for a country or region is not always the same for each year. However, because the sales manager for a country or region does not always change annually, we do not want to overly increase granularity to the level of customer/year because this would create unnecessary duplicates of some customers. In this scenario, our ideal granularity falls somewhere between customer (which is too low to account for changing managers) and customer/year (which is too high to account for the years in which the manager remained the same). This granularity depends on how many times the manager of the customer's country or region changed.

Let us start by finding the correct granularity. To perform this step, you will first build the worst-case granularity. Then you will determine what the correct granularity is. Figure 5-12 shows the original table, which contains the sales managers for various countries or regions.

	CountryRegion	Manager	FromYear	ToYear
1	Australia	Paul	2007	2008
2	United States	Louise	2007	2008
3	Canada	Louise	2007	2008
4	United States	Paul	2008	2009
5	Australia	Mark	2008	2009
6	United States	Mark	2009	2010
7	Canada	Raoul	2008	2010
8	Australia	Louise	2009	2010
9	Germany	Raoul	2007	2010
10	United Kingdom	Paul	2007	2010

FIGURE 5-12 The CountryManagers table contains the columns FromYear and ToYear to indicate when the sales manager for each country or region was on duty.

To find the right granularity, you will change this model to a simpler one that contains the country or region, the sales manager, and the year by replacing the FromYear and ToYear columns with a single column that indicates the year only. By doing so, you will increase the number of rows. Many of the rows will show the same sales manager for several years. (We will cover removing those extra rows in a moment.)

First, add a new column in the table that contains the list of years that are included between FromYear and ToYear, using the `List.Numbers` function, as shown in Figure 5-13.

```
= Table.AddColumn(Managers, "Year", each List.Numbers([FromYear], [ToYear]-[FromYear]))
```

	CountryRegion	Manager	FromYear	ToYear	Year
1	Australia	Paul	2007	2008	List
2	United States	Louise	2007	2008	List
3	Canada	Louise	2007	2008	List
4	United States	Paul	2008	2009	List
5	Australia	Mark	2008	2009	List
6	United States	Mark	2009	2010	List
7	Canada	Raoul	2008	2010	List
8	Australia	Louise	2009	2010	List
9	Germany	Raoul	2007	2010	List
10	United Kingdom	Paul	2007	2010	List
11	France	Mark	2007	2010	List

List
2007
2008
2009

FIGURE 5-13 The Year column lists the years between FromYear and ToYear.

Figure 5-13 shows both the column, visible only as List in the user interface, and the column's content, which you can see in the Query Editor by clicking the cell. You can see that Paul was the manager in the United Kingdom from 2007 to 2010; thus, the list contains the three years 2007, 2008, and 2009.

Now that you have produced the list of years, you can expand the list by generating one row for each element of the list. You can also remove the FromYear and ToYear columns, which are now useless. This obtains the result shown in Figure 5-14.

	CountryRegion	Manager	Year
10	Germany	Raoul	2007
11	Germany	Raoul	2008
12	Germany	Raoul	2009
13	United Kingdom	Paul	2007
14	United Kingdom	Paul	2008
15	United Kingdom	Paul	2009
16	France	Mark	2007
17	France	Mark	2008
18	France	Mark	2009

FIGURE 5-14   In this table, United Kingdom now appears three times with the same manager.

This table now contains the worst-case granularity for the country or region, with one version for each year. Many rows will show the same value for the same country, differing only in the year. However, this table is still useful, because you will use it as a lookup when changing the granularity of the fact table. Because the table contains the historical country or region sales manager, save it under the name Historical Country Managers.

The second table you need is one that contains the actual country or region sales manager. This is somewhat easy to build, if we start from the Historical Country Managers table. You simply need to group the historical country or region sales managers by CountryRegion and Manager, which results in the distinct pairs of CountryRegion and Manager. During the grouping, you use MAX to aggregate the year to obtain the last year the sales manager was on duty for the given country or region. As shown in Figure 5-15, United Kingdom is now represented with a single row.

```
= Table.Group(Source, {"CountryRegion", "Manager"}, {{"LastYear", each List.Max([Year]), type number}})
```

	CountryRegion	Manager	LastYear
1	Australia	Paul	2007
2	United States	Louise	2007
3	Canada	Louise	2007
4	United States	Paul	2008
5	Australia	Mark	2008
6	United States	Mark	2009
7	Canada	Raoul	2009
8	Australia	Louise	2009
9	Germany	Raoul	2009
10	United Kingdom	Paul	2009
11	France	Mark	2009

FIGURE 5-15   After the grouping, the cardinality is now correct.

This table contains the distinct pairs of CountryRegion and Manager, along with the last year when the sales manager was on duty for that country or region. To transform this table into a table that contains only the current sales manager, it is enough to filter out rows that do not contain the value for the current year in the LastYear column. (In this example, the "current year" is 2009, which is the last year for which we have data in the set.) Figure 5-16 shows you the result of this second query, which we named Actual Country Managers.

	CountryRegion	Manager
4	Germany	Raoul
5	United Kingdom	Paul
6	France	Mark
7	the Netherlands	Louise
8	Greece	Raoul
9	Switzerland	Paul
10	Ireland	Mark
11	Portugal	Louise
12	Spain	Raoul
13	Italy	Paul

FIGURE 5-16 Actual Country Managers table contains only the last and current sales manager for each country or region.

At this point, you have the following two tables:

- **Actual Country Managers** This contains the current sales manager for each country or region.

- **Historical Country Managers** This contains the historical sales manager for each country or region.

The next step will be to use these two tables to update both the Customer table and the Sales table.

Fixing granularity in the dimension

You are going to use these two tables to set the right granularity on the Customer and Sales tables. Let us focus on the Customer table first. To increase the granularity, you will need to merge the original Customer table with the Historical Country Managers table. The Customer table contains the CountryRegion column. If you join the Customer table with the Historical Country Managers table based on the CountryRegion, the result will contain more rows, one for each different manager for a given customer. It will not contain a new version of the customer for each year, which would be the worst-case granularity. Instead, because of the grouping operation that is performed on the Historical Country Managers table, it will contain the right number of versions for each customer.

After you have done these two operations, the data set looks like Figure 5-17, with the OriginalCustomerKey column sorted in ascending order.

	OriginalCustomerKey	Customer Code	Name	CountryRegion	Actual Manager	Historical Manager	Year
1	1	11000	Yang, Jon	Australia	Louise	Paul	2007
2	1	11000	Yang, Jon	Australia	Louise	Mark	2008
3	1	11000	Yang, Jon	Australia	Louise	Louise	2009
4	2	11001	Huang, Eugene	Australia	Louise	Paul	2007
5	2	11001	Huang, Eugene	Australia	Louise	Mark	2008
6	2	11001	Huang, Eugene	Australia	Louise	Louise	2009
7	3	11002	Torres, Ruben	Australia	Louise	Paul	2007
8	3	11002	Torres, Ruben	Australia	Louise	Mark	2008
9	3	11002	Torres, Ruben	Australia	Louise	Louise	2009
10	4	11003	Zhu, Christy	Australia	Louise	Paul	2007
11	4	11003	Zhu, Christy	Australia	Louise	Mark	2008
12	4	11003	Zhu, Christy	Australia	Louise	Louise	2009
13	5	11004	Johnson, Elizabeth	Australia	Louise	Paul	2007

FIGURE 5-17 The new Customer table shows the adjusted granularity and the actual and historical managers denormalized.

Focus your attention on the first three lines. They represent Jon Yang, a customer in Australia who has had three different sales managers over time: Paul, Mark, and Louise. This is correctly represented in the model, but there is a problem. The column that contains the customer key (called OriginalCustomerKey) is no longer a good key for the table. In fact, that code represents the customer, whereas now we are moving toward a representation of the *versions* of the customer. Because the customer key is no longer unique, it cannot be used as our key. Thus, we need a new one.

Generally, you can build a new key by simply adding a new column with an index, which is a number starting from 1 and growing by 1 for each row. This is the preferred technique used by database managers. In our case, the granularity of the new table is at the customer/year level, where the year you use is the last year when the manager was on duty for the country. Therefore, you can safely build a new column by simply concatenating OriginalCustomerKey with Year, which is the year of the Historical Country Managers table denormalized in the new Customer table. Figure 5-18 shows the resulting table with the new key.

OriginalCustomerKey	CustomerKey	Customer Code	Name	CountryRegion	Actual Manager	Historical Manager
1	12007	11000	Yang, Jon	Australia	Louise	Paul
1	12008	11000	Yang, Jon	Australia	Louise	Mark
1	12009	11000	Yang, Jon	Australia	Louise	Louise
2	22007	11001	Huang, Eugene	Australia	Louise	Paul
2	22008	11001	Huang, Eugene	Australia	Louise	Mark
2	22009	11001	Huang, Eugene	Australia	Louise	Louise
3	32007	11002	Torres, Ruben	Australia	Louise	Paul
3	32008	11002	Torres, Ruben	Australia	Louise	Mark
3	32009	11002	Torres, Ruben	Australia	Louise	Louise
4	42007	11003	Zhu, Christy	Australia	Louise	Paul
4	42008	11003	Zhu, Christy	Australia	Louise	Mark
4	42009	11003	Zhu, Christy	Australia	Louise	Louise
5	52007	11004	Johnson, Elizabeth	Australia	Louise	Paul
5	52008	11004	Johnson, Elizabeth	Australia	Louise	Mark

FIGURE 5-18 OriginalCustomerKey is not a key. It's better to use the new CustomerKey, which contains the year.

Having reached this point, you have moved the granularity in the Customer table from the original one (that is, the customer) to the worst-case (that is, the customer and year). This table is not the final one, but it is a useful intermediate step. We saved it under the name CustomerBase.

The final step is to fix the granularity and move to the right one. This step is similar to what you did with the sales managers for the various countries or regions. Starting from CustomerBase, you remove all the columns except the granularity columns, and perform a grouping by OriginalCustomerKey, Actual Manager, and Historical Manager. You then take the MAX of CustomerKey and name it NewCustomerKey. The result is shown in Figure 5-19.

OriginalCustomerKey	Actual Manager	Historical Manager	NewCustomerKey
9	Louise	Mark	92008
9	Louise	Louise	92009
10	Louise	Paul	102007
10	Louise	Mark	102008
10	Louise	Louise	102009
11	Louise	Paul	112007
11	Louise	Mark	112008
11	Louise	Louise	112009
12	Louise	Paul	122007

FIGURE 5-19 This temporary table is now at the right level of granularity.

This grouping operation was useful to build the correct granularity, but in performing it, you had to remove all the columns from the original Customer table. The next step is to restore the needed columns. First, you remove all the columns from the table, maintaining only the NewCustomerKey column, as shown in Figure 5-20.

	1.2 NewCustomerKey
7	32007
8	32008
9	32009
10	42007
11	42008
12	42009
13	52007
14	52008

FIGURE 5-20   This table contains only the customer keys, but now it is at the correct granularity.

The final step is to merge this table with CustomerBase, based on the customer key, and to retrieve all the needed columns. The result is shown in Figure 5-21, where you can easily spot the fact that customers vary in the number of versions, depending on how many managers they had over time.

	1²3 OriginalCustomerKey	ABC 123 CustomerKey	AB C Customer Code	AB C Name	AB C CountryRegion	AB C Actual Manager	AB C Historical Manager
419	143	1432007	11142	Patterson, Eduardo	Canada	Raoul	Louise
420	143	1432009	11142	Patterson, Eduardo	Canada	Raoul	Raoul
421	144	1442007	11143	Henderson, Jonathan	United States	Mark	Louise
422	144	1442008	11143	Henderson, Jonathan	United States	Mark	Paul
423	144	1442009	11143	Henderson, Jonathan	United States	Mark	Mark
424	145	1452007	11144	Hernandez, Edward	United States	Mark	Louise
425	145	1452008	11144	Hernandez, Edward	United States	Mark	Paul
426	145	1452009	11144	Hernandez, Edward	United States	Mark	Mark
427	146	1462007	11145	Coleman, Jasmine	United States	Mark	Louise
428	146	1462008	11145	Coleman, Jasmine	United States	Mark	Paul

FIGURE 5-21   The final Customer table has the correct granularity and all the relevant columns.

Next, you will perform a similar operation with the Sales table. (Note that because you have changed the key of the Customer table, the CustomerKey column in Sales is no longer a good key to use.)

Fixing granularity in the fact table

In Sales, you cannot compute the new key based on the year of the sale. In fact, if the sales manager of a country or region did not change, then the new key does not depend on the year of the sale. Instead, you can search for the new key. The new cardinality of the dimension depends on the customer, the actual manager, and the historical manager. Given these three values, you can search in the new Customer dimension. There, you will find the new CustomerKey.

You need to perform the following steps on the Sales table to fix its granularity:

1.   In the original Sales table, add a column that contains the year of the sales.

2.   Perform a join with the CustomerBase table to obtain the customer country as well as the actual and historical managers. (You use CustomerBase because you can search for the sales year there. In the CustomerBase table, you still have one different customer per year. The table had the wrong granularity, but it now proves useful because you can easily search it using the year of the sale.)

The result of the merge operation is in the new column, as shown in Figure 5-22.

	1²₃ StoreKey	1²₃ ProductKey	1²₃ CustomerKey	ABC₁₂₃ Year	NewColumn	1²₃ OrderDateKey	1²₃ DueDateKey	1²₃ DeliveryDateKey	1²₃ Quantity	$ Unit Price	$ Un
1	306	579	2585	2007 Table		20070109	20070119	20070117	1	229	
2	306	579	2586	2007 Table		20070109	20070121	20070119	1	229	
3	306	579	2587	2007 Table		20070109	20070115	20070121	1	229	
4	306	1484	3941	2007 Table		20070109	20070120	20070121	1	208	
5	306	1484	3959	2007 Table		20070109	20070115	20070119	1	208	
6	306	1484	3962	2007 Table		20070109	20070119	20070116	1	208	
7	306	1484	3963	2007 Table		20070109	20070121	20070118	1	208	
8	306	1484	3964	2007 Table		20070109	20070115	20070120	1	206	
9	306	1484	3965	2007 Table		20070109	20070117	20070115	1	208	
10	306	1561	19037	2007 Table		20070110	20070122	20070119	1	402	
11	306	1821	2545	2007 Table		20070110	20070123	20070121	1	32	
12	306	1821	2546	2007 Table		20070110	20070117	20070116	1	32	

OriginalCustomerKey	Customer Code	Name	Education	Occupation	Continent	City	State	CountryRegion	Actual Manager	Historical Manager	Year	CustomerKey
2585	13584	Cox, Isaiah	High School	Professional	Europe	Runcorn	England	United Kingdom	Paul	Paul	2007	25852007

FIGURE 5-22 You need to merge Sales with CustomerBase to retrieve the actual and historical managers.

Having reached this point, you can expand the actual and historical managers. You can then use them to perform a second join with the Customer table, which has the right granularity. Then search for the customer that has the same customer code, actual manager, and historical manager. This final lookup will let you retrieve the new customer key and will solve the granularity on the fact table.

Figure 5-23 shows an extract of the Sales table after the processing. The first highlighted row is about a customer whose manager was first Mark and then changed to Louise. Thus, that customer will have different versions, and the individual row (related to 2007, when the manager was still Mark) points to the 2007 version of the customer. In the second row, the sales manager never changed, so there is only one row for the customer (marked 2009, the last year). In addition, the sale—even if it happened in 2007—points to the 2009 version of the customer. In the final version of the Sales table, the lookup column will no longer be present; it is only part of the processing.

ABC₁₂₃ CustomerKeyLookup	Aᴮ_C NewColumn.Actual Manager	Aᴮ_C NewColumn.Historical Manager	ABC₁₂₃ NewColumn.Year	ABC₁₂₃ NewColumn.CustomerKey
1752007	Mark	Louise	2007	1752007
1782007	Mark	Louise	2007	1782007
1802007	Mark	Louise	2007	1802007
1812007	Mark	Louise	2007	1812007
1822007	Mark	Louise	2007	1822007
2062009	Mark	Mark	2009	2062009
2072009	Mark	Mark	2009	2072009
3022007	Mark	Louise	2007	3022007
3022007	Mark	Louise	2007	3022007
3392007	Raoul	Raoul	2007	3392009
3392007	Raoul	Raoul	2007	3392009

FIGURE 5-23 The two highlighted rows show the different handling of customers who changed sales managers versus customers who did not.

Loading SCDs requires a lot of care. The following is a brief recap of the steps you've performed so far:

1. You defined the new granularity of the SCD. The new granularity depended on the attributes of the dimension that were expected to change over time.

2. You modified the dimension so it used the right granularity. This required complex queries and, most importantly, the definition of a new customer code to use as the foundation of the relationship.

3. You modified the fact table so that it used the new code. Because the new code could not be easily computed, you had to search for its value in the new dimension by performing a lookup. All the slowly changing attributes were used to define the granularity.

We went through the whole process of describing how to handle SCDs with the Query Editor of Power BI Desktop. (You can perform the same steps in Excel 2016.) We wanted to show the level of complexity involved in handling SCDs. The next section describes rapidly changing dimensions. As you will discover, the management of rapidly changing dimensions is far simpler than that of SCDs. However, rapidly changing dimensions are not the optimal solution from a storage and performance point of view. Also, you can safely use the easier pattern of rapidly changing dimensions for slowly changing ones if your data model is small enough (that is, in the range of a few million rows).

Rapidly changing dimensions

As their name implies, slowly changing dimensions typically change slowly and do not produce too many versions of the entity they represent. We deliberately used customers under different sales managers as an example of an SCD that might potentially change every year. Because the changing attribute is owned by all customers, the number of new versions created is somewhat high. A more traditional example of an SCD might be tracking the current and historical address of a customer, as customers are not generally expected to update their address every year. We chose to use the sales manager example rather than the address one because the resulting model can be easily created with Excel or Power BI Desktop.

Another attribute that you might be interested in tracking—one that always changes each year—is the customer's age. For example, suppose you want to analyze sales by age range. If you do not handle the customer's age as an SCD, you cannot store it in the customer dimension. The customer's age changes, and you need to track the age when the sale was made rather than the current age. You could use the pattern described in the previous section to handle age. However, this section shows a different way of handling changes in a dimension: implementing the pattern for rapidly changing dimensions.

Suppose you have 10 years of data in your model. Chances are, if you have used SCDs, you have 10 different versions of the same customer in your table. If even more attributes must be monitored for changes, this number might easily increase up to a point where handling it becomes cumbersome. To address this, focus your attention on the fact that the whole dimension does not change. Rather, what changes is one attribute of the dimension. If an attribute changes too frequently, the best option is to store the attribute as a dimension by itself, which removes it from the customer dimension.

The starting model is shown in Figure 5-24, where the current age of the customer is saved in the Customer table.

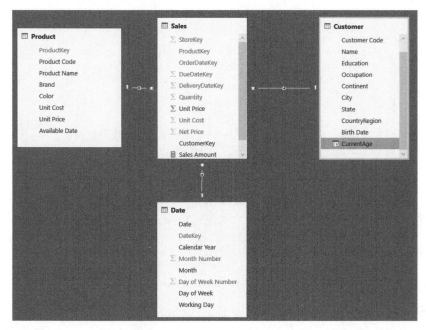

FIGURE 5-24 The age of the customer is stored as an attribute of the Customer table.

The ages stored in the Customer table are the current ages of each customer. They are updated every day, based on the current date. But what about the customer's historical age—that is, his or her age when the sale was made? Because the customer's age is changing quickly, a good way to model it is to store the historical age in the fact table by using a calculated column. Try the following code:

```
Sales[Historical Age] =
DATEDIFF (
    RELATED ( Customer[Birth Date] ),
    RELATED ( 'Date'[Date] ),
    YEAR
)
```

At the time of the sale, this column computes the difference between the customer's birth date and the date of the sale. The resulting value stores the historical age in a very simple and convenient way. If you store the data in the fact table and denormalize it there, you are not creating a dimension. This approach models the age without the whole process of data transformation that is required to handle an SCD.

This column, alone, is already useful to build charts. For example, Figure 5-25 shows a histogram with the sales divided by age.

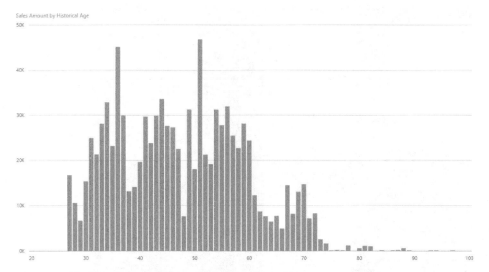

Sales Amount by Historical Age

FIGURE 5-25 The historical age works perfectly fine to show histograms and charts.

The age, as a number, works fine for charts. But you might also be interested in grouping the age into different ranges to obtain different insights. In such a case, the best option is to create a real dimension and use the age in the fact table as a foreign key to point to the dimension. This will result in a data model like the one shown in Figure 5-26.

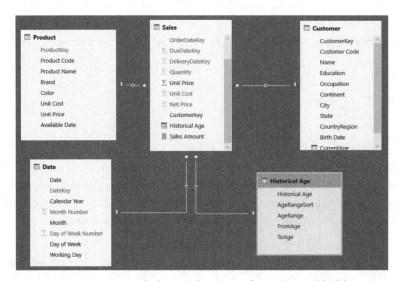

FIGURE 5-26 You can turn the historical age into a foreign key and build a proper age dimension.

In the Historical Age dimension, you can store age ranges or other interesting attributes. This enables you to build reports that slice by age range instead of an individual age. For example, the report shown in Figure 5-27 shows sales amount, the number of customers in that age range, and the average spent in that age range.

AgeRange	Sales Amount	NumOfCustomers	AverageSale
	2.870.569,69	352	$8.155,03
25-40	281.923,90	615	$458,41
40-50	252.664,85	556	$454,43
50-60	272.339,29	525	$518,74
Over 60	146.787,88	310	$473,51
Total	**3.824.285,61**	**2.353**	**$1.625,28**

FIGURE 5-27 With a proper dimension, you can easily slice by age range.

You can obtain a good data model by separating the rapidly changing attribute from the original dimension and storing it as a value in the fact table or, if needed, building a proper dimension on top of the attribute. The resulting loading process is much easier—and the data model is much simpler—than with a fully featured SCD.

Choosing the right modeling technique

In this chapter, we have shown two different methods for handling changing dimensions. The canonical way is to create a fully featured SCD with a rather complex loading process. The simpler way is to store the slowly changing attribute as a column in the fact table, and, if needed, to build a proper dimension on top of the attribute.

The latter solution is much simpler to develop, so sometimes it will be the best way to handle SCDs, especially if you can easily isolate one slowly changing attribute. However, if the number of attributes is larger, you might end up having too many dimensions, making the data model difficult to browse. As often happens in data modeling, you should always think carefully before choosing one solution over the other. For example, if you want to track, for the customer, several historical attributes like age, full address (country/region, state, and continent), country or region sales manager, and possibly other attributes, you can end up building many dimensions for the sole purpose of tracking all those attributes. On the other hand, no matter how many changing attributes you have in a dimension, if you go for the fully featured SCD, then you will have to maintain only a single dimension.

Let us go back to the example used throughout this chapter: the handling of the current and historical sales manager. If, instead of focusing on the dimension, you focus on the attribute alone, you can easily solve the scenario by using the model shown in Figure 5-28.

Building the model is straightforward. You only need to compute, for each sale, the sales manager assigned to the customer's country or region at the time of the sale. You can obtain this with a couple of merge operations—and, most importantly, without having to update the granularity of either the fact table or the dimension.

Regarding SCDs, here is a simple rule of thumb: If possible, try to isolate the slowly changing attribute (or set of attributes) and build a separate dimension for those attributes. You do not need to update the granularity. If the number of attributes is too large, then the best option is to go for the much more complex process of building a full SCD.

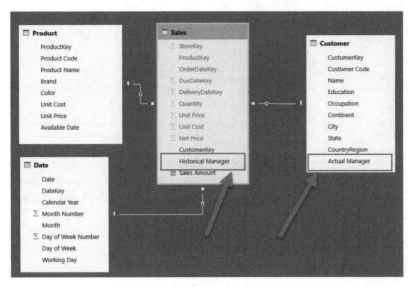

FIGURE 5-28 Denormalizing the historical manager in the fact table leads to a simple model.

Conclusions

SCDs are not easy to manage. Yet, in many cases, it is important to use them because you want to track what happened in a relationship and attempt to predict what might happen in the future. The following are the important points to remember from this chapter:

- What changes is not the dimension. It is a set of attributes of a dimension. Thus, the proper way of expressing the changing nature of your data is to understand what the slowly changing attributes are.

- You use historical attributes when analyzing the past. You use current attributes when projecting the current data to forecast the future.

- If you have a small set of slowly changing attributes, you can safely denormalize them in the fact table. If a dimension is needed for those attributes, you can build a historical dimension as a separate one.

- If the number of attributes is too large, you must follow the SCD pattern, knowing that the loading process will be much more complex and error-prone.

- If you build an SCD, you must move the granularity of both the fact table and the dimension to the version of the entity instead of the original entity.

- When you manage SCDs, most of the counting calculations must be adjusted to handle the new granularity, typically by using a distinct count instead of simple counts.

CHAPTER 6

Using snapshots

A *snapshot* is a kind of table that is often used in the modeling of data. In the first chapters of this book, you became familiar with the idea of dividing a model by fact tables and dimensions, and you learned that a fact is a type of event—that is, something that happens. Then, you aggregated values from the fact table by using an aggregation function, like SUM, COUNT or DISTINCTCOUNT. But the truth is, sometimes a fact is *not* an event. Sometimes, a fact stores something that has been measured, like the temperature of an engine, the daily average number of customers who entered a store each month, or the quantity on-hand of a product. In all these cases, you store a measurement at a point in time instead of the measure of an event. All these scenarios are typically modeled as snapshots. Another kind of snapshot is the balance of a current account. The fact is an individual transaction in the account, and a snapshot states what the balance was, at a given point in time.

A snapshot is not a fact. It is a measure taken at some point in time. In fact, when it comes to snapshots, time is a very important part of the equation. Snapshots might appear in your model because the more granular information is too large or it is unavailable.

In this chapter, we analyze some kinds of snapshots to give you a good level of understanding on how to handle them. As always, keep in mind that your model is likely to be slightly different from anything we will ever be able to describe as a standard pattern. Be prepared to adjust the content of this book to your specific needs, and use some creativity in developing your model.

Using data that you cannot aggregate over time

Suppose you periodically perform an inventory in your stores. The table that contains the inventory is a fact table. However, this time, the fact is not something that happened; it is something that holds true at a given point in time. What you are saying in the fact table is, "at this date, the quantity of this product available in this store is *x*." The next month, when you perform the same operation, you can state another fact. This is a snapshot—that is, a measure of what was available at that time. From an operational point of view, the table is a fact table because you are likely to compute values on top of the table, and because the table is linked to dimensions. The difference here has more to do with the nature of the fact than with the structure.

Another example of a snapshot is the exchange rate of a currency. If you need to store the exchange rate of a currency, you can store it in a table that contains the date, the currency, and its value compared to some other reference currency, like USD. It is a fact table because it is related to dimensions, and it contains numbers that you will use for an aggregation. However, it does not store an event that happened. Rather, it stores a value that has been measured at a given point in time. We will provide a complete lesson of how to manage exchange rates later in Chapter 11, "Working with multiple currencies." For the purposes of this chapter, it is enough to note that a currency exchange rate is a kind of snapshot.

It is useful to differentiate between the following kinds of snapshots:

- **Natural snapshots**   These are data sets in which the data is, by its nature, in the form of a snapshot. For example, a fact table that measures the temperature of the water in an engine on a daily basis is a natural snapshot. In other words, the fact is the measure, and the event is the measurement.

- **Derived snapshots**   These are data sets that look like snapshots, but are treated as such only because we tend to think of them as snapshots. Think, for example, of a fact table that contains the balance of the current accounts on a monthly basis. Every month, the measure is the balance, but in reality, the balance of the account is derived from the sum of all the transactions (either positive or negative) that previously occurred. Thus, the data is in the form of a snapshot, but it can also be computed by a simpler aggregation of the raw transactions.

The difference is important. In fact, as you will learn in this chapter, handling snapshots comes with both advantages and disadvantages. You must find the correct balance between them to choose the best possible representation for your data. Sometimes, it is better to store balances; other times, it is better to store transactions. In the case of derived snapshots, you have the freedom (and the responsibility) to make the right choice. With natural snapshots, however, the choice is limited, because the data comes in naturally as a snapshot.

Aggregating snapshots

Let us start the analysis of snapshots by learning the details on how to correctly aggregate data from snapshots. As an example, let us consider an Inventory fact that contains weekly snapshots of the on-hand quantity for each product and store. The full model is shown in Figure 6-1.

Initially, this looks like a simple star schema with two fact tables (Sales and Inventory) and no issues at all. Indeed, both fact tables have the same day, product, and store granularity dimensions. The big difference between the two tables is that Inventory is a snapshot, whereas Sales is a regular fact table.

> **Note**   As you will learn in this section, computing values on top of snapshot tables hides some complexity. In fact, in the process of building the correct formula, we will make many mistakes, which we will analyze together.

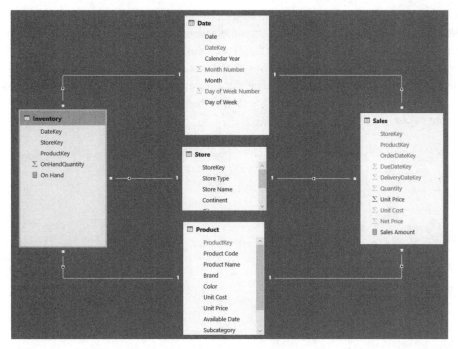

FIGURE 6-1 The Inventory table contains snapshots of on-hand quantity, created on a weekly basis.

For now, let us focus on the Inventory table. As we mentioned, Inventory contains weekly snapshots of the on-hand quantity for every product and store. You can easily create a measure that aggregates the On Hand column by using the following code:

```
On Hand := SUM ( Inventory[OnHandQuantity] )
```

Using this measure, you can build a matrix report in Power BI Desktop to analyze the values for an individual product. Figure 6-2 shows a report with the details of one type of stereo headphones in different stores in Germany.

Product Name	Calendar Year	Month	Giebelstadt Store	Munich Store	obamberg Store	Total
☐ NT Bluetooth Active Headphones E202 Black	CY 2007	January		6		6
☐ NT Bluetooth Active Headphones E202 Red		February		18		18
☐ NT Bluetooth Active Headphones E202 Silver		March			8	8
☐ NT Bluetooth Active Headphones E202 White		April	8	8	24	40
■ NT Bluetooth Stereo Headphones E52 Black		May	24	18		42
☐ NT Bluetooth Stereo Headphones E52 Blue		June			6	6
☐ NT Bluetooth Stereo Headphones E52 Pink		July			20	20
☐ NT Bluetooth Stereo Headphones E52 Yellow		October	6	6	6	18
☐ NT Wireless Bluetooth Stereo Headphones E10...		November	18	18	18	54
☐ NT Wireless Bluetooth Stereo Headphones E10...		**Total**	**56**	**74**	**82**	**212**
☐ NT Wireless Bluetooth Stereo Headphones E10...	CY 2008	May		34		34
☐ NT Wireless Bluetooth Stereo Headphones E30...		June	18	63		81
☐ NT Wireless Bluetooth Stereo Headphones E30...		July	42	42		84
☐ NT Wireless Bluetooth Stereo Headphones E30...		**Total**	**60**	**139**		**199**
☐ NT Wireless Bluetooth Stereo Headphones E30...	CY 2009	November			20	20
☐ NT Wireless Bluetooth Stereo Headphones M4...		December			27	27
☐ NT Wireless Bluetooth Stereo Headphones M4...		**Total**			**47**	**47**
☐ NT Wireless Bluetooth Stereo Headphones M4...						
☐ NT Wireless Bluetooth Stereo Headphones M4...	**Total**		**116**	**213**	**129**	**458**

FIGURE 6-2 This report shows the on-hand quantity for one product in different stores in Germany.

Looking at the totals in the report, you can easily spot the problem. The total for each store at the year level is wrong. In fact, if in the Giebelstadt store there were 18 headphones available in November and none in December, then the total value for 2007 is obviously not 56. The correct value should be zero, as there were none on-hand after November 2007. Because the snapshot is a weekly one, if you expand the month to the date level, you will notice that even at the month level, the value reported is incorrect. You can see this in Figure 6-3, where the total at the month level is shown as the sum of the individual date values.

Calendar Year	Month	Date	Giebelstadt Store	Munich Store	obamberg Store	Total
CY 2007	January	1/27/2007		6		6
		Total		**6**		**6**
	February	2/3/2007		6		6
		2/10/2007		6		6
		2/17/2007		6		6
		Total		**18**		**18**
	March	3/3/2007			8	8
		Total			**8**	**8**
	April	4/7/2007			6	6
		4/14/2007			6	6
		4/21/2007	8	8	6	22
		4/28/2007			6	6
		Total	**8**	**8**	**24**	**40**
	May	5/5/2007	8	6		14
		5/12/2007	8	6		14
		5/26/2007	8	6		14
		Total	**24**	**18**		**42**

FIGURE 6-3 The total at the month level is generated by summing the individual dates, resulting in an incorrect value.

When handling snapshots, remember that snapshots do not generate additive measures. An *additive measure* is a measure that can be aggregated by using SUM over all the dimensions. With snapshots, you must use SUM when you aggregate over the stores, for example, but you cannot use SUM to aggregate over time. Snapshots contain sets of information that are valid at a given point in time. However, at the grand-total level, you typically don't aggregate over dates by using a sum—for example, showing the sum of all the individual days. Instead, you should consider the last valid value, the average, or some other kind of aggregation to display a meaningful result.

This is a typical scenario in which you must use the semi-additive pattern, where you show the values from the last period for which there is some information. If you focus on April, for example, the last date for which there is data is the 28th. There are multiple ways to handle this calculation by using DAX. Let us explore them.

The canonical semi-additive pattern uses the LASTDATE function to retrieve the last date in a period. Such a function is not useful in this example because, when you select April, LASTDATE will return the 30th of April, for which there is no data. In fact, if you modify the On Hand measure with the following code, the result will clear out the monthly totals:

```
On Hand :=
CALCULATE (
    SUM ( Inventory[OnHandQuantity] ),
    LASTDATE ( 'Date'[Date] )
)
```

You can see this in Figure 6-4, where the totals at the month level are blank.

Calendar Year	Month	Date	Giebelstadt Store	Munich Store	obamberg Store	Total
CY 2007	January	1/27/2007		6		6
		Total				
	February	2/3/2007		6		6
		2/10/2007		6		6
		2/17/2007		6		6
		Total				
	March	3/3/2007			8	8
		Total				
	April	4/7/2007			6	6
		4/14/2007			6	6
		4/21/2007	8	8	6	22
		4/28/2007			6	6
		Total				

FIGURE 6-4 If you use LASTDATE to retrieve the last date in a period, the totals disappear.

The date you need to use is the last date for which there is data, which might not correspond to the last date of the month. In this case, DateKey in the Inventory table is a date, so you might try a different formulation. Instead of using LASTDATE on the Date table, which contains all the dates, you might be tempted to use LASTDATE on the Inventory date column in the Inventory table, which contains only the available dates. We have seen these kinds of formulas multiple times in naïve models. Unfortunately, however, they result in incorrect totals. This is because it violates one of the best practices of DAX, that is to apply filters on dimensions instead of applying them on the fact table, for columns belonging to a relationship. Let us analyze the behavior by looking at the result in Figure 6-5, where the measure has been modified with the following code:

```
On Hand :=
CALCULATE (
    SUM ( Inventory[OnHandQuantity] ),
    LASTDATE ( Inventory[DateKey] )
)
```

Calendar Year	Month	Date	Giebelstadt Store	Munich Store	obamberg Store	Total
CY 2007	January	1/27/2007		6		6
		Total		6		6
	February	2/3/2007		6		6
		2/10/2007		6		6
		2/17/2007		6		6
		Total		6		6
	March	3/3/2007			8	8
		Total			8	8
	April	4/7/2007			6	6
		4/14/2007			6	6
		4/21/2007	8	8	6	22
		4/28/2007			6	6
		Total	8	8	6	6

FIGURE 6-5 Using LASTDATE on the Inventory date column still results in wrong numbers.

Look at the totals for April. Notice that in Giebelstadt and Munich, the value shown is from the 21st of April, whereas for Obamberg, the value is from the 28th. However, the grand total for all three stores is only 6, which matches the total of the values for all three stores on the 28th. What is happening?

Instead of counting the values from the last date for Munich and Giebelstadt (the 21st) and the value for the last date for Obamberg (the 28th), the grand total counts only the values from the 28th because that is the last date among the three stores. In other words, the value given—that is, 6—is not the grand total, but rather the partial total at the store level. In fact, because there are no quantities on the 28th for Giebelstadt and Munich, their monthly total should show a zero, not the last available value. Thus, a correct formulation of the grand total should search for the last date for which there are values for at least one shop. The standard solution for this pattern is as follows:

```
On Hand := CALCULATE (
    SUM ( Inventory[OnHandQuantity] ),
    CALCULATETABLE (
        LASTNONBLANK ( 'Date'[Date], NOT ( ISEMPTY ( Inventory ) ) ),
        ALL ( Store )
    )
)
```

Or, in this specific case, as follows:

```
On Hand := CALCULATE (
    SUM ( Inventory[OnHandQuantity] ),
    LASTDATE (
        CALCULATETABLE (
            VALUES ( Inventory[Date] ),
            ALL ( Store )
        )
    )
)
```

Both versions work fine. You decide which one to use depending on the data distribution and some peculiarities of the model, which are not worth investigating here. The point is that using this version of the on-hand calculation, you obtain the desired result, as shown in Figure 6-6.

Calendar Year	Month	Date	Giebelstadt Store	Munich Store	obamberg Store	Total
CY 2007	January	1/27/2007		6		6
		Total		6		6
	February	2/3/2007		6		6
		2/10/2007		6		6
		2/17/2007		6		6
		Total				
	March	3/3/2007			8	8
		Total				
	April	4/7/2007			6	6
		4/14/2007			6	6
		4/21/2007	8	8	6	22
		4/28/2007			6	6

FIGURE 6-6 The last formula yields the correct results at the total level.

This code runs just fine, but it has one major drawback: It must scan the Inventory table whenever it searches for the last date for which there is data. Depending on the number of dates in the table, and on data distribution, this might take some time, and could result in poor performance. In such a case, a good solution is to anticipate the calculation of which dates are to be considered valid dates for the inventory at process time when your data is loaded in memory. To do this, you can create a calculated column in the Date table that indicates whether the given date is present in the Inventory table. Use the following code:

```
Date[RowsInInventory] := CALCULATE ( NOT ISEMPTY ( Inventory ) )
```

The column is a Boolean with only two possible values: TRUE or FALSE. Moreover, it is stored in the Date table, which is always a tiny table. (Even if you had 10 years of data, the Date table would account for only around 3,650 rows.) The consequence of this is that scanning a tiny table is always a fast operation, whereas scanning the fact table—which potentially contains millions of rows—might not be. After the column is in place, you can change the calculation of the on-hand value as follows:

```
On Hand := CALCULATE (
    SUM ( Inventory[OnHandQuantity] ),
    LASTDATE (
        CALCULATETABLE (
            VALUES ( 'Date'[Date] ),
            'Date'[RowsInInventory] = TRUE
        )
    )
)
```

Even if the code looks more complex, it will be faster because it needs to search for the inventory dates in the Date table, which is smaller, filtering by a Boolean column.

This book is not about DAX. It is about data modeling. So why did we spend so much time analyzing the DAX code to compute a semi-additive measure? The reason is that we wanted to point your attention to the following details, which do in fact relate to data modeling:

- **A snapshot table is not like a regular fact table**   Its values cannot be summed over time. Instead, they must use non-additive formulas (typically LASTDATE).

- **Snapshot granularity is seldom that of the individual date**   A table snapshotting the on-hand quantity for each product every day would quickly turn into a monster. It would be so large that performance would be very bad.

- **Mixing changes in granularity with semi-additivity can be problematic**   The formulas tend to be hard to write. In addition, if you do not pay attention to the details, performance will suffer. And of course, it is very easy to author code that does not compute the totals in the right way. It is always good to double-check all the numbers before considering them correct.

- **To optimize the code, precompute information whenever possible**   You should precompute the information about which dates are present in the snapshot by using a calculated column in the date table. This small change results in much better performance.

What you learned in this section applies to nearly all kinds of snapshots. You might need to handle the price of a stock, the temperature of an engine, or any kind of measurement. They all fall in the same category. Sometimes, you will need the value at the beginning of the period. Other times, it will be the value at the end. However, you will seldom be able to use a simple sum to aggregate values from the snapshot.

Understanding derived snapshots

A *derived snapshot* is a pre-aggregated table that contains a concise view of the values. Most of the time, snapshots are created for performance reasons. If you need to aggregate billions of rows every time you want to compute a number, then it might be better to precompute the value in a snapshot to reduce the computational effort of your model.

Often, this is a good idea, but you must carefully balance the pros and cons before choosing a snapshot for your model. Imagine, for example, that you must build a report that shows the number of customers for every month, dividing them into new customers and returning ones. You can leverage a precomputed table, like the one shown in Figure 6-7, which contains the three values you need for every month.

DateKey	Customers	NewCustomers	ReturningCustomers
20070131	182	182	0
20080131	40	27	13
20090131	21	10	11
20070228	154	147	7
20080229	54	40	14
20090228	47	39	8
20070331	152	148	4
20080331	61	56	5
20090331	49	42	7
20070430	185	177	8
20080430	100	94	6
20090430	26	19	7
20070531	153	143	10
20080531	43	38	5

FIGURE 6-7   This table contains new and returning customers as a snapshot.

This pre-aggregated table, named NewCustomers, can be added to the model and joined through relationships with the Date table. This will enable you to build reports on top of it. Figure 6-8 shows the resulting model.

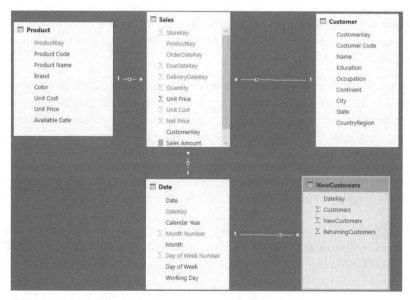

FIGURE 6-8   NewCustomers is a snapshot table linked in the model.

This snapshot contains only one row per month, for a total of 36 rows. When compared to the millions of rows in the fact table, it looks like a great deal. In fact, you can easily build a report that shows the sales amount along with the precomputed values, as shown in Figure 6-9.

Calendar Year	Month	Sales Amount	Customers	NewCustomers	ReturningCustomers
CY 2007	January	101,097.12	182	182	0
CY 2007	February	108,553.20	154	147	7
CY 2007	March	119,707.83	152	148	4
CY 2007	April	121,085.74	185	177	8
CY 2007	May	123,413.41	153	143	10
CY 2007	June	121,707.44	86	75	11
CY 2007	July	139,381.00	113	106	7
CY 2007	August	87,384.31	119	114	5
CY 2007	September	155,275.94	81	73	8
CY 2007	October	99,872.65	70	60	10
CY 2007	November	122,522.86	106	98	8
CY 2007	December	159,214.45	97	86	11
CY 2008	January	64,601.67	40	27	13
CY 2008	February	61,157.39	54	40	14

FIGURE 6-9 A monthly report is very easy to generate with a snapshot.

From a performance point of view, this report is great because all the numbers are precomputed and available in a matter of milliseconds. Nevertheless, in a scenario like this, speed comes at a cost. In fact, the report has the following issues:

- **You cannot generate subtotals** As with the snapshot shown in the previous section, you cannot generate subtotals by aggregating with SUM. Worse, in this case, the numbers are all computed with distinct counts—meaning you cannot aggregate them by using LASTDATE or any other technique.

- **You cannot slice by any other attribute** Suppose you are interested in the same report, but limited to customers who bought some kind of product. In that case, the snapshot is of no help. The same applies to the date or any other attribute that goes deeper than the month.

In such a scenario, because you can obtain the same calculation by using a measure, the snapshot is not the best option. If you must handle tables that have less than a few hundred million rows, then making derived snapshots is not a good option. Calculations on the fly typically provide good performance and much more flexibility.

With that said, there are scenarios in which you don't want flexibility or need to avoid it. In those scenarios, snapshots play a very important role in the definition of the data model, even if they are derived snapshots. In the next section, we analyze one of these scenarios, the transition matrix.

Understanding the transition matrix

A *transition* matrix is a very useful modeling technique that makes extensive use of snapshots to create powerful analytical models. It is not an easy technique, but we think it is important that you understand at least the basic concepts of the transition matrix. It can be a useful tool for your modeling tool belt.

Suppose you assign a ranking to your customers based on how much they bought in a month. You have three categories of customers—low, medium, and high—and you have a Customer Rankings configuration table that you use to store the boundaries of each category, as shown in Figure 6-10.

Rating	MinSale	MaxSale
Low	0	100
Medium	100	500
High	500	999999999

FIGURE 6-10 The Customer Rankings configuration table for the rating of a customer.

Based on this configuration table, you can build a calculated table in the model that ranks each customer on a monthly basis, by using the following code:

```
CustomerRanked =
SELECTCOLUMNS (
    ADDCOLUMNS (
        SUMMARIZE ( Sales, 'Date'[Calendar Year], 'Date'[Month], Sales[CustomerKey] ),
        "Sales", [Sales Amount],
        "Rating", CALCULATE (
            VALUES ( 'Rating Configuration'[Rating] ),
            FILTER (
                'Ranking Configuration',
                AND (
                    'Ranking Configuration'[MinSale] < [Sales Amount],
                    'Ranking Configuration'[MaxSale] >= [Sales Amount]
                )
            )
        ),
        "DateKey", CALCULATE ( MAX ( 'Date'[DateKey] ) )
    ),
    "CustomerKey", [CustomerKey],
    "DateKey", [DateKey],
    "Sales", [Sales],
    "Rating", [Rating]
)
```

This query looks rather complex, but in reality, its result is simple. It produces a list of month, year, and customer keys. Then, based on the configuration table, it assigns to each customer a monthly rating. The resulting CustomerRanked table is shown in Figure 6-11.

DateKey ↓	CustomerKey	Sales	Rating
20070228	11567	$1,136.46	High
20070228	11601	$2,302.68	High
20070228	4550	$607.96	High
20070228	6126	$627.00	High
20070228	10056	$3,383.15	High
20070228	6124	$313.50	Medium
20070228	6125	$313.50	Medium
20070228	6336	$313.50	Medium
20070228	6337	$313.50	Medium
20070228	6341	$313.50	Medium
20070228	956	$103.55	Medium

FIGURE 6-11 The rating snapshot stores the ratings of customers on a monthly basis.

Depending on how much a customer buys, that customer may be rated differently in different months. Or, there may be several months when the customer has no rating at all. (This only means the customer did not buy anything in those months.) If you add the table to the model and build the proper set of relationships, you will obtain the data model shown in Figure 6-12. If, at this point, you think we are building a derived snapshot, you are right. CustomerRanked is a derived snapshot that precomputes a metric based on Sales, which actually stores the facts.

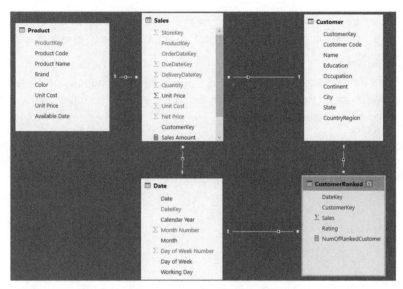

FIGURE 6-12   The snapshot, as always, looks like another fact table in the model.

You can use this table to build a simple report that shows the number of customers rated in different months and years. It is worth noting that this snapshot must be aggregated by using a distinct count, to consider each customer only once at the total level. The following formula is used to generate the measure found in the report shown in Figure 6-13:

```
NumOfRankedCustomers :=
CALCULATE (
    DISTINCTCOUNT ( CustomerRanked[CustomerKey] )
)
```

Calendar Year	Month	Low	Medium	High	Total
CY 2007	January	87	40	55	182
	February	53	47	54	154
	March	43	55	54	152
	April	60	61	64	185
	May	41	46	66	153
	June	41	6	39	86
	July	35	22	56	113
	August	76	14	29	119
	September	12	23	46	81
	October	16	29	25	70
	November	38	22	46	106
	December	24	24	49	97
	Total	526	389	583	1498

FIGURE 6-13   Using a snapshot to count the number of customers for a given rating is straightforward.

So far, we have built a snapshot table that looks very similar to the example in the previous section, which ended with a suggestion not to use a snapshot for that scenario. What is different here? The following are some important differences:

- The rating is assigned, depending on how much the customer spent, no matter what product was purchased. Because the definition of the rating is independent from the external selection, it makes sense to precompute it and to store it once and forever.

- Further slicing at the day level, for example, does not make much sense because the rating is assigned based on the sales of the whole month. Therefore, the very concept of month is included in the rating assigned.

Those considerations are already strong enough to make the snapshot a good solution. Nevertheless, there is a much stronger reason to do it. You can turn this snapshot into a transition matrix and perform much more advanced analyses.

A transition matrix aims to answer questions like, what is the evolution of the ranking of customers who were ranked medium in January 2007? The report required is like the one shown in Figure 6-14. It contains the customers who had a medium ranking in January 2007, and shows how their rankings changed over time.

Year Month

January 2007   ∨

Rating

Medium   ∨

Calendar Year	Month	Low	Medium	High	Total
CY 2007	January		40		40
	April			1	1
	May	1			1
	November			1	1
	Total	**1**	**40**	**2**	**40**
CY 2009	June	4			4
	Total	**4**			**4**
Total		**5**	**40**	**2**	**40**

FIGURE 6-14 The transition matrix provides very powerful insights in your customer analysis.

Figure 6-14 shows that in January 2007, 40 customers had a medium ranking. Of those customers, one was ranked high in April, one low in May, and one high in November. In 2009, four of those 40 customers had a low ranking in June. As you see, you set a filter for a given ranking in one month. This filter identifies a set of customers. You can then analyze how that set of customers behaved in other periods.

To build the transition matrix, you must perform the following two distinct operations:

1. Identify the customers who were ranked with a given ranking and date.

2. Check how they were ranked in different periods.

Let us start with the first operation. We want to isolate the customers with a given rating in one month. Because we want to use a slicer to fix the snapshot date and rating, we need a helper table to use as the filter. This point is important to understand. As an example, think about filtering the date of the snapshot (January 2007, in this example). If you use the Date table as a filter, then you use the same table that will be used also to show the evolution over time. In other words, if you use the Date table to filter January 2007, that filter will be effective on the entire model, making it impossible (or, rather, very hard) to build the report because you will not be able to see the evolution in, for example, February 2007.

Because you cannot use the Date table as a filter for the snapshot, the best option is to build a new table to serve as the source of the slicers. Such a table contains two columns: one with the different ratings and one with the months referenced by the fact table. You can build it using the following code:

```
SnapshotParameters =
SELECTCOLUMNS (
    ADDCOLUMNS (
        SUMMARIZE (
            CustomerRanked,
            'Date'[Calendar Year],
            'Date'[Month],
            CustomerRanked[Rating]
        ),
        "DateKey", CALCULATE ( MAX ( 'Date'[DateKey] ) )
    ),
    "DateKey", [DateKey],
    "Year Month", FORMAT (
        CALCULATE ( MAX ( 'Date'[Date] ) ),
        "mmmm YYYY"
    ),
    "Rating", [Rating]
)
```

Figure 6-15 shows the resulting table (SnapshotParameters).

DateKey	Year Month	Rating
20070131	January 2007	Medium
20080131	January 2008	Medium
20090131	January 2009	Medium
20070228	February 2007	Medium
20080229	February 2008	Medium
20090228	February 2009	Medium
20070331	March 2007	Medium
20080331	March 2008	Medium
20090331	March 2009	Medium

FIGURE 6-15   The SnapshotParameters table contains three columns.

The table contains both the date key (as an integer) and the year month (as a string). You can put the string in a slicer and grab the corresponding key that will be useful when moving the filter to the snapshot table.

This table should not be related to any other table in the model. It is merely a helper table, used as the source of two slicers: one for the snapshot date and one for the snapshot rating. The data model is now in place. You can select a starting point for the ranking and put the years and months in the rows of a matrix. The following DAX code will compute the desired number—that is the number of customers who had a given rating in the selection from the slicer and a different rating in different periods:

```
Transition Matrix =
CALCULATE (
    DISTINCTCOUNT ( CustomerRanked[CustomerKey] ),
    CALCULATETABLE(
        VALUES ( CustomerRanked[CustomerKey] ),
        INTERSECT (
            ALL ( CustomerRanked[Rating] ),
            VALUES ( SnapshotParameters[Rating] )
        ),
        INTERSECT (
            ALL ( CustomerRanked[DateKey] ),
            VALUES ( SnapshotParameters[DateKey] )
        ),
        ALL ( CustomerRanked[RatingSort] ),
        ALL ( 'Date' )
    )
)
```

This code is not easy to understand at first sight, but we suggest you to spend some time studying it carefully. It expresses so much power in so few lines that you will probably grasp some new ideas from understanding it.

The core of the code is the CALCULATETABLE function, which uses two INTERSECT calls. INTERSECT is used to apply the selection from SnapshotParameters (the table used for the slicers) as a filter of CustomerRanked. There are two INTERSECT calls: one for the date, one for the ranking. When this filter is in place, CALCULATETABLE returns the keys of the customers who were ranked with the given rating at the given date. Thus, the outer CALCULATE will compute the number of customers ranked in different periods, but limit the count to only the ones selected by CALCULATETABLE. The resulting report is the one already shown in Figure 6-14.

From a modeling point of view, it is interesting that you need a snapshot table to perform this kind of analysis. In fact, in this case, the snapshot is used to determine the set of customers who had a specific rating in a given month. This information is further used as a filter to perform an analysis of their behavior over time.

You have seen the following important points so far:

- A snapshot makes perfect sense when you want to freeze the calculation. In this example, you wanted to focus on customers with a given ranking in one specific month. The snapshot offers you an easy way to do this.

- If you need to filter the snapshot date but you don't want this filter to propagate to the model, you can keep the table unrelated and use INTERSECT to activate the filter on demand.

- You can use the snapshot as a tool to compute a filter over the customers. In the example, you wanted to examine the behavior of those customers in other periods of time.

One of the interesting aspects of the transition matrix is that you can use it to compute more complex numbers.

Conclusions

Snapshots are useful tools to reduce the size of a table at the price of granularity. By pre-aggregating data, your formulas will be much faster. In addition, as you have seen with the transition matrix pattern, you open a whole set of analytical possibilities by snapshotting the data. With that said, a snapshot comes with an increased complexity in the model. This chapter explored the following important points:

- Snapshots almost always require aggregations other than a simple sum. You must carefully analyze the kind of aggregation you require or, at worst, fully avoid subtotals.

- The granularity of snapshots is always different from the granularity of normal fact tables. You must take this into account when building reports, as speed comes with limitations.

- You can often avoid derived snapshots if your model is not too large. Use derived snapshots as a last resource if optimizing your DAX code does not lead to acceptable performance.

- As you saw with the transition matrix, snapshots open new possibilities in the analysis of data. There are many more possibilities you can explore, depending on the kind of business you need to analyze.

Using snapshots is not easy. This chapter provided some simple and advanced scenarios. We suggest you learn the simple scenarios, spend some time thinking about how you can benefit from the harder ones, and move slowly through the use of snapshots and transition matrixes. Even seasoned data modelers will find it hard to author some of the code in this chapter. Nevertheless, if needed, transition matrixes are extremely powerful for grabbing insights from your data.

CHAPTER 7

Analyzing date and time intervals

Chapter 4, "Working with date and time," discussed time intelligence and calculations over time. This chapter will show you several models that, again, use time as the primary analytical tool. This time, however, we are not interested in discussing calculations like year-to-date (YTD) and year-over-year. Instead, we want to discuss scenarios in which time is the focus of the analysis, but not necessarily the main dimension used to slice. Thus, we will show you scenarios like computing the number of working hours in a period, the number of employees available in different time frames for various projects, and the number of orders currently being processed.

What makes these models different from a standard model? In a standard model, a fact is an atomic event that happened at a very precise point in time. In these models, on the other hand, facts are typically events with durations, and they extend their effect for some time. Thus, what you store in the fact table is not the date of the event, but the point in time when the event started. Then, you must work with DAX and with the model to account for the duration of the event.

Concepts like time, duration, and periods are present in these models. However, as you will see, the focus is not only on slicing by time, but also on analyzing the facts with durations. Having time as one of the numbers to aggregate or to consider during the analysis makes these models somewhat complex. Careful modeling is required.

Introduction to temporal data

Having read this book so far, you are very familiar with the idea of using a date dimension to slice your data. This allows you to analyze the behavior of facts over time, by using the date dimension to slice and dice your values. When we speak about facts, we usually think about events with numbers associated with them, such as the number of items sold, their price, or the age of a customer. But sometimes, the fact does not happen at a given point in time. Instead, it starts at a given point in time, and then its effect has a duration.

Think, for example, about a normal worker. You can model the fact that, on a given date, that worker was working, produced some amount of work, and earned a specific amount of money. All this information is stored as normal facts. At the same time, you might store in the model the number of hours that person worked, to be able to summarize them at the end of the month. In such a case, a simple model like the one shown in Figure 7-1 looks correct. There, you have two dimensions, Workers and Date, and a Schedule fact table with the relevant keys and values.

FIGURE 7-1 This figure shows a simple data model for handling working schedules.

It might be the case that workers are paid at a different rate, depending on the time of the day. Night shifts, for example, are typically paid more than day shifts. You can see this effect in Figure 7-2, which shows the Schedule table content, where the hourly wage for shifts starting after 6:00 p.m. is higher. (You can obtain such a rate dividing Amount by HoursWorked.)

WorkerId	Date	TimeStart	HoursWorked	Amount
1	1/1/2016	9:00:00 AM	8	160
1	1/15/2016	6:00:00 PM	6	180
1	1/31/2016	9:00:00 PM	9	360
2	1/1/2016	9:00:00 AM	8	160
2	1/15/2016	6:00:00 PM	5	150
2	1/31/2016	9:00:00 PM	8	320
1	2/1/2016	9:00:00 AM	4	80
1	2/15/2016	6:00:00 PM	3	90
1	2/29/2016	9:00:00 PM	8	320
2	2/1/2016	9:00:00 AM	6	120
2	2/15/2016	6:00:00 PM	5	150
2	2/29/2016	9:00:00 PM	8	320

FIGURE 7-2 This figure shows the contents of the Schedule table.

You can now use this simple dataset to build a report that shows the hours worked on a monthly basis and the amount earned by the workers. The matrix is shown in Figure 7-3.

Year	Month Name	Michelle	Paul	Total
2016	January	21	23	**44**
	February	19	15	**34**
	Total	**40**	**38**	**78**
Total		**40**	**38**	**78**

FIGURE 7-3 This figure shows a simple matrix report on top of the schedule data model.

At first sight, the numbers look correct. However, look again at Figure 7-2, focusing your attention on the days at the end of each period (either January or February). You'll notice that at the end of January, the shifts start at 9:00 p.m., and because of their duration, they extend into the next day. Moreover, because it is the end of the month, they also extend to the next month. It would be much more accurate to state that some of the amount of January 31st needs to be accounted for in February, and some of the amount of February 29th needs to be accounted for in March. The data model does not produce this result. Instead it looks like all the hours are being worked in the day that the shift started, even if we know this is not the case.

Because this is only an introductory section, we do not want to dive into the details of the solution. These will be shown throughout the rest of the chapter. The point here is that the data model is not accurate. The problem is that each of the events stored in the fact table has a duration, and this duration extends its effects outside of the granularity that is defined in the fact table itself. In other words, the fact table has a granularity at the day level, but the facts it stores might contain information related to different days. Because of this, we have (again!) a granularity issue. A very similar scenario happens whenever you have to analyze durations. Each fact that has a duration falls into a similar scenario and needs to be handled with a lot of care. Otherwise, you end up with a data model that does not accurately represent the real world.

This is not to say that the data model is wrong. It all depends on the kinds of questions you want your data model to answer. The current model is totally fine for many reports, but it is not accurate enough for certain kinds of analysis. You might decide that the full amount should be shown in the month when the shift starts, and in most scenarios, this would be perfectly reasonable. However, this is a book about data modeling, so we need to build the right model for different requirements.

In this chapter, we will deal with scenarios like the one in the example, carefully studying how to model them to correctly reflect the data they need to store.

Aggregating with simple intervals

Before diving into the complexity of interval analysis, let us start with some simpler scenarios. In this section, we want to show you how to correctly define a time dimension in your model. In fact, most of the scenarios we are managing require time dimensions, and learning how to model them is very important.

In a typical database, you will find a DateTime column that stores both the date and the time in the same column. Thus, an event that started at 09:30 a.m. on January 15, 2017 will contain a single column with that precise point in time. Even if this is the data you find in the source database, we urge you to split it into two different columns in your data model: one for the date and one for the time. The reason is that Tabular, which is the engine of both Power Pivot and Power BI, works much better with small dimensions than with larger ones. If you store date and time in the same column, you will need a much larger dimension because, for every single day, you need to store all the different hours and minutes. By splitting the information into two columns, the date dimension contains only the day granularity, and the time dimension contains only the time granularity. To host 10 years of data, for example, you need around 3,650 rows in the date dimension, and 1,440 rows in the time dimension, if you are working at the individual minute level. On the other hand, a single date/time dimension would require around 5,256,000 rows, which is 3,650 times 1,440. The difference in terms of query speed is tremendous.

Of course, you need to perform the operation of splitting the date/time column into two columns before the data enters your model. In other words, you can load a date/time column in your model, and then build two calculated columns on which to base the relationship—one for the date and one for the time. With that said, the memory used for the date/time column is basically a waste of resources because you will never use that column. You can obtain the same result with much less memory consumption by performing the split using the Excel or Power BI Query Editor or, for more advanced users, using a SQL view that performs the splitting. Figure 7-4 shows a very simple time dimension.

Time	Hour	Minute	HourMinute	TimeIndex
00.00	00	00	00:00	0
00.01	00	01	00:01	1
00.02	00	02	00:02	2
00.03	00	03	00:03	3
00.04	00	04	00:04	4
00.05	00	05	00:05	5
00.06	00	06	00:06	6
00.07	00	07	00:07	7
00.08	00	08	00:08	8
00.09	00	09	00:09	9
00.10	00	10	00:10	10

FIGURE 7-4 This figure shows a very basic time dimension at the minute granularity.

If the time dimension contained only hours and minutes, it would not be of much use unless you needed to perform an analysis at a very detailed level. You are likely to add some attributes to the dimension to be able to group the data in different buckets. For example, in Figure 7-5, we added two columns so we could group the time in day periods (night, morning, and so on) and in hourly buckets. We then reformatted the Time column.

Time	Hour	Minute	HourMinute	TimeIndex	Hour Range	Day Period
00.00	00	00	00:00	0	From 00:00 to 01:00	Night
00.01	00	01	00:01	1	From 00:00 to 01:00	Night
00.02	00	02	00:02	2	From 00:00 to 01:00	Night
00.03	00	03	00:03	3	From 00:00 to 01:00	Night
00.04	00	04	00:04	4	From 00:00 to 01:00	Night
00.05	00	05	00:05	5	From 00:00 to 01:00	Night
00.06	00	06	00:06	6	From 00:00 to 01:00	Night
00.07	00	07	00:07	7	From 00:00 to 01:00	Night
00.08	00	08	00:08	8	From 00:00 to 01:00	Night
00.09	00	09	00:09	9	From 00:00 to 01:00	Night
00.10	00	10	00:10	10	From 00:00 to 01:00	Night

FIGURE 7-5 You can group time in different buckets by using simple calculated columns.

You must take particular care when analyzing time buckets. In fact, even if it looks very natural to define a time dimension at the minute level and then group it using buckets, you may be able to define the dimension at the bucket level. In other words, if you are not interested in analyzing data at the minute level (which will usually be the case), but only want to perform an analysis at the half-hour level, then using the dimension at the minute level is a waste of space and time. If you store the dimension at the half-hour level, the whole dimension will use 48 rows instead of 1,440. This gives you two orders of magnitude and a tremendous saving in terms of RAM and query speed because of the savings applied to the larger fact table. Figure 7-6 shows you the same time dimension as Figure 7-5, but in this case, it is stored at the half-hour level.

Of course, if you store the time at the half-hour level, you will need to compute a column in the fact table that acts as an index for the table. In Figure 7-6, we used Hours × 60 + Minutes as the index instead of using a simple auto-increment column. This makes it much easier to compute the time key in the fact table, by starting from the date/time. You can obtain it by using simple math, without the need to perform complex ranged lookups.

Time	Hour	Minute	HourMinute	TimeIndex	Hour Range	Day Period
03.00	03	00	03:00	180	From 03:00 to 04:00	Night
03.30	03	30	03:30	210	From 03:00 to 04:00	Night
04.00	04	00	04:00	240	From 04:00 to 05:00	Night
04.30	04	30	04:30	270	From 04:00 to 05:00	Night
05.00	05	00	05:00	300	From 05:00 to 06:00	Night
05.30	05	30	05:30	330	From 05:00 to 06:00	Night
06.00	06	00	06:00	360	From 06:00 to 07:00	Night
06.30	06	30	06:30	390	From 06:00 to 07:00	Night
07.00	07	00	07:00	420	From 07:00 to 08:00	Morning
07.30	07	30	07:30	450	From 07:00 to 08:00	Morning
08.00	08	00	08:00	480	From 08:00 to 09:00	Morning
08.30	08	30	08:30	510	From 08:00 to 09:00	Morning

FIGURE 7-6   By storing at the half-hour level, the table becomes much smaller.

Let us repeat this very important fact: Date and time must be stored in separate columns. After many years of consulting different customers with different needs, we have yet to find many cases where storing a single date/time column is the best solution. This is not to say that it is forbidden to store a date/time column. In very rare cases, using a date/time column is the only viable option. However, it is so rare to find a good case for a date/time column that we always default to splitting the columns—although we are ready to change our minds if (and only if) there is a strong need to do so. Needless to say, this does not typically happen.

Intervals crossing dates

In the previous section, you learned how to model a time dimension. It is now time to go back to the introduction and perform a deeper analysis of the scenario in which events happen, and they have a duration that might span to the next day.

As you might recall, we had a Schedule table that contained the worked hours. Because a worker might start a shift in the late evening (or even at night), the working day could span to the next day, making it difficult to perform analysis on it. Let us recall the data model, which is shown in Figure 7-7.

FIGURE 7-7   This figure shows a simple data model for handling working schedules.

First, let us see how to perform the analysis on this model in the right way by using some DAX code. Be aware that using DAX is not the optimal solution. We use this example only to show how complex the code might become if you do not work with the correct model.

In this very specific example, a shift might span over two days. You can obtain the real working hours by first computing the working hours in the day and then removing from the day the shift hours that might be in the next day. After this first step, you must sum the potential working hours of the previous day that spanned to the current day. This can be accomplished by the following DAX code:

```
Real Working Hours =
--
-- Computes the working hours in the same day
--
SUMX (
    Schedule,
    IF (
        Schedule[TimeStart] + Schedule[HoursWorked] * ( 1 / 24 ) <= 1,
        Schedule[HoursWorked],
        ( 1 - Schedule[TimeStart] ) * 24
    )
)
--
-- Check if there are hours today, coming from a previous day that overlapped here
--
+ SUMX (
    VALUES ( 'Date'[Date] ),
    VAR
        CurrentDay = 'Date'[Date]
    RETURN
        CALCULATE (
            SUMX (
                Schedule,
                IF (
                    Schedule[TimeStart] + Schedule[HoursWorked] * ( 1 / 24 ) > 1,
                    Schedule[HoursWorked] - ( 1 - Schedule[TimeStart] ) * 24
                )
            ),
            'Date'[Date] = CurrentDay - 1
        )
)
```

Now the code returns the correct number, as shown in Figure 7-8.

Year ▼	Month Name	Date	Michelle	Paul	Total
2016	January	1/1/2016	8	8	16
		1/15/2016	5	6	11
		1/31/2016	3	3	6
		Total	**16**	**17**	**33**
	February	2/1/2016	11	10	21
		2/15/2016	5	3	8
		2/29/2016	3	3	6
		Total	**19**	**16**	**35**
	March	3/1/2016	5	5	10
		Total	**5**	**5**	**10**
	Total		**40**	**38**	**78**
Total			**40**	**38**	**78**

FIGURE 7-8 The new measure shows the working hours in the correct day.

The problem appears to have been solved. However, at this point, the real question is whether you really want to write such a measure. We had to because we are writing a book and we needed to demonstrate how complex it is, but you are not, and you might have better options. The chances of making mistakes with such a complex piece of code are very high. Moreover, this works only in the very special case in which an event spans two consecutive days. If an event has a duration of more than two days, this code becomes much more complex, thus increasing the chances of making mistakes.

As is usually the case in this book (and in the real world), the solution is not writing complex DAX code. The best solution is to change the data model so that it reflects, in a more precise way, the data you need to model. Then, the code will be simpler (and faster).

There are several options for changing this model. As we anticipated earlier in this chapter, the problem is that you are storing data at the wrong granularity level. In fact, you must change the granularity if you want to be able to slice by the hours the employees actually worked in a day and if you are considering the night shift as belonging to the calendar day. Instead of storing a fact that says, "Starting on this day, the worker worked for some hours," you must store a fact that says, "On this given day, the worker worked for so many hours." For example, if a worker starts a shift on September 1st and ends it on September 2nd, you will store two rows: one with the hours on September 1st and one with the hours on September 2nd, effectively splitting the single row into multiple ones.

Thus, an individual row in the previous fact table might as well be transformed into multiple rows in the new data model. If a worker starts a shift during the late evening, then you will store two rows for the shift—one for the day when the work started, with the correct starting time, and another on the next day, starting at midnight, with the remaining hours. If the shift spans multiple days, then you can generate multiple rows. This, of course, requires a more complicated data preparation, which we do not show in the book because it involves quite complex M code. However, you can see this in the companion content, if you are interested. The resulting Schedule table is shown in Figure 7-9, where you can see several days starting at midnight, which are the continuation of the previous days. The hours worked have been adjusted during Extract, Transform, Load (ETL).

WorkerId	Amount	Date	TimeStart	HoursWorked
1	160	1/1/2016	9:00:00 AM	8
1	180	1/15/2016	6:00:00 PM	6
1	360	1/31/2016	9:00:00 PM	3
1	360	2/1/2016	12:00:00 AM	6
1	80	2/1/2016	9:00:00 AM	4
1	90	2/15/2016	6:00:00 PM	3
1	320	2/29/2016	9:00:00 PM	3
1	320	3/1/2016	12:00:00 AM	5
2	160	1/1/2016	9:00:00 AM	8
2	150	1/15/2016	6:00:00 PM	5
2	320	1/31/2016	9:00:00 PM	3
2	320	2/1/2016	12:00:00 AM	5
2	120	2/1/2016	9:00:00 AM	6
2	150	2/15/2016	6:00:00 PM	5
2	320	2/29/2016	9:00:00 PM	3
2	320	3/1/2016	12:00:00 AM	5

FIGURE 7-9 The Schedule table now has a lower granularity at the day level.

Because of this change in the model, which is correcting the granularity, now you can easily aggregate values by using a simple SUM. You will obtain the correct result and will avoid the complexity shown in the previous DAX code.

A careful reader might notice that we fixed the field containing HoursWorked, but we did not perform the same operation for Amount. In fact, if you aggregate the current model that shows the sum of the amount, you will obtain a wrong result. This is because the full amount will be aggregated for different days that might have been created because of midnight crossing. We did that on purpose because we wanted to use this small mistake to investigate further on the model.

An easy solution is to correct the amount by simply dividing the hours worked during the day by the total hours worked in the shift. You should obtain the percentage of the amount that should be accounted for the given day. This can be done as part of the ETL process, when preparing the data for analysis. However, if you strive for precision, then it is likely that the hourly rate is different depending on the time of the day. There might be shifts that mix different hourly rates. If this is the case, then, again, the data model is not accurate enough.

If the hourly price is different, then you must change, again, the data model to a lower level of granularity (that is, a higher level of detail) by moving the granularity to the hourly level. You have the option of making it easy by storing one fact per hour, or by pre-aggregating values when the hourly rate does not change. In terms of flexibility, moving to the hourly level gives you more freedom and easier-to-produce reports because, at that point, you also have the option of analyzing time across different days. This would be much more complex in a case where you pre-aggregate the values. On the other hand, the number of rows in the fact table grows if you lower the granularity. As is always the case in data modeling, you must find the perfect balance between size and analytical power.

In this example, we decided to move to the hourly level of granularity, generating the model shown in Figure 7-10.

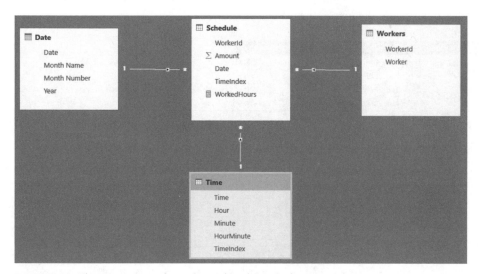

FIGURE 7-10 The new measure shows the working hours in the correct day.

In this new model, the fact basically says, "This day, at this hour, the employee worked." We increased the detail to the lowest granularity. At this point, computing the number of hours worked does not even require that we perform a SUM. In fact, it is enough to count the number of rows in Schedule to obtain the number of worked hours, as shown in the following WorkedHours measure:

```
WorkedHours := COUNTROWS ( Schedule )
```

In case you have a shift starting in the middle of the hour, you can store the number of minutes worked in that hour as part of the measure and then aggregate using SUM. Alternatively, in very extreme cases, you can move the granularity to a lower level—to the half-hour or even the minute level.

As mentioned, one of the big advantages of splitting date and time is to be able to analyze the time as a dimension by itself, unrelated to dates. If you want to analyze the shifts for which a worker is mostly employed, you can build a simple matrix like the one shown in Figure 7-11. In this figure, we used a version of the time dimension that includes, as indicated earlier in the chapter, day periods that contain only 24 rows. This is because we are interested in the hours only.

Day Period	Michelle	Paul	Total
Morning	8	8	**16**
Afternoon	6	4	**10**
Evening	16	15	**31**
Night	10	11	**21**
Total	**40**	**38**	**78**

FIGURE 7-11   This figure shows an analysis of time periods that are unrelated to dates.

At this point, you can compute the hourly rate (which will probably require some sort of configuration table) and perform a much finer analysis on the model. Nevertheless, in this demonstration, we were mainly focused on finding the correct granularity. We can stop analyzing this example here.

The important part of this demo is that, by finding the correct granularity, we moved from a very complex DAX expression to a much simpler one. At the same time, we increased the analytical power of our data model. We are perfectly aware of how many times we repeat the same concept. But this way, you can see how important it is to perform a deep analysis of the granularity needed by your model, depending on the kind of analysis you want to perform.

It does not matter how the original data is shaped. As a modeler, you must continue massaging your data until it reaches the shape needed by your model. Once it reaches the optimal format, all the numbers come out quickly and easily.

Modeling working shifts and time shifting

In the previous example, we analyzed a scenario where the working shifts were easy to get. In fact, the time at which the worker started the shift was part of the model. This is a very generic scenario, and it is probably more complex than what the average data analyst needs to cover.

In fact, having a fixed number of shifts during the day is a more common scenario. For example, if a worker normally works eight hours a day, there can be three different shifts that are alternately assigned to a worker during the month. It is very likely that one of these shifts will cross into the next day, and this makes the scenario look very similar to the previous one.

Another example of time shifting appears in a scenario where you want to analyze the number of people who are watching a given television channel, which is commonly used to understand the composition of the audience of a show. For example, suppose a show starts at 11:30 p.m., and it is two hours long, meaning it will end the next day. Nevertheless, you want it to be included in the previous day. And what about a show that starts at half past midnight? Do you want to consider it in competition with the previous show that started one hour earlier? Most likely, the answer is yes, because no matter when the two shows started, they were playing at the same time. It is likely an individual chose either one or the other.

There is an interesting solution to both these scenarios that requires you to broaden your definition of time. In the case of working shifts, the key is to ignore time completely. Instead of storing in the fact table the starting time, you can simply store the shift number, and then perform the analysis using the shift number only. If you need to consider time in your analysis, then the best option is to lower the granularity and use the previous solution. However, in most cases, we solved the model by simply removing the concept of time from the model.

The audience analysis scenario is somewhat different, and the solution, although strange, is very simple. You might want to consider the events happening right after midnight as belonging to the previous day so that when you analyze the audience of one day, you consider in the total what happened after midnight. To do so, you can easily implement a time-shifting algorithm. For example, instead of considering midnight as the beginning of the day, you can make the day start at 02:00 a.m. You can then add two more hours to the standard time so that the time ranges from 02:00 to 26:00 instead of going from 00:00 to 24:00. It is worth noting that, for this specific example, using the 24-hour format (26, to be precise) works much better than using a.m./p.m.

Figure 7-12 shows a typical report that uses this time-shifting technique. Note that the custom period starts at 02:00 and ends at 25:59. The total is still 24 hours, but by shifting time in this way, when you analyze the audience of one day, you also include the first two hours of the next day.

Date

4/7/2007 ∨			
CustomPeriod ▲	Elementary Schoool	Middle School	University
02:00 - 06:59	10,067.46	25,018.60	1,415.84
07:00 - 08:59	18,475.77	48,784.07	7,690.13
09:00 - 11:59	47,470.48	95,504.44	14,268.88
12:00 - 14:59	65,762.05	119,570.51	11,174.80
15:00 - 17:59	71,332.52	109,397.22	19,694.87
18:00 - 20:29	73,224.83	133,068.51	19,587.23
20:30 - 22:29	56,335.09	80,823.25	19,095.64
22:30 - 25:59	41,825.78	64,199.56	11,762.30
Total	**45,129.44**	**79,795.58**	**11,925.10**

FIGURE 7-12 By using the time-shifting technique, the day starts at 02:00 instead of starting at midnight.

Obviously, when loading the data model for such a scenario, you will need to perform a transformation. However, you will not be able to use DateTime columns because there is no such time as 25:00 in a normal date/time.

Analyzing active events

As you have seen, this chapter mainly covers fact tables with the concept of duration. Whenever you perform an analysis of these kinds of events, one interesting model is one that analyzes how many events were active in a given period. An event is considered active if it is started and not yet finished. There are many different kinds of these events, including orders in a sales model. An order is received, it is processed, and then it is shipped. In the period between the date of receipt and the date of shipment, the order is active. (Of course, in performing this analysis, you can go further and think that between shipment and delivery to the recipient, the order is still active, but in a different status.)

For the sake of simplicity, we are not going to perform a complex analysis of those different statuses. Here, we are mainly interested in discovering how you can build a data model to perform an analysis of active events. You can use such a model in different scenarios, like insurance policies (which have a start and end date), insurance claims, orders growing plants, or building items with a type of machinery. In all these cases, you record as a fact the event (such as the plants grown, the order placed, or the full event). However, the event itself has two or more dates identifying the process that has been executed to bring the event to its conclusion.

Before starting to solve the scenario, let us look at the first consideration you must account for when analyzing orders. The data model we used through most of this book stores sales at the granularity of the product, date, and customer level. Thus, if a single order contains 10 different products, it is represented with 10 different lines in the Sales table. Such a model is shown in Figure 7-13.

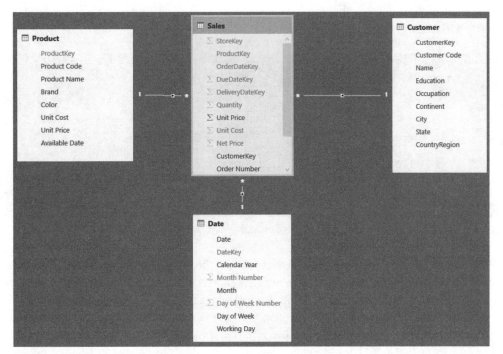

FIGURE 7-13 The fact table in this model stores individual sales.

If you want to count the number of orders in this model, you will need to perform a distinct count of the Order Number column in Sales, because a given order number will be repeated for multiple rows. Moreover, it is very likely that, if an order was shipped in multiple packages, different lines in the same order might have different delivery dates. So, if you are interested in analyzing the open orders, the granularity of the model is wrong. In fact, the order as a whole is to be considered delivered only when all its products have been delivered. You can compute the date of delivery of the last product in the order with some complex DAX code, but in this case, it is much easier to generate a new fact table containing only the orders. This will result in a lower granularity, and it will reduce the number of rows. Reducing the number of rows has the benefit of speeding up the calculation and avoiding the need to perform distinct counts.

The first step is to build an Orders table, which you can do with SQL, or, as we are doing in the example, with a simple calculated table that uses the following code:

```
Orders =
SUMMARIZECOLUMNS (
    Sales[Order Number],
    Sales[CustomerKey],
    "OrderDateKey", MIN ( Sales[OrderDateKey] ),
    "DeliveryDateKey", MAX ( Sales[DeliveryDateKey] )
)
```

This new table has fewer rows and fewer columns. It also already contains the first step of our calculation, which is the determination of the effective date of delivery, by taking into account the last delivery date of the order as a whole. The resulting data model, once the necessary relationships are created, is shown in Figure 7-14.

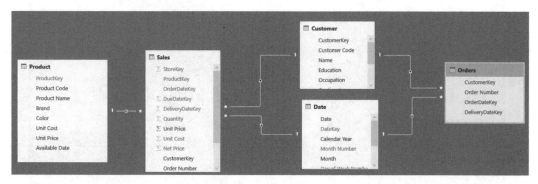

FIGURE 7-14 The new data model contains two fact tables at different granularities.

You can see that the Orders table has no relationships with Product. It is worth noting that you can also model such a scenario using a standard header/detail table, with Orders as the header and Sales as the detail. In such a case, you should take into account all the considerations we already made in Chapter 2, "Using header/detail tables." In this section, we ignore the header/detail relationship because we are mainly interested in using the Orders table only. Thus, we will use a simplified model, as shown in Figure 7-15. (Note that in the companion file, the Sales table is still present, because Orders depends on it. However, we will focus on these three tables only.)

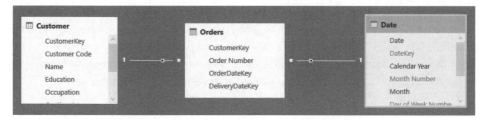

FIGURE 7-15 This figure shows the simplified model we use for this demo.

After the model is in place, you can easily build a DAX measure that computes the number of open orders by using the following code:

```
OpenOrders :=
CALCULATE (
    COUNTROWS ( Orders ),
    FILTER (
        ALL ( Orders[OrderDateKey] ),
        Orders[OrderDateKey] <= MIN ( 'Date'[DateKey] )
    ),
    FILTER (
        ALL ( Orders[DeliveryDateKey] ),
        Orders[DeliveryDateKey] > MAX ( 'Date'[DateKey] )
    ),
    ALL ( 'Date' )
)
```

The code itself is not complex. The important point is that because there is a relationship between Orders and Date that is based on OrderDateKey, you must remove its effects by using ALL on the Date table. Forgetting to do so will return a wrong number—basically the same number as the orders placed. The measure itself works just fine, as you can see in Figure 7-16, which shows both the number of orders received and the number of open orders.

Calendar Year	Month	Date	OrdersReceived	OpenOrders
CY 2007	January	2/1/07	10	10
		3/1/07	10	20
		4/1/07	15	35
		5/1/07	2	37
		6/1/07		37
		7/1/07	6	43
		8/1/07		42
		9/1/07	9	50
		10/1/07	15	61
		11/1/07	5	62
		12/1/07	9	66
		13/1/07	6	64
		14/1/07		60
		15/1/07	9	61

FIGURE 7-16 The report shows the number of orders received and the number of open orders.

To check the measure, it would be useful to show both the orders received and the orders shipped in the same report. This can be easily accomplished by using the technique you learned in Chapter 3, "Using multiple fact tables," which is adding a new relationship between Orders and Date. This time, the relationship will be based on the delivery date and kept inactive to avoid model ambiguity. Using this new relationship, you can build the OrdersDelivered measure in the following way:

```
OrdersDelivered :=
CALCULATE (
    COUNTROWS ( Orders ),
    USERELATIONSHIP ( Orders[DeliveryDateKey], 'Date'[DateKey] )
)
```

At this point, the report looks easier to read and check, as shown in Figure 7-17.

Calendar Year	Month	Date	OrdersReceived	OrdersDelivered	OpenOrders
CY 2007	January	2/1/07	10		10
		3/1/07	10		20
		4/1/07	15		35
		5/1/07	2		37
		6/1/07			37
		7/1/07	6		43
		8/1/07		1	42
		9/1/07	9	1	50
		10/1/07	15	4	61
		11/1/07	5	4	62
		12/1/07	9	5	66
		13/1/07	6	8	64
		14/1/07		4	60
		15/1/07	9	8	61

FIGURE 7-17 Adding the OrdersDelivered measure makes the report easier to understand.

This model provides the correct answers at the day level. However, at the month level (or on any other level above the day level), it suffers from a serious drawback. In fact, if you remove the date from the report and leave only the month, the result is surprising: The OpenOrders measure always shows a blank, as shown in Figure 7-18.

Calendar Year	Month	OrdersReceived	OrdersDelivered	OpenOrders
CY 2007	January	194	134	
	February	167	184	
	March	170	176	
	April	203	165	
	May	174	187	
	June	108	139	
	July	132	122	
	August	136	137	
	September	104	114	
	October	93	82	
	November	124	126	
	December	121	130	
	Total	**1726**	**1696**	

FIGURE 7-18 At the month level, the measure produces the wrong (blank) results.

The issue is that no orders lasted for more than one month, and this measure returns the number of orders received before the first day of the selected period and delivered after the end of that period (in this case, a month). Depending on your needs, you must update the measure to show the value of open orders at the end of the period, or the average value of open orders during the period. For example, the version that computes the open orders at the end of the period is easily produced with the following code, where we simply added a filter for LASTDATE around the original formula.

```
OpenOrders :=
CALCULATE (
    CALCULATE (
        COUNTROWS ( Orders ),
        FILTER (
            ALL ( Orders[OrderDateKey] ),
            Orders[OrderDateKey] <= MIN ( 'Date'[DateKey] )
        ),
        FILTER (
            ALL ( Orders[DeliveryDateKey] ),
            Orders[DeliveryDateKey] > MAX ( 'Date'[DateKey] )
        ),
        ALL ( 'Date' )
    ),
    LASTDATE ( 'Date'[Date] )
)
```

With this new formula, the result at the month level is as desired, as shown in Figure 7-19.

Calendar Year	Month	OrdersReceived	OrdersDelivered	OpenOrders
CY 2007	January	194	134	60
	February	167	184	43
	March	170	176	37
	April	203	165	75
	May	174	187	62
	June	108	139	31
	July	132	122	41
	August	136	137	40
	September	104	114	30
	October	93	82	41
	November	124	126	39
	December	121	130	30
	Total	**1726**	**1696**	**30**

FIGURE 7-19   This report shows, at the month level, the orders that were open on the last day of the month.

This model works just fine, but in older versions of the engine (that is, in Excel 2013 and in SQL Server Analysis Services 2012 and 2014), it might result in very bad performance. The new engine in Power BI and Excel 2016 is much faster, but this measure is still not a top performer. Explaining the exact reason for this poor performance is beyond the scope of this book, but in a few words, we can say that the problem is in the fact that the condition of filtering does not make use of relationships. Instead, it forces the engine to evaluate the two conditions in its slower part, known as the *formula engine*. On the other hand, if you build the model in such a way that it relies only on relationships, then the formula will be faster.

To obtain this result, you must change the data model, modifying the meaning of the facts in the fact table. Instead of storing the duration of the order by using the start and end date, you can store a simpler fact that says, "this order, on this date, was still open." Such a fact table needs to contain only two columns: Order Number and DateKey. In our model, we moved a bit further, and we also added the customer key so that we could slice the orders by customer, too. The new fact table can be obtained through the following DAX code:

```
OpenOrders =
SELECTCOLUMNS (
    GENERATE (
        Orders,
        VAR CurrentOrderDateKey = Orders[OrderDateKey]
        VAR CurrentDeliverDateKey = Orders[DeliveryDateKey]
        RETURN
            FILTER (
                ALLNOBLANKROW ( 'Date'[DateKey] ),
                AND (
                    'Date'[DateKey] >= CurrentOrderDateKey,
                    'Date'[DateKey] < CurrentDeliverDateKey
                )
            )
    ),
    "CustomerKey", [CustomerKey],
    "Order Number", [Order Number],
    "DateKey", [DateKey]
)
```

 Note Although we provide the DAX code for the table, it is more likely that you can produce such data using the Query Editor or a SQL view. Because DAX is more concise than SQL and M, we prefer to publish DAX code, but please do not assume that this is the best solution in terms of performance. The focus of this book is on the data model itself, not on performance considerations about how to build it.

You can see the new data model in Figure 7-20.

FIGURE 7-20 The new Open Orders table only contains an order when it is open.

In this new data model, the whole logic of when an order is open is stored in the table. Because of this, the resulting code is much simpler. In fact, the Open Orders measure is the following single line of DAX:

```
Open Orders := DISTINCTCOUNT ( OpenOrders[Order Number] )
```

You still need to use a distinct count because the order might appear multiple times, but the whole logic is moved into the table. The biggest advantage of this measure is that it only uses the fast engine of DAX, and it makes much better use of the cache system of the engine. The OpenOrders table is larger than the original fact table, but with simpler data, it is likely to be faster. In this case, as in the case of the previous model, the aggregation at the month level produces unwanted results. In fact, at the month level, the previous model returned orders that were open at the beginning and not closed until the end, resulting in blank values. In this model, on the other hand, the result at the month level is the total number of orders that were open on at least one day during the month, as shown in Figure 7-21.

Calendar Year	Month	Open Orders
CY 2007	January	194
	February	227
	March	213
	April	240
	May	249
	June	170
	July	163
	August	177
	September	144
	October	123
	November	165
	December	160
	Total	**1726**

FIGURE 7-21 This new model returns, at the month level, the orders that were open sometime during the month.

You can easily change this to the average number of open orders or to the open orders at the end of the month by using the following two formulas:

```
Open Orders EOM := CALCULATE ( [Open Orders], LASTDATE ( ( 'Date'[Date] ) ) )
Open Orders AVG := AVERAGEX ( VALUES ( 'Date'[DateKey] ), [Open Orders] )
```

You can see an example of the resulting report in Figure 7-22.

Calendar Year	Month	Open Orders	Open Orders EOM	Open Orders AVG
CY 2007	January	194	60	56
	February	218	43	61
	March	207	37	55
	April	236	75	60
	May	240	62	57
	June	166	31	42
	July	154	41	42
	August	173	40	44
	September	143	30	38
	October	119	41	30
	November	160	39	42
	December	154	30	39
	Total	**1726**	**30**	**47**

FIGURE 7-22 This report shows the total, average, and end-of-month number of open orders.

It is worth noting that computing open orders is a very CPU-intensive operation. It might result in slow reports if you have to handle several million orders. In such a case, you might also think about moving more computational logic into the table, removing it from the DAX code. A good example might be that of pre-aggregating the values at the day level by creating a fact table that contains the date and the number of open orders. In performing this operation, you obtain a very simple (and small) fact table that has all the necessary values already precomputed, and the code becomes even easier to author.

You can create a pre-aggregated table with the following code:

```
Aggregated Open Orders =
FILTER (
    ADDCOLUMNS (
        DISTINCT ( 'Date'[DateKey] ),
        "OpenOrders", [Open Orders]
    ),
    [Open Orders] > 0
)
```

The resulting table is tiny because it has the same granularity as the date table. Thus, it contains a few thousand rows. This model is the simplest of the set of models that we analyzed for this scenario because, having lost the order number and the customer key, the table has a single relationship with the date. You can see this in Figure 7-23. (Again, note that the companion file contains more tables. This is because it contains the whole model, as will be explained later in this section.)

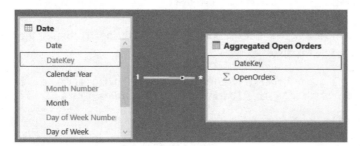

FIGURE 7-23   Pre-aggregating open orders produces an amazingly simple data model.

In this model, the number of open orders is computed in the simplest way, because you can easily aggregate the OpenOrders column by SUM.

At this point, the careful reader might object that we went several steps back in our learning of data modeling. In fact, at the very beginning of the book, we said that working with a single table where everything is already precomputed is a way to limit your analytical power. This is because if a value is not present in the table, then you lose the capability to slice at a deeper level or to compute new values. Moreover, in Chapter 6, "Using snapshots," we said that this pre-aggregation in snapshots is seldom useful—and now we are snapshotting open orders to improve the performance of a query!

To some extent, these criticisms are correct, but we urge you to think more about this model. The source data is still available. What we did this time does not reduce the analytical power. Instead, seeking top performance, we built a snapshot table using DAX that includes most of the computational logic.

In this way, heavy-to-compute numbers like the value of open orders can be gathered from the pre-aggregated table while, at the same time, more lightweight values like the total amount sold can still be recovered from the original fact table. Thus, we are not losing expressivity in the model. Instead, we are increasing it by adding fact tables when needed. Figure 7-24 shows you the whole model we built in this section. Obviously, you will never build all these tables in a single model. The intent is only to show all the fact tables we created in this long journey to analyze how open orders can co-exist and provide different insights in your model.

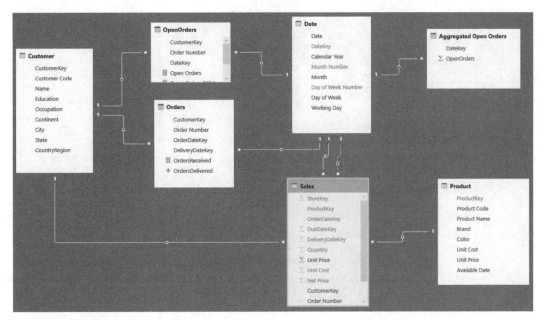

FIGURE 7-24 The whole model, with all the fact tables together, is pretty complex.

Depending on the size of your data model and the kind of insights you need, you will build only parts of this whole model. As we have said multiple times, the intent is to show you different ways to build a data model and how the DAX code becomes easier or harder depending on how well the model fits your specific needs. Along with the DAX code, flexibility also changes in each approach. As a data modeler, it is your task to find the best balance and, as always, to be prepared to change the model if the analytical needs change.

Mixing different durations

When handling time and duration, you will sometimes have several tables that contain information that is valid for some period in time. For example, when handling employees, you might have two tables. The first table contains the store at which the employee is working and an indication of when this is happening. The second one might come from a different source and contain the gross salary of the employee. The start and end date of the two tables do not need to match. The employee's salary could change on one date, and the employee could switch to a different store on a different date.

If you face such a scenario, then you can either write very complex DAX code to solve it or change the data model so it stores the correct information and makes the code much easier to use. Let us start by looking at the data model shown in Figure 7-25.

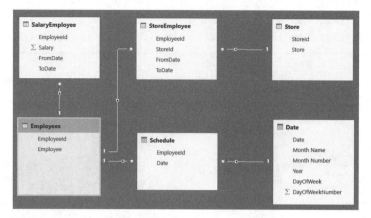

FIGURE 7-25 This data model shows employees with different store assignments and different salaries.

This time, the model is somewhat complex. A more complete description follows:

- **SalaryEmployee**   This contains the salary of an employee, with the start and end date. Thus, each salary has a duration.

- **StoreEmployee**   This contains the store assignment of an employee, again with the start and end date. Thus, there is also a duration in this case, which might be different from the one in SalaryEmployee.

- **Schedule**   This contains the days that the employee worked.

The other tables (Store, Employees, and Date) are simple tables containing employee names, store names, and a standard calendar table.

The data model contains all the necessary information to produce a report that shows, over time, the amount paid to the employee. It gives the user the ability to slice by store or by employee. With that said, the DAX measures that you must write are very complex because, given a date, you must perform the following:

1. Retrieve the salary that was effective on the date by analyzing FromDate and ToDate in SalaryEmployee of the given employee. If the selection contains multiple employees, then you will need to perform this operation for each employee separately, one by one.

2. Retrieve the store that was assigned to the employee at the given time.

Let us start with a simple report that works straight out of the model: the number of working days per employee, sliced by year. It works because the relationships are set so you can slice Schedule based on both the calendar year and the employee name. You can author a simple measure like the following:

```
WorkingDays := COUNTROWS ( Schedule )
```

With the measure in place, the first part of the report is straightforward, as shown in Figure 7-26.

Employee	Year	WorkingDays
Michelle	2015	261
Michelle	2016	119
Paul	2015	261
Paul	2016	42
Total		**683**

FIGURE 7-26 This figure shows the number of working days, sliced by year and employee.

First, let us determine the amount paid to Michelle, who is employee 2, in 2015. The SalaryEmployee table with the salaries contains the values shown in Figure 7-27.

EmployeeId	Salary	FromDate	ToDate	DailySalary
1	100000	1/1/2015	6/30/2015	$274.00
1	125000	7/1/2015	11/30/2015	$342.00
1	150000	12/1/2015	2/29/2016	$411.00
2	120000	1/1/2015	6/30/2015	$329.00
2	160000	7/1/2015	6/15/2016	$438.00

FIGURE 7-27 Depending on the date, the salary changes for each employee.

Michelle has two different salary amounts in 2015. Thus, the formula needs to iterate on a day-by-day basis and determine what the current daily salary was for each day. This time, you cannot rely on relationships because the relationships must be based on a between condition. The salary has a range defined by FromDate and ToDate columns, including the current date.

The code is not exactly easy to write, as you can see in the following measure definition:

```
SalaryPaid =
SUMX (
    'Schedule',
    VAR SalaryRows =
        FILTER (
            SalaryEmployee,
            AND (
                SalaryEmployee[EmployeeId] = Schedule[EmployeeId],
                AND (
                    SalaryEmployee[FromDate] <= Schedule[Date],
                    SalaryEmployee[ToDate] > Schedule[Date]
                )
            )
        )
    RETURN
        IF ( COUNTROWS ( SalaryRows ) = 1, MAXX ( SalaryRows, [DailySalary] ) )
)
```

The complexity comes from the fact that you must move the filter through a complex FILTER function that evaluates the between condition. Additionally, you must make sure that a salary exists and is unique, and you must verify your findings before returning them as the result of the formula. The formula works, provided the data model is correct. If, for any reason, the dates of the salary table overlap, then the result might be wrong. You would need further logic to check it and to correct the possible error.

With this code in place, you can enhance the report, displaying the salary paid in each period, as shown in Figure 7-28.

Employee	Year	WorkingDays	SalaryPaid
Michelle	2015	261	$99,928.00
Michelle	2016	119	$51,684.00
Paul	2015	261	$81,461.00
Paul	2016	42	$16,851.00
Total		**683**	**$249,924.00**

FIGURE 7-28   This figure shows the number of working days, sliced by year and employee.

The scenario becomes more complex if you want to be able to slice by store. In fact, when you slice by store, you want to account for only the period when each employee was working for the given store. You must consider the filter on the store and use it to filter only the rows from Schedule when the employee was working there. Thus, you must add a FILTER around the Schedule table by using the following code:

```
SalaryPaid =
SUMX (
    FILTER (
        'Schedule',
        AND (
            Schedule[Date] >= MIN ( StoreEmployee[FromDate] ),
            Schedule[Date] <= MAX ( StoreEmployee[ToDate] )
        )
    ),
    VAR SalaryRows =
        FILTER (
            SalaryEmployee,
            AND (
                SalaryEmployee[EmployeeId] = Schedule[EmployeeId],
                AND (
                    SalaryEmployee[FromDate] <= Schedule[Date],
                    SalaryEmployee[ToDate] > Schedule[Date]
                )
            )
        )
    RETURN
        IF ( COUNTROWS ( SalaryRows ) = 1, MAXX ( SalaryRows, [DailySalary] ) )
)
```

This formula works correctly, as shown in Figure 7-29, but it is extremely complex and might return incorrect results if it is not used in the proper way.

Employee	Store	Year	SalaryPaid
Michelle	Miami	2015	$99,928.00
Michelle	Indianapolis	2016	$51,684.00
Paul	Indianapolis	2015	$38,523.00
Paul	Miami	2015	$42,938.00
Paul	Seattle	2016	$16,851.00
Total			**$249,924.00**

FIGURE 7-29 The last version of SalaryPaid returns the correct numbers when sliced by store.

The problem with this model is that the relationship between stores, salary, and employees is complex. And using DAX to navigate through it results in very complex code, which is extremely error-prone. As before, the solution is to move complexity from the DAX code to the loading process, moving toward a star schema.

For each row in Schedule, you can easily compute which store the employee is working at and what the daily salary for that day of work is. As always, a correct denormalization removes complexity from the aggregation formulas, moving it to the fact table and resulting in a much simpler model to work with.

You should create two calculated columns in Schedule: one containing the daily salary and another containing the store ID. You can do this by using the following code:

```
Schedule[DailySalary] =
VAR CurrentEmployeeId = Schedule[EmployeeId]
VAR CurrentDate = Schedule[Date]
RETURN
    CALCULATE (
        VALUES ( SalaryEmployee[DailySalary] ),
        SalaryEmployee[EmployeeId] = CurrentEmployeeId,
        SalaryEmployee[FromDate] <= CurrentDate,
        SalaryEmployee[ToDate] > CurrentDate
    )

Schedule[StoreId] =
VAR CurrentEmployeeId = Schedule[EmployeeId]
VAR CurrentDate = Schedule[Date]
RETURN
    CALCULATE (
        VALUES ( StoreEmployee[StoreId] ),
        StoreEmployee[EmployeeId] = CurrentEmployeeId,
        StoreEmployee[FromDate] <= CurrentDate,
        StoreEmployee[ToDate] >= CurrentDate
    )
```

When the two columns are ready, you can get rid of most of the relationships with the SalaryEmployee and StoreEmployee tables, and you can transform the data model into the simpler star schema shown in Figure 7-30.

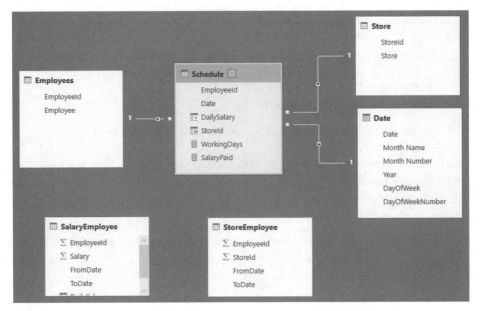

FIGURE 7-30 The denormalized model is a star schema.

Note We intentionally left SalaryEmployee and StoreEmployee visible in the figure of the model to highlight the fact that these tables, which were used to compute the calculated columns, have no relationships with the remaining ones. In a production model, you would likely hide these tables to prevent users from even seeing them. They do not contain useful information from a user point of view.

With the new model, the code to compute the salary paid is as easy as the following one:

```
SalaryPaid = SUM ( Schedule[DailySalary] )
```

Once again, you have seen that a proper denormalization strategy leads to the best data model. Maintaining complex relationships in the model does not help the code, which tends to be very complex and error-prone. On the other hand, denormalizing the values by using SQL or DAX and calculated columns splits the more complex scenario into smaller ones. Thus, each single formula is much simpler and easier to write and debug, and the final aggregation formulas become extremely easy to write and fast to execute.

Conclusions

This chapter deviated from the standard models to perform a deeper analysis of scenarios in which duration is the primary concept. As you have seen, duration forces you to think in a slightly different way, redefining the very concept of a fact. You might store a fact along with its duration, but in doing so, you will need to reconsider the concept of time because a single fact might extend its effects into different periods. The following is a brief overview of what you learned in this chapter:

- Date and time must be separate columns.

- Aggregating simple intervals is easy. You should only try to reduce the cardinality of the facts to the best one that satisfies your analytical needs, and at the same time, reduce the cardinality of the Time column.

- When you store duration (or intervals) that cross the time dimension, you must define the model in the right way. There are many options, and you are responsible for finding the best one. The good news is that you can move from one solution to another by simply changing the data model. Then, you can use the one that works best for your specific scenario.

- Sometimes, changing the way you think about time might help. If your day does not end at midnight, you can model it the way you want—for example, making it start at 2:00 a.m. You are not a slave of the model. Instead, it is the model that must change according to your needs.

- Analysis of active events is a very common scenario that is frequently used in many businesses. You learned multiple ways of solving this scenario. The more tailored the model, the easier the DAX code, but at the same time, the more complex the data-preparation steps.

- When you have multiple tables where each one defines its own set of durations, trying to solve the problem with a single DAX measure makes the code very complex. On the other hand, pre-computing the values in a calculated column or a calculated table and obtaining the right degree of denormalization will lead to much simpler DAX code, which you can trust more.

The main takeaway is nearly always the same: If the DAX code becomes too complex, then it is a very good indicator that you might need to work on the model. Although it is true that the model should not be built for a single report, it is also true that a good model is the key to an efficient solution.

CHAPTER 8

Many-to-many relationships

M any-to-many relationships are an important tool in the data analyst's toolbelt. Often, they are viewed as problematic because many-to-many relationships tend to make the model more complex than usual. However, we suggest you start thinking about many-to-many relationships as an opportunity instead. In fact, it's easy to handle many-to-many relationships. You only need to learn the basic technique and then use it at your convenience.

As you will learn in this chapter, many-to-many relationships are extremely powerful and let you build great data models—even if they hide some complexity both in the modeling and in the interpretation of the results. Moreover, many-to-many relationships are present in nearly every data model. For example, simple star schemas contain many-to-many relationships. We want to show you how to recognize these relationships and—most importantly—how to take advantage of them to derive good insights from your data.

Introducing many-to-many relationships

Let us start by introducing many-to-many relationships. There are scenarios where the relationship between two entities cannot be expressed with a simple relationship. The canonical example is that of a current account. The bank stores transactions related to the current account. However, the current account can be owned by multiple individuals at the same time. Conversely, one individual might possess multiple current accounts. Thus, you cannot store the customer key in the Accounts table, and at the same time, you cannot store the account key in the Customers table. This kind of relationship is, by its very nature, that of many entities related to many other entities, and it cannot be expressed with a single column.

> **Note** There are a lot of other scenarios in which many-to-many relationships appear, such as sales agents with orders, where an order can be overseen by multiple sales agents. Another example could be house ownership, where an individual might possess multiple houses, and the same house might be owned by multiple individuals.

The canonical way of modeling a many-to-many relationship is to use a bridge table that contains the information about which account is owned by which individual. Figure 8-1 shows you an example of a model with many-to-many relationships based on the current account scenario.

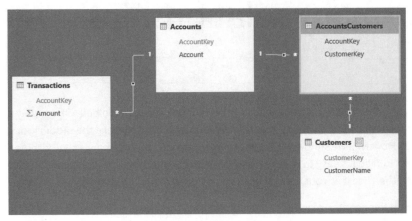

FIGURE 8-1 The relationship between Customers and Accounts is through a bridge table, AccountsCustomers.

The first important thing to note about many-to-many relationships is that they are a different kind of relationship from the point of view of the data model, but when implemented, are transformed into a pair of standard one-to-many relationships. Thus, many-to-many is more of a concept than a physical relationship. We speak of, think about, and work with many-to-many as a kind of relationship, but we implement it as a pair of relationships.

Note that the two relationships that link Customers and Accounts with the bridge table are in opposite directions. In fact, both relationships start from the bridge table and reach the two dimensions. The bridge table is always on the many side.

Why is many-to-many more complex than other kinds of relationships? Here are several reasons:

- **Many-to-many does not work by default in a data model**   To be precise, it might or might not work, depending on the version of Tabular you are using and its settings. In Power BI, you can enable bidirectional filtering, whereas in Microsoft Excel (up to and including Excel 2016), you will need to author some DAX code to make formulas traverse many-to-many relationships the right way.

- **Many-to-many typically generates non-additive calculations**   This makes the numbers returned when using many-to-many slightly more difficult to understand, and makes debugging your code a little trickier.

- **Performance might be an issue**   Depending on the size of the many-to-many filtering, the traversal of two relationships in opposite directions might become expensive. Thus, when working with many-to-many, you might face performance issues that require more attention.

Let us analyze all these points in more detail.

Understanding the bidirectional pattern

By default, a filter on a table moves from the one side to the many side, but it does not move from the many side to the one side. Thus, if you build a report and slice by customer, the filter will reach the bridge table, but at that point, the filter propagation stops. Consequently, the Accounts table will not receive the filter coming from Customers, as shown in Figure 8-2.

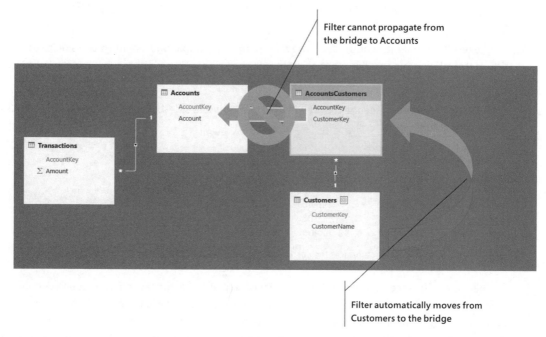

FIGURE 8-2 The filter can move from the one side to the many side, but not from the many side to the one side.

If you build a report that contains the customers on the rows and a simple SUM of the Amount column as the value, the same number is repeated for all the rows. This is because the filter coming from Customers is not working against Accounts, and from there to the transactions. The result is shown in Figure 8-3.

CustomerName	Amount
Luke	€ 5,000
Mark	€ 5,000
Paul	€ 5,000
Robert	€ 5,000
Total	**€ 5,000**

FIGURE 8-3 You cannot filter the amount per customer because of the many-to-many relationship.

You can solve this scenario by setting the propagation of the filter on the relationship between the bridge table and the Accounts table as bidirectional. This is a simple setting in Power BI, where bidirectional filtering is available as part of the modeling tools. In Excel, however, you must use DAX.

One approach is to activate bidirectional filtering in the model, in which case it will be active for all the calculations. Alternatively, you can use the CROSSFILTER function as a parameter of CALCULATE to activate bidirectional filtering for the duration of CALCULATE. You can see this in the following code:

```
SumOfAmount :=
CALCULATE (
    SUM ( Transactions[Amount] ),
    CROSSFILTER ( AccountsCustomers[AccountKey], Accounts[AccountKey], BOTH )
)
```

The result is the same in both cases. The filter permits propagation from the many side to the one side of the relationship that links the accounts with the bridge. Thus, the Accounts table will show only the rows that belong to the selected customer.

In Figure 8-4, you can see the report with this new measure side-by-side with the previous one that uses a simple SUM.

CustomerName	Amount	SumOfAmount
Luke	$5,000.00	$800.00
Mark	$5,000.00	$2,800.00
Paul	$5,000.00	$1,700.00
Robert	$5,000.00	$1,700.00
Total	**$5.000.00**	**$5.000.00**

FIGURE 8-4 SumOfAmount computes the correct value, whereas Amount always shows the grand total.

There is a difference between setting the relationship as bidirectional and using the DAX code. In fact, if you set the relationship as bidirectional, then any measure will benefit from the automatic propagation of the filter from the many side to the one side. However, if you rely on DAX code, then you need to author all the measures using the same pattern to force the propagation. If you have lots of measures, then it is somewhat annoying to have to use the three lines of the bidirectional pattern for all of them. On the other hand, setting the bidirectional filtering on a relationship might make the model ambiguous. For this reason, you cannot always set the relationship as bidirectional, and you will need to write some code.

With that said, Excel does not offer you bidirectional relationships, thus you have no choice. In Power BI, on the other hand, you can choose the technique you prefer. In our experience, bidirectional relationships are more convenient and tend to lower the number of errors in your code.

You can obtain a similar effect to that of CROSSFILTER by leveraging table expansion in DAX. Explaining table expansion in detail would require a full chapter by itself; we discuss it in more detail in our book *The Definitive Guide to DAX*, where this topic is covered in detail. Here, we only want to note that, by using table expansion, you can write the previous measure in the following way:

```
SumOfAmount :=
CALCULATE (
    SUM ( Transactions[Amount] ),
    AccountsCustomers
)
```

The result is nearly the same as before. You still obtain the filter propagation, but this time, it happens through table expansion. The main difference between using bidirectional filtering and table expansion is that the pattern with table expansion always applies the filter, whereas the bidirectional filtering works only when the filter is active. To see the difference, let us add a new row to the Transactions table, which is not related to any account. This row has 5,000 USD and, not being related to any account, it does not belong to any customer. Figure 8-5 shows you the result.

CustomerName	SumOfAmount CrossFilter	SumOfAmount Table Expansion
Luke	$800.00	$800.00
Mark	$2,800.00	$2,800.00
Paul	$1,700.00	$1,700.00
Robert	$1,700.00	$1,700.00
Total	**$10,000.00**	**$5,000.00**

FIGURE 8-5 CROSSFILTER and table expansion lead to different results in the grand total.

The difference between the two measures is exactly 5,000 USD, which is the amount that is not related to any customer. It is reported at the grand total in the CROSSFILTER version, but it is not reported in the table expansion one. When you use the CROSSFILTER version at the grand total when no filter on the customer is active, the fact table shows all the rows. On the other hand, the filter is always activated when using table expansion, showing only the rows in the fact table that can be reached through one of the customers. Thus, the additional row is hidden and does not contribute to the grand total.

As it often happens in these cases, it is not that one value is more correct than the other. They are reporting different numbers following different calculations. You only need to be aware of the difference so you can use the correct formula depending on your needs. From a performance point of view, because the filter is not applied if it is not necessary, you can expect the version with CROSSFILTER to be slightly faster than the version with table expansion. CROSSFILTER and bidirectional filtering, on the other hand, report the same numbers, and behave the same way in terms of performance.

Understanding non-additivity

The second important point about many-to-many relationships is that typically, measures aggregated through a many-to-many relationship are non-additive. This is not an error in the model; it is the nature of many-to-many that makes these relationships non-additive. To better understand this, look at the report in Figure 8-6 that shows both the Accounts and the Customers tables on the same matrix.

Account	Luke	Mark	Paul	Robert	Total
Luke	$800.00				**$800.00**
Mark		$800.00			**$800.00**
Mark-Paul		$1,000.00	$1,000.00		**$1,000.00**
Mark-Robert		$1,000.00		$1,000.00	**$1,000.00**
Paul			$700.00		**$700.00**
Robert				$700.00	**$700.00**
Total	**$800.00**	**$2,800.00**	**$1,700.00**	**$1,700.00**	**$10,000.00**

FIGURE 8-6 Many-to-many relationships generate non-additive calculations.

You can easily see that the column totals are correct, meaning that the total is the sum of all the rows in that column. The row totals, however, are incorrect. This is because the amount of the account is shown for all the customers who own that account. The account Mark-Paul, for example, is owned by Mark and Paul together. Individually, they have 1,000 USD each, but when you consider them together, the total is still 1,000.

Non-additivity is not a problem. It is the correct behavior whenever you work with many-to-many relationships. However, you need to be aware of non-additivity because you can easily be fooled if you do not take it into account. For example, you might iterate over the customers, compute the sum of the amount, and then aggregate it at the end, which obtains a result that is different from the calculation done for the grand total. This is demonstrated in the report in Figure 8-7, which shows the result of the following two calculations:

```
Interest := [SumOfAmount] * 0.01
Interest SUMX := SUMX ( Customers, [SumOfAmount] * 0.01 )
```

CustomerName ▲	Account	SumOfAmount	Interest	Interest SUMX
Luke	Luke	$800.00	$8.00	$8.00
	Total	**$800.00**	**$8.00**	**$8.00**
Mark	Mark	$800.00	$8.00	$8.00
	Mark-Paul	$1,000.00	$10.00	$10.00
	Mark-Robert	$1,000.00	$10.00	$10.00
	Total	**$2,800.00**	**$28.00**	**$28.00**
Paul	Mark-Paul	$1,000.00	$10.00	$10.00
	Paul	$700.00	$7.00	$7.00
	Total	**$1,700.00**	**$17.00**	**$17.00**
Robert	Mark-Robert	$1,000.00	$10.00	$10.00
	Robert	$700.00	$7.00	$7.00
	Total	**$1,700.00**	**$17.00**	**$17.00**
Total		**$5,000.00**	**$50.00**	**$70.00**

FIGURE 8-7 The grand total of the two interest calculations is different because of many-to-many.

The version with SUMX forced the additivity by moving the sum out of the calculation. In doing so, it computes a wrong number. When handling many-to-many, you need to be aware of its nature and act accordingly.

Cascading many-to-many

As you saw in the previous section, there are different ways to handle many-to-many relationships. Once you learn them, these kinds of relationships can be easily managed. One scenario that requires slightly more attention is where you have chains of many-to-many relationships, which we call *cascading many-to-many*.

Let us start with an example. Using our previous model about current accounts, suppose we now want to store, for each customer, the list of categories to which the customer belongs. Every customer might belong to multiple categories, and in turn, each category is assigned to multiple customers. In other words, there is a many-to-many relationship between customers and categories.

The data model is a simple variation of the previous one. This time it includes two bridge tables: one between Accounts and Customers, and another between Customers and Categories, as shown in Figure 8-8.

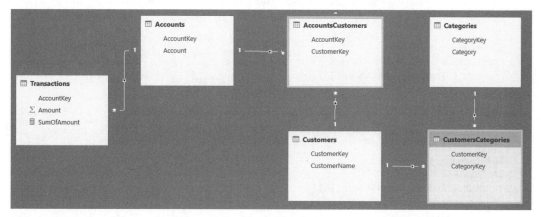

FIGURE 8-8 In the cascading many-to-many patterns, there are two chained bridge tables.

You can easily make this model work by setting the relationships between Accounts and Accounts-Customers and between Customers and CustomersCategories to bidirectional. By doing so, the model becomes fully functional, and you can produce reports like the one in Figure 8-9, which shows the amount available sliced by category and customer.

Category	Luke	Mark	Paul	Robert	Total
House Owner		$2,800.00	$1,700.00		**$3,500.00**
Married		$2,800.00		$1,700.00	**$3,500.00**
Premium Customer		$2,800.00	$1,700.00		**$3,500.00**
Single	$800.00		$1,700.00		**$2,500.00**
Standard Customer	$800.00			$1,700.00	**$2,500.00**
Total	**$800.00**	**$2,800.00**	**$1,700.00**	**$1,700.00**	**$5,000.00**

FIGURE 8-9 Cascading many-to-many with bidirectional filtering is non-additive over rows and columns.

Obviously, you lose additivity over any dimension that is browsed through a many-to-many relationship. Thus, as you can easily spot, additivity is lost on both rows and columns, and numbers become harder to interpret.

If, instead of using bidirectional filtering, you use the CROSSFILTER pattern, then you need to set cross-filtering on both relationships by using the following code:

```
SumOfAmount :=
CALCULATE (
    SUM ( Transactions[Amount] ),
    CROSSFILTER ( AccountsCustomers[AccountKey], Accounts[AccountKey], BOTH ),
    CROSSFILTER ( CustomersCategories[CustomerKey], Customers[CustomerKey], BOTH )
)
```

If, on the other hand, you opted for the table expansion pattern, then you need to take additional care when authoring your code. In fact, the evaluation of the table filters needs to be done in the right order: from the farthest table from the fact table to the nearest one. In other words, first you need to move the filter from Categories to Customers, and only later move the filter from Customers to Accounts. Failing to follow the correct order produces wrong results. The correct pattern is as follows:

```
SumOfAmount :=
CALCULATE (
    SUM ( Transactions[Amount] ),
    CALCULATETABLE ( AccountsCustomers, CustomersCategories )
)
```

If you don't pay attention to this detail, you might author the code in the following way:

```
SumOfAmount :=
CALCULATE (
    SUM ( Transactions[Amount] ),
    AccountsCustomers,
    CustomersCategories
)
```

However, the result is wrong because the filter propagation has not been executed in the right order, as shown in Figure 8-10.

Category	Luke	Mark	Paul	Robert	Total
House Owner	$800.00	$2,800.00	$1,700.00	$1,700.00	**$5,000.00**
Married	$800.00	$2,800.00	$1,700.00	$1,700.00	**$5,000.00**
Premium Customer	$800.00	$2,800.00	$1,700.00	$1,700.00	**$5,000.00**
Single	$800.00	$2,800.00	$1,700.00	$1,700.00	**$5,000.00**
Standard Customer	$800.00	$2,800.00	$1,700.00	$1,700.00	**$5,000.00**
Total	**$800.00**	**$2,800.00**	**$1,700.00**	**$1,700.00**	**$5,000.00**

FIGURE 8-10 If you do not follow the right order, table expansion produces the wrong results.

This is one of the reasons we prefer to declare the relationship as bidirectional (if possible), so that your code will work without the need to pay attention to these details. It is very easy to write the wrong code, and this, added to the complexity of non-additivity, might be challenging to debug and check.

Before leaving the topic of cascading many-to-many, it is worth mentioning that the model with cascading many-to-many can be created most of the time with a single bridge table. In fact, in the model we have seen so far, we have two bridges: one between Categories and Customers, and one between Customers and Accounts. A good alternative is to simplify the model and build a single bridge that links the three tables, as shown in Figure 8-11.

There is nothing complex in a bridge table that links three dimensions, and the data model looks somewhat easier to analyze—at least once you get used to the shape of data models with many-to-many relationships. Moreover, a single relationship needs to be set as bidirectional. In the case of CROSSFILTER or table expansion, a single parameter is needed, again lowering the chances of errors in your code.

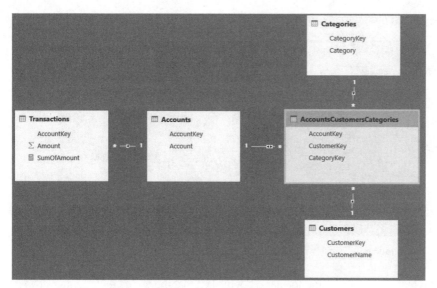

FIGURE 8-11 A single bridge table can link multiple tables together.

> **Note** This model that links three tables together is also used for categorized many-to-many, which is a many-to-many relationship that has another table used to filter it. For example, you might have different kinds of relationships between entities (different kinds of owners of current accounts, where one is the primary account and others are secondary accounts). You can model them with a bridge table that also contains a link to the category. It is a simple model, yet it is extremely powerful and effective.

Obviously, you will need to build such a super-bridge table. In the example, we used a simple calculated table built with DAX, but, as usual, you can use SQL or the query editor to obtain a similar result.

Temporal many-to-many

In the previous section, you learned that you can model many-to-many relationships even in cases where the bridge links multiple tables. When the bridge links three tables, you can consider each of the three tables as a separate filter, and at the end, you can find the rows in the fact table that satisfy all the conditions. A variation of this scenario happens when the many-to-many relationship has a condition, but this condition cannot be expressed with a simple relationship. Instead, it is expressed by a duration. Such a relationship is known as a *temporal many-to-many*, and it is an interesting mix between duration handling (covered in Chapter 7, "Analyzing date and time intervals") and many-to-many (the topic of this chapter).

You can use these kinds of relationships to model, for example, a team of people that might change over time. An individual might belong to different teams and change his or her team over time, so the relationship between individuals and teams has a duration. The starting model is shown in Figure 8-12.

As you can see, it is a standard many-to-many model.

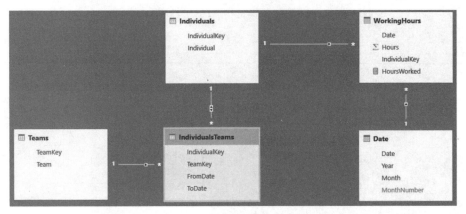

FIGURE 8-12 A single bridge table can link multiple tables together.

The key of this model is not the many-to-many, but the fact that the bridge table contains two dates (FromDate and ToDate) that determine in which period the individual was working with the team. In fact, if you use this model as it is and slice the number of worked hours by team and individual, you obtain an incorrect result. This is because you need to carefully use the time constraints to correctly map individuals to teams in any given period. A simple filter by individual will not work. To better understand what happens, see Figure 8-13, which depicts the bridge table and highlights the rows pertinent to Catherine.

FromDate	ToDate	Individual ↓	Team
1/1/2015	1/31/2015	Catherine	Developers
2/1/2015	12/31/2015	Catherine	Sales
1/1/2016		Catherine	Testers
1/1/2015		Louis	Testers
1/1/2015	12/31/2015	Michelle	Testers
1/1/2016		Michelle	Sales
1/1/2015	2/28/2015	Paul	Developers
3/1/2015	9/30/2015	Paul	Testers
8/1/2015	12/31/2015	Paul	Sales
1/1/2016		Paul	Developers
1/1/2015	4/30/2015	Thomas	Developers
5/1/2015	5/31/2015	Thomas	Sales
6/1/2015	12/31/2015	Thomas	Developers
1/1/2016		Thomas	Testers

FIGURE 8-13 Filtering the bridge by Catherine, you obtain all the teams for which she worked at any time.

If you filter by name, you obtain all the teams for which Catherine worked. But when you look at 2015, for example, you want to obtain only the first two rows. Moreover, because Catherine worked for two different teams in 2015, you want to account January to the Developers team, and February through December to the Sales team.

Temporal many-to-many relationships are complex models to solve, and usually, they are very hard to optimize. In fact, it is extremely easy to fall into the many traps they hide. You might be tempted to simply apply a temporal filter to the many-to-many to show only the rows that are considered valid during the period selected. But imagine you restrict the rows to only Catherine in the year 2015. You will still see two different teams (Developers and Sales).

To solve the scenario, you need to perform the following steps in the right way:

1. Determine the periods during which each individual worked for a given team.

2. Move the filter on the dates to the fact table, taking care to intersect it with any other filter that is already applied on the fact table.

These two operations need to be executed inside an iteration at the individual level because different individuals might have different periods to take into account. You can do this with the following code:

```
HoursWorked :=
SUMX (
    ADDCOLUMNS (
        SUMMARIZE (
            IndividualsTeams,
            Individuals[IndividualKey],
            IndividualsTeams[FromDate],
            IndividualsTeams[ToDate]
        ),
        "FirstDate", [FromDate],
        "LastDate", IF ( ISBLANK ( [ToDate] ), MAX ( WorkingHours[Date] ), [ToDate] )
    ),
    CALCULATE (
        SUM ( WorkingHours[Hours] ),
        DATESBETWEEN ( 'Date'[Date], [FirstDate], [LastDate] ),
        VALUES ( 'Date'[Date] )
    )
)
```

In this scenario, you have no way of modeling the many-to-many relationship in the data model because the duration of the relationship forces you to rely on DAX code to transfer the filter from the bridge table to the fact table. The code is not simple, and it requires you to have a deep understanding of how filter context propagates through relationships. Moreover, because of its complexity, this code is sub-optimal. Still, it works just fine, and you can use it to produce reports like the one shown in Figure 8-14, which demonstrates how the filter on the periods is correctly moved to the fact table.

Individual	Year Team	2015 January	February	March	April	May	June	July
Catherine	Developers	60						
	Sales		54	68	54	67	57	65
	Testers							
Louis	Testers	60	56	64	60	60	60	61
Michelle	Sales							
	Testers	64	54	65	61	60	60	64
Paul	Developers	62	54					
	Sales							
	Testers			64	60	61	61	62
Thomas	Developers	66	54	61	62		64	61
	Sales					59		
	Testers							

FIGURE 8-14 The report shows the number of hours worked by individuals on different teams.

As you have seen, the code is very complex. Moreover, it is worth noting that in this specific model, many-to-many is probably the wrong tool. We deliberately chose a model where many-to-many seemed like the right choice, but after looking closer at the model, it becomes clear that there are better choices. In fact, even if it is true that over time an individual might belong to different teams, on a given day that person should belong to a single team. If this condition is met, then the correct way of modeling this scenario is to consider the team as a dimension unlinked from the individuals, and to use the fact table to store the relationship between teams and individuals. In the model we are using as an example, this condition is not met, as shown in Figure 8-15, which reveals that Paul, during August and September 2015, was on two different teams.

Individual	Year Team	2015 June	July	August	September	October	November
Paul	Sales			62	58	63	59
	Testers	61	62	62	58		

FIGURE 8-15   In August and September 2015, Paul is working for two different teams.

We are going to use this scenario to introduce the next topic, which is the reallocation factors in the many-to-many.

Reallocating factors and percentages

As the report in Figure 8-15 showed, it looks like Paul accounted for 62 hours in August for both the Sales and the Testers teams. These figures are clearly wrong. Paul cannot have worked for both teams at the same time. In this scenario—that is, when the many-to-many relationship generates overlaps—it is usually a good practice to store in the relationship a correction factor that indicates how much of Paul's total time is to be allocated to each team. Let us see the data in more detail with the aid of Figure 8-16.

FromDate	ToDate	Individual	Team
1/1/2015	1/31/2015	Catherine	Developers
2/1/2015	12/31/2015	Catherine	Sales
1/1/2016		Catherine	Testers
1/1/2015		Louis	Testers
1/1/2015	12/31/2015	Michelle	Testers
1/1/2016		Michelle	Sales
1/1/2015	2/28/2015	Paul	Developers
3/1/2015	9/30/2015	Paul	Testers
8/1/2015	12/31/2015	Paul	Sales
1/1/2016		Paul	Developers
1/1/2015	4/30/2015	Thomas	Developers
5/1/2015	5/31/2015	Thomas	Sales
6/1/2015	12/31/2015	Thomas	Developers
1/1/2016		Thomas	Testers

FIGURE 8-16   In August and September 2015, Paul is working for Testers and Sales.

The data in this model does not look correct. To avoid assigning 100 percent of Paul's time to both teams, you can add a value to the bridge table that represents the percentage of time that needs to be assigned to each team. This requires splitting and storing the periods in multiple rows, as shown in Figure 8-17.

FromDate	ToDate	Individual	Team	Perc
1/1/2015	1/31/2015	Catherine	Developers	100.00 %
2/1/2015	12/31/2015	Catherine	Sales	100.00 %
1/1/2016		Catherine	Testers	100.00 %
1/1/2015		Louis	Testers	100.00 %
1/1/2015	12/31/2015	Michelle	Testers	100.00 %
1/1/2016		Michelle	Sales	100.00 %
1/1/2015	2/28/2015	Paul	Developers	100.00 %
3/1/2015	7/30/2015	Paul	Testers	100.00 %
8/1/2015	9/30/2015	Paul	Testers	60.00 %
8/1/2015	9/30/2015	Paul	Sales	40.00 %
10/1/2015	12/31/2015	Paul	Sales	100.00 %
1/1/2016		Paul	Developers	100.00 %
1/1/2015	4/30/2015	Thomas	Developers	100.00 %
5/1/2015	5/31/2015	Thomas	Sales	100.00 %
6/1/2015	12/31/2015	Thomas	Developers	100.00 %
1/1/2016		Thomas	Testers	100.00 %

FIGURE 8-17 By duplicating some rows, you can avoid overlaps, and you can add percentages that allocate the hours.

Now Paul's overlapping periods are divided into non-overlapping periods. In addition, a percentage was added to indicate that 60 percent of the total time should be allocated to the Testers team and 40 percent of the total time should be allocated to the Sales team.

The final step is to take these numbers into account. To do that, it is enough to modify the code of the measure so it uses the percentage in the formula. The final code is as follows:

```
HoursWorked :=
SUMX (
    ADDCOLUMNS (
        SUMMARIZE (
            IndividualsTeams,
            Individuals[IndividualKey],
            IndividualsTeams[FromDate],
            IndividualsTeams[ToDate],
            IndividualsTeams[Perc]
        ),
        "FirstDate", [FromDate],
        "LastDate", IF ( ISBLANK ( [ToDate] ), MAX ( WorkingHours[Date] ), [ToDate] )
    ),
    CALCULATE (
        SUM ( WorkingHours[Hours] ),
        DATESBETWEEN ( 'Date'[Date], [FirstDate], [LastDate] ),
        VALUES ( 'Date'[Date] )
    ) * IndividualsTeams[Perc]
)
```

As you can see, we added the Perc column to SUMMARIZE. We then used it as a multiplier in the final step of the formula to correctly allocate the percentage of hours to the team. Needless to say, this operation made the code even harder than before.

In Figure 8-18, you can see that in August and September, Paul's hours are correctly split between the two teams he worked with.

Individual	Year Team	2015 June	July	August	September	October	November
Catherine	Sales	57	65	61	58	64	56
Louis	Testers	60	61	62	60	63	60
Michelle	Testers	60	64	60	58	65	57
Paul	Sales			25	23	63	59
	Testers	61	61	37	35		
Thomas	Developers	64	61	61	58	64	60

FIGURE 8-18   The report shows correctly that Paul was in two teams in August and September, and splits hours between them.

Nevertheless, in doing this operation, we moved to a slightly different data model that transformed the overlapping periods into percentages. We had to do this because we did not want to obtain a non-additive measure. In fact, while it is true that many-to-many relationships are non-additive, it is also true that, in this specific case, we wanted to guarantee additivity because of the data we are representing.

From the conceptual point of view, this important step helps us introduce the next step in the optimization of the model: the materialization of many-to-many relationships.

Materializing many-to-many

As you saw in the previous examples, many-to-many relationships could have temporal data (or, in general, with a complex filter), percentages, and allocation factors. That tends to generate very complex DAX code. In the DAX world, complex typically means slow. In fact, the previous expressions are fine if you need to handle a small volume of data, but for larger datasets or for heavy environments, they are too slow. The next section covers some performance considerations with many-to-many relationships. In this section, however, we want to show you how you can get rid of many-to-many relationships if you are seeking better performance, and as usual, easier DAX.

As we anticipated, most of the time, you can remove many-to-many relationships from the model by using the fact table to store the relationship between the two dimensions. In fact, in our example, we have two different dimensions: Teams and Individuals. They are linked by a bridge table, which we need to traverse and filter every time we want to slice by team. A more efficient solution would be to store the team key straight in the fact table by materializing the many-to-many relationship in the fact table.

Materializing the many-to-many relationship requires that you denormalize the columns from the bridge table to the fact table, and at the same time increase the number of rows in the fact table. In the case of Paul's hours that need to be assigned to two different teams during August and September, you will need to duplicate the rows, adding one row for each team. The final model will be a perfect star schema, as shown in Figure 8-19.

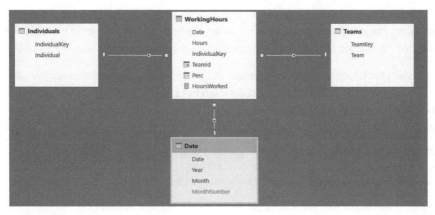

FIGURE 8-19   Once you remove the many-to-many relationship, you obtain a normal star schema.

Increasing the row count requires some steps of ETL. This is usually done through a SQL view, or by using the query editor. Performing the same operation with DAX proves to be very complex, since DAX is not intended as a data manipulation language, but it is primarily a query language.

The good news is that, once the many-to-many is materialized, the formula becomes extremely simple to author because you only need to compute the sum of the hours multiplied by the percentage. As an additional option, you can also compute the hours multiplied by the percentage during extract, transform, load (ETL) to avoid the multiplication at query time.

Using the fact tables as a bridge

One curious aspect of many-to-many relationships is that they often appear where you don't expect them. In fact, the main characteristic of many-to-many relationships is the bridge table, which is a table with two relationships in the opposite direction that link two dimensions. This schema is much more frequent than you might expect. In fact, it is present in any star schema. In Figure 8-20, for example, you can see one of the star schemas we have used multiple times in the demos for this book.

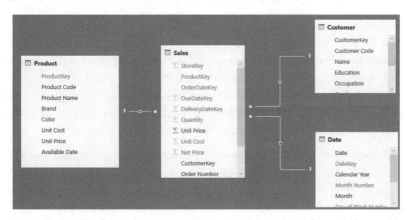

FIGURE 8-20   This figure shows a typical many-to-many relationship with the number of rows in each table.

At first sight, it looks like there is no many-to-many relationship in this model. However, if you carefully consider the nature of many-to-many relationships, you can see that the Sales table has multiple relationships in opposite directions, linking different dimensions. It has the same structure as a bridge table.

For all effects, a fact table can be considered as a bridge between any two dimensions. We have used this concept multiple times in this book, even if we did not clearly state that we were traversing a many-to-many relationship. However, as an example, if you think about counting the number of customers who bought a given product, you can do the following:

- Enable bidirectional filtering on the relationship between Sales and Customer.

- Use CROSSFILTER to enable the bidirectional relationship on demand.

- Use the bidirectional pattern with CALCULATE (COUNTROWS (Customer), Sales).

Any one of these three DAX patterns will provide the correct answer, which is that you filter a set of products, and you can count and/or list the customers who bought some of those articles. You might have recognized in the three patterns the same technique we have used to solve the many-to-many scenario.

In your data-modeling career, you will learn how to recognize these patterns in different models and start using the right technique. Many-to-many is a powerful modeling tool, and as you have seen in this short section, it appears in many different scenarios.

Performance considerations

Earlier, we discussed different ways to model complex many-to-many relationships. We concluded that if you need to perform complex filtering or multiplication by some allocation factors, then the best option, from both a performance and a complexity point of view, is to materialize the many-to-many relationship in the fact table.

Unfortunately, there is not enough space in this book for a detailed analysis of the performance of many-to-many relationships. Still, we want to share with you some basic considerations to give you a rough idea of the speed you might expect from a model containing many-to-many relationships.

Whenever you work with a many-to-many model, you have three kinds of tables: dimensions, fact tables, and bridge tables. To compute values through a many-to-many relationship, the engine needs to scan the bridge table using the dimension as a filter, and then, with the resulting rows, perform a scan of the fact table. Scanning the fact table might take some time, but it is not different from scanning it to compute a value when the dimension is directly linked to it. Thus, the additional effort required by the many-to-many relationship does not depend on the size of the fact table. A larger fact table slows down all the calculations; many-to-many relationships are not different from other relationships.

The size of the dimension is typically not an issue unless it contains more than 1,000,000 rows, which is very unlikely for self-service BI solutions. Moreover, as already happened with the fact table, the engine needs to scan the dimension anyway, even if it is directly linked to the fact table. Thus, the second point is that the performance of many-to-many relationships does not depend on the size of the dimension linked to the table.

The last table to analyze is the bridge. The size of the bridge, unlike the other tables, matters. To be precise, it is not the actual size of the bridge table that matters, but the number of rows that are used to filter the fact tables. Let us use some extreme examples to clarify things. Suppose you have a dimension with 1,000 rows, a bridge with 100,000 rows, and 10,000 rows in the second dimension, as shown in Figure 8-21.

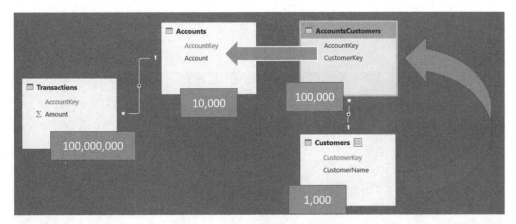

FIGURE 8-21 This figure shows a typical many-to-many relationship with the number of rows in each table.

As mentioned, the size of the fact table is not useful. It has 100,000,000 rows, but this should not be intimidating. What changes the performance is the selectivity of the bridge table over the Accounts table. If you are filtering 10 customers, the bridge filters only around 100 accounts. Thus, you have a fairly balanced distribution, and performance will be very good. Figure 8-22 shows this scenario.

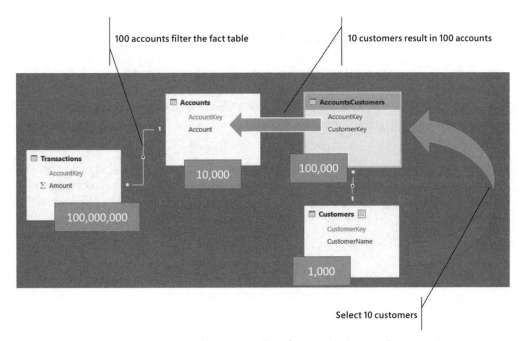

FIGURE 8-22 If the number of accounts filtered is small, performance is very good.

On the other hand, if the filtering of the bridge is much less selective, then performance will be worse depending on the number of resulting accounts. Figure 8-23 shows you an example where filtering 10 customers results in 10,000 accounts. In that case, performance will start to suffer.

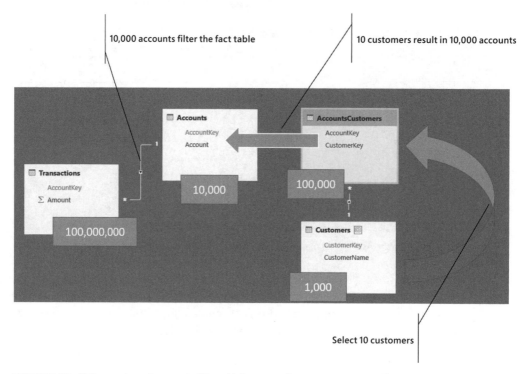

FIGURE 8-23 If the number of accounts filtered is large, performance starts to suffer.

In short, the higher the selectivity of the bridge table, the better the performance. Typically, because bridge tables tend to have a normal selectivity, this translates to a simpler statement: The larger the bridge table, the worse the performance. It is somewhat incorrect to state it this way, but we also understand that it is much easier to remember and apply, and to some extent, it gives you the correct figures.

In our experience, bridge tables up to 1,000,000 rows work just fine, but larger bridge tables require much more attention and some effort in trying to reduce their size. The point to remember here is to not spend time reducing the size of the fact table. Instead, try to work on the bridge table and reduce its size. This will guide you in the right direction in optimizing the many-to-many behavior.

Conclusions

You must learn how to take advantage of many-to-many relationships because they provide incredible power of analysis. That said, learning how to use this type of relationship means understanding the limitations and complexity, both in terms of DAX code and ease of use. Review the following highlights:

- You can manage many-to-many relationships using three main patterns: bidirectional relationships, CROSSFILTER, or table expansion. The choice depends on the version of DAX you are using and the results you want to obtain.

- Basic many-to-many does not require much effort. Once you understand its non-additivity nature and how to set the relationships the correct way, it works just fine.

- Cascading many-to-many relationships and filtered many-to-many relationships are a bit more complex in their handling, especially if you rely on table expansion. In that case, flattening them all in a single bridge might help you write easier code.

- Temporal many-to-many and many-to-many with reallocation factors are complex by their nature. They are powerful but hard to manage.

- If you need to handle very complex many-to-many relationships, your best choice might be to remove the many-to-many altogether. By materializing the relationship in the fact table, you can nearly always get rid of many-to-many relationships, even if this requires you to carefully study the new fact table, increase its number of rows, and probably revise some of the code you wrote earlier.

- When thinking about performance, reducing the size of the bridge is your first goal. You reduce the bridge to increase its selectivity. If your bridge is large, but highly selective when you use it, then you are already on the fast track of DAX.

CHAPTER 9

Working with different granularity

We talked a lot about granularity in previous chapters, and you have seen how important it is to always have the data at the right granularity. But sometimes, data is stored in different fact tables at a different granularity, and the data model cannot be changed. For each table, the granularity is right. In that case, it might be painful to build calculations that use both tables.

In this chapter, we will perform a deeper analysis of how to handle different granularities, looking at different modeling options and a different kind of DAX code. All these models have one thing in common: Granularity cannot be fixed by changing the model. In most cases, the issue comes from having different levels of granularity in different tables, but for each table, the granularity is the right one. You start having problems when you mix both tables in the same report.

Introduction to granularity

Granularity is the level of detail at which you store information. In a typical star schema, granularity is defined by the dimensions—*not* by the fact table. The more dimensions, the higher the granularity. Likewise, the more detailed the dimensions, the higher the granularity. Look, for example, at the model shown in Figure 9-1.

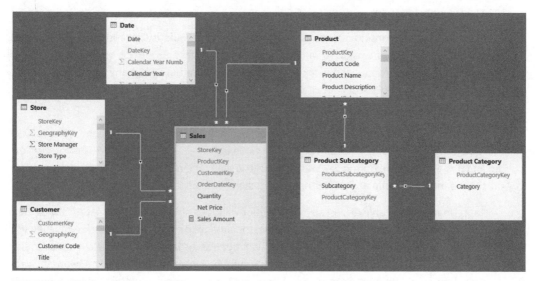

FIGURE 9-1 This is a simple snowflake model with four dimensions and one fact table.

In this model, the granularity is defined by the presence of Date, Store, Customer, and Product. Product Subcategory and Product Category, being snowflaked dimensions, do not contribute to the granularity. The Sales table needs to contain at most one row for each unique combination of the values in the dimension. If two rows exist in Sales with the same combination of dimensional keys, they can be merged into a single row with no loss in expressivity. For example, look at the content of the Sales table, which is shown in Figure 9-2. Notice that there are multiple rows containing the very same set of keys and values.

StoreKey	ProductKey	CustomerKey	OrderDateKey	Quantity	Net Price
306	2490	19075	20091023	1	$11.99
306	2490	19075	20091023	1	$11.99
306	2490	19075	20091023	1	$11.99
306	2490	19075	20091023	1	$11.99
306	2490	19075	20091023	1	$11.99
306	2490	19075	20091023	1	$11.99
306	2490	19075	20091023	1	$11.99
306	2490	19075	20091023	1	$11.99
306	2496	19075	20091016	1	$7.99
306	2496	19075	20091016	1	$7.99
306	2496	19075	20091016	1	$7.99
306	2496	19075	20091016	1	$7.99
306	2496	19075	20091016	1	$7.99
306	2496	19075	20091016	1	$7.99
306	2496	19075	20091016	1	$7.99

FIGURE 9-2 The first eight rows of this table are totally identical.

There is no way to differentiate between these rows in a report. If you slice by any dimension, their values will always be aggregated together. You can compress the first eight rows in a single line that contains 8 for the quantity and with all the remaining columns identical. It looks strange at first, but it is correct. The expressivity of the model does not change in any way if you reduce the number of rows to the most detailed granularity needed. Having more rows only results in a waste of space.

Obviously, if you add a dimension, things change. For example, it might be the case that these eight rows had a difference in the promotional discount applied. If you add a new Promotion dimension, then you change the granularity, increasing it.

Snowflaked dimensions do not count when defining the granularity because they are at a lower level of detail than the dimension to which they are linked. In fact, Product is on the many side of the relationship between Product and Product Subcategory. Thus, there are many products with the same category. If you add the Product Subcategory key to the fact table, you are not going to change its size, in terms of rows.

Whenever you build a new model, always take these considerations into account. After you define the dimensions, try to reduce the size of the fact table to its natural granularity, by performing grouping and pre-aggregation during the extraction of the data. The result is a smaller model, or more precisely, a model of optimal size: Neither too small nor too large, simply perfect.

Notice that the fact table discussed in this section includes no detailed information about the order number. If you put the order number in the table, then many rows will become different, even if they share the same set of dimensions. For example, two identical orders for the same customer could be grouped if you do not take into account the order number. However, as soon as you want the order number, they can no longer be grouped together. Thus, the presence of detailed information in the fact table changes the granularity of the table itself. You might have good reasons to store this detailed information in the fact table. It is only important to understand that its presence has a high cost in terms of size and memory use. Store these fields only if they are really needed for your reports.

Relationships at different granularity

Now that we have set the common terminology about granularity, let us see examples where granularity is different between fact tables. A great example is a budgeting scenario.

Analyzing budget data

When you need to analyze a budget, you are likely to check the difference between the actual sales (either in the past or in the current year) and the forecasted, budgeted figures. This leads to interesting key performance indicators (KPIs) and reports. To do this, however, you must face the problem of granularity. In fact, it is very unlikely that you have forecasted sales in the budget for each product and day. However, you have sales at the product and day level. Let us explore this with an example. Figure 9-3 shows a data model with a standard star schema for Sales and a Budget table, which contain the figures for the next year.

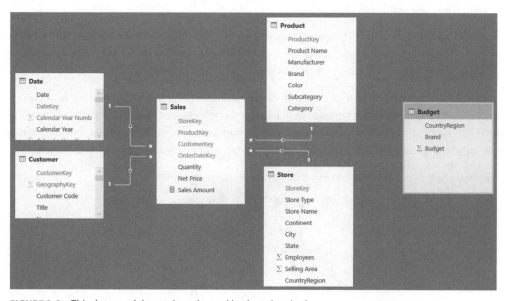

FIGURE 9-3 This data model contains sales and budget data in the same structure.

The budget information is present at the country/region and brand level. Obviously, it does not make sense to provide a day-by-day budget. When you forecast numbers, you do so at a higher level. The same applies at the product level. You cannot forecast the sales of individual products (unless you have very few sales). In the example shown in Figure 9-3 the budgeting manager focused on only two attributes: the country/region and the brand.

If you try to build a report that shows Sales and Budget in the same structure, you will find yourself in trouble because of the missing relationships. As you can see in Figure 9-4, you can slice sales in 2009 by brand using the product brand (that is, the Brand column in the Product table), but you cannot slice budget information using the same column, because there are no relationships between Product and Budget.

Brand	Sales 2009	Budget 2009
A. Datum	$36,200.51	$1,141,350.00
Adventure Works	$32,581.41	$1,141,350.00
Contoso	$132,922.31	$1,141,350.00
Fabrikam	$110,962.34	$1,141,350.00
Litware	$102,200.93	$1,141,350.00
Northwind Traders	$2,505.23	$1,141,350.00
Proseware	$67,563.50	$1,141,350.00
Southridge Video	$35,644.43	$1,141,350.00
Total	**$629,836.71**	**$1,141,350.00**

FIGURE 9-4 The product brand does not slice the Budget table because there are no relationships between Product and Budget.

You might remember that we dealt with a similar scenario in Chapter 1, "Introduction to data modeling." At that time, you did not have the knowledge you have now, so we can now discuss in more detail the different options available to solve it.

It is important to note that the granularity issue is not a mistake in the model. The budget exists at its own granularity, whereas sales are present at a different one. Both tables are modeled the right way. However, it is not so easy to slice by both of them.

The first option we want to analyze is the easiest way of making the budget model a working one: reducing the granularity of both tables to match by removing details in Sales that are not present in Budget. You can easily do this by modifying the queries that load Sales and removing tables referenced by Sales that are at a level of detail not supported by the budget. The resulting model is shown in Figure 9-5.

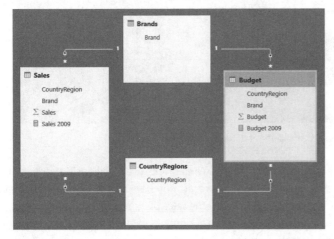

FIGURE 9-5 By simplifying both tables, you can obtain a simple star schema.

To obtain the simplified model, we reduced the granularity of Sales by removing all the details. We had to remove the date references, the product key (replaced by the brand), and the StoreKey (replaced by the CountryRegion). We precomputed the amount of sales while grouping. All the dimensions are gone, replaced by two simple dimensions containing the brands and the country/region. The resulting model is straightforward and, as shown in Figure 9-6, it works just fine. You can slice Sales and Budget by the brand, obtaining meaningful figures.

Brand	Sales 2009	Budget 2009
A. Datum	$33,315.51	$48,500.00
Adventure Works	$31,766.41	$67,100.00
Contoso	$132,785.98	$239,500.00
Fabrikam	$99,675.86	$169,500.00
Litware	$106,393.85	$143,000.00
Northwind Traders	$2,505.23	$64,500.00
Proseware	$65,963.93	$115,500.00
Southridge Video	$36,392.89	$61,500.00
Total	**$617,297.77**	**$1,141,350.00**

FIGURE 9-6 Because the model is based on a star schema, it now produces meaningful numbers.

The problem with this solution is that to make it work, we had to pay a huge price in terms of analytical power. That is, we had to remove all the detailed information about sales. On the date, for example, we had to restrict data to only 2009. In addition, we are no longer able to slice the sales by month and quarter, or by product color. Thus, even if the solution works from a technical point of view, it is far from being correct. What we would like to achieve is a way to slice the budget without losing any analytical capability in Sales.

Using DAX code to move filters

The next technique we want to analyze to solve the scenario is based on DAX. The problem with the data model in Figure 9-3 is that you can filter by brand using the Brand column in the Product table, but because there are no relationships between Product and Budget, the filter will not be able to reach the Budget table.

By using a DAX filter, you can force the filter from the Brand column in Products to the Brand column in Budget. The filter must be written in different ways, depending on the version of DAX you have available. In Power BI and Excel 2016 and later, you can leverage set functions. In fact, if you author the code of the Budget 2009 measure by using the following expression, it will correctly slice by brand and country/region:

```
Budget 2009 :=
CALCULATE (
    SUM ( Budget[Budget] ),
    INTERSECT ( VALUES ( Budget[Brand] ), VALUES ( 'Product'[Brand] ) ),
    INTERSECT ( VALUES ( Budget[CountryRegion] ), VALUES ( Store[CountryRegion] ) )
)
```

The INTERSECT function performs a set intersection between the values of Product[Brand] and the values of Budget[Brand]. Because the Budget table, having no relationships, is not filtered, the result will be a set intersection between all the values of Brand in Budget and the visible ones in Product. In other words, the filter on Product will be moved to the Budget table, for the Brand column. Because there are two such filters, both the filter on Brand and the filter on CountryRegion will be moved to Budget, starting from Product and Store.

The technique looks like the dynamic segmentation pattern covered in Chapter 10, "Segmentation data models." In fact, because we do not have a relationship and we cannot create it, we rely on DAX to mimic it so that the user thinks the relationship is in place, even if there is none.

In Excel 2013, the INTERSECT function is not available. You must use a different technique, based on the CONTAINS function, as in the following code:

```
Budget 2009 Contains =
CALCULATE (
    SUM ( Budget[Budget] ),
    FILTER (
        VALUES ( Budget[Brand] ),
        CONTAINS (
            VALUES ( 'Product'[Brand] ),
            'Product'[Brand],
             Budget[Brand]
        )
    ),
    FILTER (
        VALUES ( Budget[CountryRegion] ),
        CONTAINS (
            VALUES ( Store[CountryRegion] ),
            Store[CountryRegion],
            Budget[CountryRegion]
        )
    )
)
```

This code is much more complex than the simple INTERSECT used in the previous expression, but if you need to use such a pattern in Excel 2010 or Excel 2013, it is your best option. Figure 9-7 shows how the two measures return the very same number, even if they use a slightly different technique to obtain the result.

The technique discussed here does not require you to change the data model because it relies only on the use of DAX. It works just fine, but the code tends to be somewhat complex to write, especially if you are using an older version of Excel. With that said, the version using set functions might easily become too complex if, instead of only two, you start to have a significant number of attributes in the Budget table. In fact, you will need to add a new INTERSECT function call for each of the columns that define the granularity of the budget table.

Brand	Sales 2009	Budget 2009	Budget 2009 Contains
A. Datum	$36,200.51	$48,500.00	$48,500.00
Adventure Works	$32,581.41	$67,100.00	$67,100.00
Contoso	$132,922.31	$239,500.00	$239,500.00
Fabrikam	$110,962.34	$169,500.00	$169,500.00
Litware	$102,200.93	$143,000.00	$143,000.00
Northwind Traders	$2,505.23	$64,500.00	$64,500.00
Proseware	$67,563.50	$115,500.00	$115,500.00
Southridge Video	$35,644.43	$61,500.00	$61,500.00
Tailspin Toys	$9,439.22	$28,000.00	$28,000.00
The Phone Company	$31,975.17	$78,750.00	$78,750.00
Wide World Importers	$67,841.67	$125,500.00	$125,500.00
Total	**$629,836.71**	**$1,141,350.00**	**$1,141,350.00**

FIGURE 9-7 Budget 2009 and Budget 2009 Contains compute the very same result.

Another issue with this measure is performance. The INTERSECT function will rely on the slower part of the DAX language, so for large models, performance might be suboptimal. Fortunately, in January 2017, DAX was extended with a specific function to handle these scenarios: TREATAS. In fact, with the latest versions of the DAX language, you can write the measure as follows:

```
Budget 2009 :=
CALCULATE (
    SUM ( Budget[Budget] ),
    TREATAS ( VALUES ( Budget[Brand] ), 'Product'[Brand] ),
    TREATAS ( VALUES ( Budget[CountryRegion] ), Store[CountryRegion] )
)
```

The TREATAS function works in a similar way to INTERSECT. It is faster than INTERSECT, but much slower than the relationship version we are about to show in the next section.

Filtering through relationships

In the previous section, we solved the scenario of budgeting by using DAX code. In this section, we will work on the same scenario, but instead of using DAX, we will solve it by changing the data model to rely on relationships that propagate the filter in the right way. The idea is to mix the first technique, which is the reduction of granularity of Sales and the creation of two new dimensions, with a snowflake model.

First, we can use the following DAX code to create two new dimensions: Brands and CountryRegions.

```
Brands =
DISTINCT (
    UNION (
        ALLNOBLANKROW ( Product[Brand] ),
        ALLNOBLANKROW ( Budget[Brand] )
    )
)
```

```
CountryRegions =
DISTINCT (
    UNION (
        ALLNOBLANKROW ( Store[CountryRegion] ),
        ALLNOBLANKROW ( Budget[CountryRegion] )
    )
)
```

After the tables are created, you can set up the relationships by making them a snowflake (for Sales) and direct dimensions (for Budget), as in the data model shown in Figure 9-8.

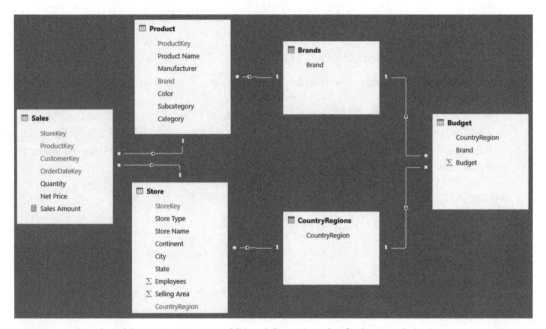

FIGURE 9-8 Brands and CountryRegions are additional dimensions that fix the granularity issue.

With this model in place, which is a perfect star schema, you can use the Brand column in Brands or the CountryRegion column in CountryRegions to slice both Sales and Budget at the same time. You need to be very careful to use the right column, however. If you use the Brand column in Product, it will not be able to slice Brands or, by extension, Budget, because of the direction of relationship cross-filtering. For this reason, it is a very good practice to hide the columns that filter the model in a partial (and unwanted) way. If you were to keep the previous model, then you should hide the CountryRegion column in both Budget and Store, as well as the Brand column in Product and Budget.

The good news is that, in Power BI, you have full control over the propagation of relationship cross-filtering. Thus, you can choose to enable bidirectional filtering on the relationship between Product, Brands, and CountryRegions. The model you obtain is shown in Figure 9-9.

At first, there seems to be no difference between Figure 9-8 and Figure 9-9. But even if the models contain the very same tables, the difference is in how the relationships are set. The relationship between Product and Brands has a bidirectional filter, exactly like the one between Store and CountryRegions.

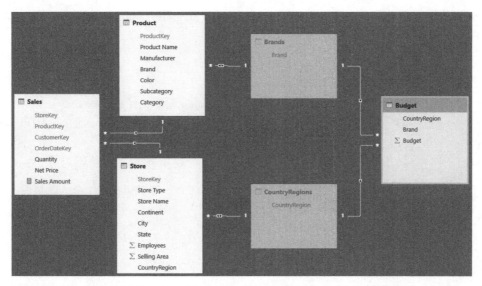

FIGURE 9-9 In this model, Brands and CountryRegions are hidden, and their relationships with Product and Store are set as bidirectional.

Moreover, both the Brands and CountryRegions tables are hidden. This is because they now became helper tables (that is, tables that are used in formulas and code but are not useful for the user to look at). After you filter the Brand column in Product, the bidirectional filter in the relationship moves the filter from Product to Brands. From there, the filter will flow naturally to Budget. The relationship between Store and CountryRegions exhibits the same behavior. Thus, you built a model where a filter on either Product or Store filters Budget, and because the two technical tables are hidden, the user will have a very natural approach to it.

This technique offers significant performance advantages. In fact, being based on relationships, it improves the use of the fastest part of the DAX engine, and it applies filters and uses filter propagation only when necessary. (This is not the case with the solution described in the previous section, where we used a FILTER function regardless of an existing selection on affected dimensions.) This results in optimal performance. Finally, because the granularity issue is handled in the model, the measures become simple SUM operations, with no CALCULATE operations or filtering happening inside. From a maintainability point of view, this is extremely important because it means that any new formula will not need to repeat the filtering pattern that was mandatory in the previous models.

Hiding values at the wrong granularity

In previous sections, we attempted to address the granularity issue by moving Sales to the lower granularity of Budget, losing expressivity. Then we managed to merge the two fact tables in a single data model by using intermediate, hidden snowflaked dimensions, which let the user seamlessly browse Budget and Sales. Nevertheless, even if the user can browse budget values slicing by the product brand, he or she will not be able to slice by, say, product color. In fact, color has a different distribution than brand, and Budget does not contain information at the color granularity. Let us examine this with an example. If you build a simple report that slices Sales and Budget by color, you obtain a result similar to what is shown in Figure 9-10.

Color	Sales Amount	Budget 2009
Azure	$6,362.32	$48,500.00
Black	$337,734.90	$1,141,350.00
Blue	$92,449.76	$1,062,600.00
Brown	$115,653.60	$806,100.00
Gold	$17,447.49	$625,750.00
Green	$64,720.29	$934,000.00
Grey	$246,243.30	$1,076,850.00
Orange	$33,211.29	$726,000.00
Pink	$27,358.17	$958,750.00
Purple	$60.60	$600,500.00
Red	$48,697.27	$1,014,100.00
Silver	$285,768.49	$1,141,350.00
Silver Grey	$18,238.76	$457,500.00
Transparent	$178.75	$239,500.00
White	$453,935.43	$1,092,850.00
Yellow	$4,311.34	$662,000.00
Total	**$1,752,371.77**	**$1,141,350.00**

FIGURE 9-10 Sales Amount is additive, whereas Budget 2009 is not. The sum of the rows is much higher than the grand total.

You might notice a pattern like that in the many-to-many relationship. In fact, this is exactly what is happening. The report is not showing the budget for products of a given color because the Budget fact table does not contain any information about the products. It only knows about brands. In fact, the number shown is the value of Budget for any brand that has at least one product of the given color. This number has at least two problems. First, it is wrong. Second, it is difficult to spot that it is wrong.

You don't want such a report to come out of your models. The best-case scenario is that users might complain about numbers. The worst-case scenario is that they might make decisions based on wrong figures. As a data modeler, it is your responsibility to make sure that if a number cannot be computed out of the model, you clearly show the error and do not provide any answer. In other words, your code needs to contain some logic to make sure that if a number is returned by your measures, that number is the right one. Returning a wrong result is, to state the obvious, not an option.

As you might imagine, the next question is this: How do you know that you should not return any value? This is easy, even if it requires some DAX knowledge. You must determine whether the PivotTable (or the report in general) is browsing data beyond the granularity at which the number still makes sense. If it is above the granularity, then you are aggregating values, which is fine. If it is below the granularity, then you are splitting values based on the granularity, even if you are showing them at a more detailed level. In such a case, you should return a BLANK result to inform the user that you do not know the answer.

The key to solving this scenario is being able to count the number of products (or stores) selected at the Sales granularity and compare them with the number of products selected at the Budget granularity.

If the two numbers are equal, then the filter induced by the products will produce meaningful values in both fact tables. If, on the other hand, the numbers are different, then the filter will produce an incorrect result on the table with the lower granularity. To achieve this, you define the following two measures:

```
ProductsAtSalesGranularity := COUNTROWS ( Product )

ProductsAtBudgetGranularity :=
CALCULATE (
    COUNTROWS ( Product ),
    ALL ( Product ),
    VALUES ( Product[Brand] )
)
```

ProductsAtSalesGranularity counts the number of products at the maximum granularity—that is, the product key. Sales is linked to Product at this granularity. ProductsAtBudgetGranularity, on the other hand, counts the number of products, taking into account only the filter on Brand and removing any other existing filters. This is the very definition of the granularity of Budget. You can appreciate the difference between the two measures if you build a report like the one shown in Figure 9-11, which slices the two measures by brand and color.

Brand	Color	ProductsAtBudgetGranularity	ProductsAtSalesGranularity
A. Datum	Azure	132	14
	Black	132	18
	Blue	132	4
	Gold	132	4
	Green	132	14
	Grey	132	18
	Orange	132	18
	Pink	132	18
	Silver	132	18
	Silver Grey	132	6
	Total	**132**	**132**
Adventure Works	Black	192	54
	Blue	192	12
	Brown	192	15
	Grey	192	14
	Red	192	6
	Silver	192	39
	White	192	52
	Total	**192**	**192**

FIGURE 9-11 This report shows the number of products at different granularities.

The two measures report the same value only when there is a filter on the brand and no other filter is applied. In other words, the two numbers are equal only when the Product table is sliced at the Budget granularity. The same needs to be done for Store, too, where the granularity is country/region. You define two measures to check the granularity at the store level by using the following code:

```
StoresAtSalesGranularity := COUNTROWS ( Store )

StoresAtBudgetGranularity :=
CALCULATE (
    COUNTROWS ( Store ),
    ALL ( Store ),
    VALUES ( Store[CountryRegion] )
)
```

When you use them in a report, the two measures return the same number at the budget granularity and above, as shown in Figure 9-12.

Continent	CountryRegion	State	StoresAtBudgetGranularity	StoresAtSalesGranularity ▼
North America	United States	Texas	198	35
		Wisconsin	198	22
		Colorado	198	21
		Washington	198	20
		Massachusetts	198	19
		New Jersey	198	18
		New York	198	14
		Florida	198	13
		Maryland	198	11
		Connecticut	198	8
		Virginia	198	8
		Maine	198	6
		South Carolina	198	2
		Alaska	198	1
		Total	**198**	**198**
	Canada	Ontario	11	5
		British Columbia	11	3
		Quebec	11	2
		Alberta	11	1
		Total	**11**	**11**
	Total		**209**	**209**
Total			**209**	**209**

FIGURE 9-12 This report shows the number of stores at different granularities.

In fact, the numbers are identical not only at the country/region level, but also at the continent level. This is correct because Continent has higher granularity than CountryRegion, and the value of the Budget, at the Continent level, is correct.

The last step, to make sure you show only meaningful numbers for Budget, is to blank out the Budget measure when the measures we have written so far do not match. This can be easily accomplished by using a conditional formula as in the following code:

```
Budget 2009 :=
IF (
    AND (
        [ProductsAtBudgetGranularity] = [ProductsAtSalesGranularity],
        [StoresAtBudgetGranularity] = [StoresAtSalesGranularity]
    ),
    SUM ( Budget[Budget] )
)
```

The additional condition ensures that a value is returned if and only if the report is not browsing below the granularity of Budget. The result is shown in Figure 9-13, where Budget is correctly reported at the brand level, and is blanked at the color level.

Note Whenever you have fact tables at different granularity, it is very important to recognize when a value should not be shown because of granularity issues. Otherwise, the report will always produce a number—and it is likely to be the wrong one.

Brand	Color	Sales 2009	Budget 2009
A. Datum	Azure	$2,300.20	
	Black	$9,084.43	
	Gold	$1,014.00	
	Green	$5,138.80	
	Grey	$3,103.05	
	Orange	$5,306.96	
	Pink	$1,378.92	
	Silver	$1,726.35	
	Silver Grey	$7,147.80	
	Total	**$36,200.51**	**$48,500.00**
Adventure Works	Black	$15,303.77	
	Blue	$520.47	
	Silver	$8,622.21	
	White	$8,134.95	
	Total	**$32,581.41**	**$67,100.00**

FIGURE 9-13 This report blanks the value of Budget below the correct granularity.

Allocating values at a higher granularity

In the previous examples, you learned how to hide values when the user is browsing at a granularity that is no longer supported by the data model. This technique is useful to avoid showing a wrong number. For some specific scenarios, however, you can do more than this. You can compute the value at the higher granularity using an allocation factor. For example, suppose you do not know the budget of blue products at a company called Adventure Works. (You only know the budget for the total of Adventure Works.) You can ascertain this by taking a percentage of the total budget, which you can compute on the fly. This percentage is the allocation factor.

A good allocation factor can be, for example, the percentage of sales of blue products against the totality of colors in the previous year. Rather than trying to describe it with words, it is much simpler to look at the final report shown in Figure 9-14.

Brand	Color	Sales 2008	AllocationFactor	Budget 2009	Allocated Budget
A. Datum	Azure	$4,062.12	9.33 %		$4,526.04
	Black	$681.90	1.57 %		$759.78
	Blue	$1,587.60	3.65 %		$1,768.91
	Green	$3,450.30	7.93 %		$3,844.35
	Grey	$1,800.00	4.14 %		$2,005.57
	Orange	$6,424.10	14.76 %		$7,157.77
	Pink	$12,566.60	28.87 %		$14,001.78
	Silver	$9,557.72	21.96 %		$10,649.28
	Silver Grey	$3,398.40	7.81 %		$3,786.52
	Total	**$43,528.75**	**100.00 %**	**$48,500.00**	**$48,500.00**
Adventure Works	Black	$27,481.25	29.36 %		$19,703.50
	Blue	$8,603.64	9.19 %		$6,168.64
	Brown	$7,549.63	8.07 %		$5,412.93
	Grey	$4,644.90	4.96 %		$3,330.30
	Red	$5,592.00	5.98 %		$4,009.35
	Silver	$18,013.27	19.25 %		$12,915.15
	White	$21,702.32	23.19 %		$15,560.13
	Total	**$93,587.00**	**100.00 %**	**$67,100.00**	**$67,100.00**

FIGURE 9-14 The Allocated Budget column shows values at a higher granularity by computing them dynamically.

Let us examine Figure 9-14 in more detail. In previous figures, we used Sales 2009, whereas here we are showing Sales 2008. This is because we use Sales 2008 to compute the allocation factor, which is defined here as the amount of sales in 2008 of blue products divided by the amount of sales in 2008 at the Budget granularity.

You can see, for example, that blue products from Adventure Works made $8,603.64 in sales, which, divided by $93,587.00, results in 9.19% as the share of sales in 2008. The budget of blue products is not available in 2009, but you can compute it by multiplying the budget of Adventure Works products by the share in 2008, for an expected value of $6,168.64.

Computing the value is simple when you understand the granularity details. It is a simple variation on the formulas you have seen so far, as shown in the following DAX code:

```
Sales2008AtBudgetGranularity :=
CALCULATE (
    [Sales 2008],
    ALL ( Store ),
    VALUES ( Store[CountryRegion] ),
    ALL ( Product ),
    VALUES ( Product[Brand] )
)

AllocationFactor := DIVIDE ( [Sales 2008], [Sales2008AtBudgetGranularity] )

Allocated Budget := SUM ( Budget[Budget] ) * [AllocationFactor]
```

The core of the previous formulas is Sales2008AtBudgetGranularity, which computes the sales amount after removing filters from Store and Product, apart from the columns that define the granularity at the Budget level. The remaining two measures are a simple division and a multiplication. Use the numbers shown in Figure 9-14 to produce the desired result.

The technique of reallocating at the higher granularity is very interesting, and it gives the user the feeling that numbers are present at a higher granularity than they really are. However, if you plan to use this technique, you should clearly explain how the numbers are computed to the stakeholders. At the very end, the numbers are derived from a calculation, and they are not what is entered when the budget is created.

Conclusions

Granularity is one topic you need to understand to build any data model, and has been discussed in many chapters throughout this book. This chapter went a step further to analyze some options that are available when granularity cannot be fixed because data is already stored at the right level.

The most important topics covered in this chapter are as follows:

- Granularity is defined by the level at which the dimensions are linked to the fact table.

- Different fact tables can present different levels of granularity because of the nature of their data. Usually, granularity issues are errors in the model. However, there are scenarios where fact tables are stored at the correct granularity, which is different from table to table.

- When multiple fact tables have different granularity, you must build a model that lets you slice all the tables using one dimension. You can do so either by creating a special model at the correct granularity or by moving the filter through DAX code or bidirectional relationships.

- You must be aware of granularity differences among your facts and handle them properly. You have multiple options: ignoring the problem, hiding the data when granularity becomes too high, or reallocating the values using some allocation factor.

CHAPTER 10

Segmentation data models

I n Chapter 9, "Working with different granularity," you learned how to model your data with standard
relationships: two tables related based on a single column. At the end, many-to-many relationships
were built using standard relationships. In this chapter, you will learn how to handle more complex
relationships between tables by leveraging the DAX language. Tabular models can handle simple or
bidirectional relationships between tables, which might look somewhat limited. However, by taking
advantage of the DAX language, you can create very advanced models with basically any kind of relationship, including virtual ones. When it comes to solving complex scenarios, DAX plays an important
role in the definition of the data model.

To demonstrate these kinds of relationships, we will use as examples some data models where the
main topic is that of segmenting the data. Segmentation is a common modeling pattern that happens
whenever you want to stratify your data based on some configuration table. Imagine, for example, that
you want to cluster your customers based on the age range, your products based on the amount sold,
or your customers based on the revenues generated.

The goal of this chapter is not to give you pre-built patterns that you can use in your model. Instead,
we want to show you unusual ways of using DAX to build complex models, to broaden your understanding of relationships, and to let you experience what you can achieve with DAX formulas.

Computing multiple-column relationships

The first set of relationships we will show is calculated physical relationships. The only difference
between this and a standard relationship is that the key of the relationship is a calculated column. In
scenarios where the relationship cannot be set because a key is missing, or you need to compute it with
complex formulas, you can leverage calculated columns to set up the relationship. Even if based on
calculated columns, this will still be a physical relationship.

The Tabular engine only allows you to create relationships based on a single column. It does not
support relationships based on more than one column. Yet, relationships based on multiple columns
are very useful, and appear in many data models. If you need to work with these kinds of models, use
the two following methods to do so:

- Define a calculated column that contains the composition of the keys and use it as the new key
  for the relationship.

- Denormalize the columns of the target table (the one side in a one-to-many relationship) using the LOOKUPVALUE function.

As an example, imagine you have a special "Product of the Day" promotion, where on some days, you make a special promotion for a single product with a given discount, as shown in Figure 10-1.

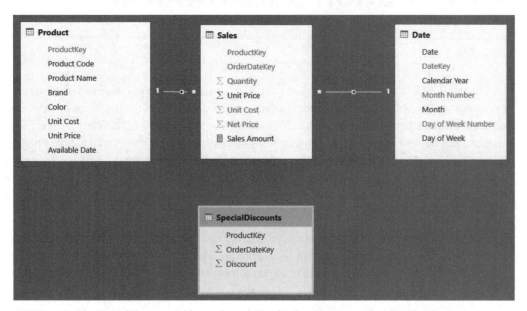

FIGURE 10-1   The SpecialDiscounts table needs a relationship based on two columns with Sales.

The table with the promotion (SpecialDiscounts) contains three columns: ProductKey, OrderDateKey, and Discount. If you need to use this information to compute, for example, the amount of the discount, you face the problem that for any given sale, the discount depends on ProductKey and OrderDateKey. Thus, you cannot create the relationship between Sales and SpecialDiscounts, because it would involve two columns, and Tabular supports only single-column relationships.

To find a possible solution to this scenario, consider that nothing prevents you from creating a relationship based on a calculated column. In fact, if the engine does not support a relationship based on two columns, you can build a new column that contains both, and then build a relationship on top of this new column. You can create a new calculated column in both the SpecialDiscount and Sales tables that contains the combination of the two columns by using the following code:

```
Sales[SpecialDiscountKey] = Sales[ProductKey] & "-" & Sales[OrderDateKey]
```

You use a similar expression in SpecialDiscount. After you define the two columns, you can finally create the relationship between the two tables. This results in the model shown in Figure 10-2.

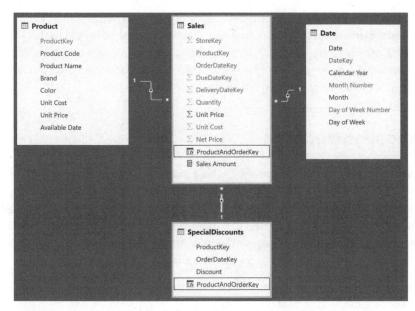

FIGURE 10-2 You can use the calculated column as the basis of the relationship.

This solution is straightforward and works just fine. However, there are several scenarios where this is not the best solution because it requires you to create two calculated columns that might have many different values. From a performance point of view, this is not advisable.

Another possible solution to the same scenario is to use the LOOKUPVALUE function. Using LOOK-UPVALUE, you can denormalize the discount directly in the fact table by defining a new calculated column in Sales that contains the following code:

```
Sales[SpecialDiscount] =
LOOKUPVALUE (
    SpecialDiscounts[Discount],
    SpecialDiscounts[ProductKey], Sales[ProductKey],
    SpecialDiscounts[OrderDateKey], Sales[OrderDateKey]
)
```

Following this second pattern, you do not create any relationship. Instead, you move the Discount value in the fact table, performing a lookup. In a more technical way, we say you denormalized the SpecialDiscount value from the SpecialDiscounts table into Sales.

Both options work fine, and the choice between them depends on several factors. If Discount is the only column you need to use from the SpecialDiscount table, then denormalization is the best option. Only a single calculated column is created, with fewer distinct values, comparatively to two calculated columns with many more distinct values. Thus, it reduces memory usage and makes the code simpler to author.

If, on the other hand, SpecialDiscounts contains many columns that you need to use in your code, then each of them would have to be denormalized in the fact table, resulting in a waste of memory and, possibly, in worse performance. In that case, the calculated column with the new composite key would be a superior method.

This first simple example is important because it demonstrates a common and important feature of DAX: the ability to create relationships based on calculated columns. This capability shows that you can create any kind of relationship, as long as you can compute it and materialize it in a calculated column. In the next example, we will show you how to create relationships based on static ranges. By extending the concept, you can create almost any kind of relationship.

Computing static segmentation

Static segmentation is a very common scenario where you have a value in a table, and, rather than being interested in the analysis of the value itself (as there might be hundreds or thousands of possible values), you want to analyze it by splitting the value into segments. Two very common examples are the analysis of sales by customer age or by list price. It is pointless to partition sales amounts by all unique values of list price because there are too many different values in list price. However, if you group different prices in ranges, then it may be possible to obtain good insight from the analysis of these groups.

In this example, you have a table, PriceRanges, that contains the price ranges. For each range, you define the boundaries of the range itself, as shown in Figure 10-3.

PriceRangeKey	PriceRange	MinPrice	MaxPrice
1	VERY LOW	0	10
2	LOW	10	30
3	MEDIUM	30	80
4	HIGH	80	150
5	VERY HIGH	150	99999

FIGURE 10-3 This is the configuration table for the price ranges.

Here, as in the previous example, you cannot create a direct relationship between the fact table, containing sales, and the PriceRanges configuration table. This is because the key in the configuration table depends on a range relationship, and range relationships are not supported by DAX. In this case, the best solution is to denormalize the price range directly in the fact table by using a calculated column. The pattern of the code is similar to the previous one, with the main difference being the following formula:

```
Sales[PriceRange] =
CALCULATE (
    VALUES ( PriceRanges[PriceRange] ),
    FILTER (
        PriceRanges,
        AND (
            PriceRanges[MinPrice] <= Sales[Net Price],
            PriceRanges[MaxPrice] > Sales[Net Price]
        )
    )
)
```

It is interesting to note the use of VALUES in this code to retrieve a single value. VALUES returns a table, not a value. However, whenever a table contains a single row and a single column, it is automatically converted into a scalar value, if needed by the expression.

Because of the way FILTER computes its result, it will always return a single row from the configuration table. Thus, VALUES is guaranteed to always return a single row, and the result of CALCULATE is the description of the price range containing the current net price. Obviously, this expression works fine if the configuration table is well designed. However, if for any reason the ranges contain holes or overlap, then VALUES will return many rows, and the expression might result in an error.

A better way to author the previous code is to leverage the error-handling function, which will detect the presence of a wrong configuration, and return an appropriate message, as in the following code:

```
Sales[PriceRange] =
VAR ResultValue =
    CALCULATE (
        IFERROR (
            VALUES ( PriceRanges[PriceRange] ),
            "Overlapping Configuration"
        ),
        FILTER (
            PriceRanges,
            AND (
                PriceRanges[MinPrice] <= Sales[Net Price],
                PriceRanges[MaxPrice] > Sales[Net Price]
            )
        )
    )
RETURN
    IF (
        ISEMPTY ( ResultValue ),
        "Wrong Configuration",
        ResultValue
    )
```

This code detects both overlapping values (with the internal IFERROR) and holes in the configuration (by checking the result value with ISEMPTY before returning it to the caller). Because it is guaranteed to always return a good value, this code is much safer to use than the previous code.

Calculated physical relationships are a very powerful tool in Power BI and Excel modeling because they let you create very advanced relationships. In addition, the computation of the relationship happens during the refresh time when you update the data, not when you query the model. Thus, they result in very good query performance regardless of their complexity.

Using dynamic segmentation

There are many scenarios where you cannot set the logical relationship between tables in a static way. In these cases, you cannot use calculated static relationships. Instead, you need to define the relationship in the measure to handle the calculations in a more dynamic way. In these cases, because the relationship does not belong to the model, we speak of virtual relationships. These are in contrast to the physical relationships you have explored so far.

This next example of a virtual relationship solves a variation of the static segmentation we showed earlier in this chapter. In the static segmentation, you assigned each sale to a specific segment using a calculated column. In dynamic segmentation, the assignment happens dynamically.

Imagine you want to cluster your customers based on the sales amount. The sales amount depends on the slicers used in the report. Therefore, the segmentation cannot be static. If you filter a single year, then a customer might belong to a specific cluster. However, if you change the year, the same customer could belong to a different cluster. In this scenario, because you cannot rely on a physical relationship, you cannot modify the data model to make the DAX code easier to author. In such a case, your only option is to roll up your sleeves and use some advanced DAX to compute the value.

You start by defining the configuration table, Segments, which is shown in Figure 10-4.

SegmentCode	Segment	MinSale	MaxSale
1	Very Low	0	75
2	Low	75	100
3	Medium	100	500
4	High	500	1000
6	Very High	1000	99999999

FIGURE 10-4 The configuration table for dynamic segmentation.

The measure to compute is the number of customers that belong to a specific cluster. In other words, you want to count how many customers belong to a segment, considering all the filters in the current filter context. The following formula looks very innocent, but it requires some attention because of its usage of context transition:

```
CustInSegment :=
COUNTROWS (
    FILTER (
        Customer,
        AND (
            [Sales Amount] > MIN ( Segments[MinSale] ),
            [Sales Amount] <= MAX ( Segments[MaxSale] )
        )
    )
)
```

To understand the formula behavior, it is useful to look at a report that shows the segments on the rows and the calendar year on columns. The report is shown in Figure 10-5.

Segment	CY 2007	CY 2008	CY 2009	Total
Very Low	351	266	255	810
Low	141	14	12	166
Medium	365	76	52	485
High	250	36	35	311
Very High	302	132	160	581
Total	1,409	524	514	2,353

FIGURE 10-5 This PivotTable shows the dynamic segmentation pattern in action.

Look at the cell that shows 76 customers belonging to the Medium cluster in 2008. The formula iterated over Customer, and for each customer it checked whether the value of Sales Amount for that customer fell between MIN of MinSale and MAX of MaxSale. The value of Sales Amount represents the sales of the individual customer, due to context transition. The resulting measure is, as expected, additive against segments and customers, and nonadditive against all other dimensions.

The formula only works if you select all of the segments. If you select, for example, only Very Low and Very High (removing the three intermediate segments from the selection), then MIN and MAX will not be the correct choice. They would enclose all the customers, which would give the wrong results in the grand total, as shown in Figure 10-6.

Segment

■ Very Low
☐ Low
☐ Medium
☐ High
■ Very High

Segment	CY 2007	CY 2008	CY 2009	Total
Very Low	351	266	255	810
Very High	302	132	160	581
Total	1,409	524	514	2,353

FIGURE 10-6 This PivotTable shows wrong values when used with a slicer with non-contiguous selections.

If you want to let the user select some of the segments, then you need to write the formula in the following way:

```
CustInSegment :=
SUMX (
    Segments,
    COUNTROWS (
        FILTER (
            Customer,
            AND (
                [Sales Amount] > Segments[MinSale],
                [Sales Amount] <= Segments[MaxSale]
            )
        )
    )
)
```

This version of the formula does not suffer from the issue of partial selection of segments, but it might result in worse performance because it requires a double iteration over the tables. The result is shown in Figure 10-7, which now yields the correct value.

Segment		Segment	CY 2007	CY 2008	CY 2009	Total
■ Very Low		Very Low	351	266	255	**810**
☐ Low		Very High	302	132	160	**581**
☐ Medium		**Total**	**653**	**398**	**415**	**1,391**
☐ High						
■ Very High						

FIGURE 10-7 At the grand total, the two measures now show different values because of the partial selection of segments.

Virtual relationships are extremely powerful. They do not actually belong to the model, even if the user perceives them as real relationships, and they are entirely computed using DAX at query time. If the formula is very complex, or if the size of the model becomes too large, performance might be an issue. However, they work absolutely fine for medium-sized models.

Tip We suggest you try to map these concepts in your specific business to see whether this pattern can be useful for any stratification you might want to pursue.

Understanding the power of calculated columns: ABC analysis

Calculated columns are stored inside the database. From a modeling point of view, this has a tremendous impact because it opens new ways of modeling data. In this section, you will look at some scenarios that you can solve very efficiently with calculated columns.

As an example of the use of calculated columns, we will show you how to solve the scenario of ABC analysis using Power BI. ABC analysis is based on the Pareto principle. In fact, it is sometimes known as ABC/Pareto Analysis. It is a very common technique to determine the core business of a company, typically in terms of best products or best customers. In this scenario, we focus on products.

The goal of ABC analysis is to identify which products have a significant impact on the overall business so that managers can focus their effort on them. To achieve this, each product is assigned a category (A, B, or C), so that the following is true:

- Products in class A account for 70 percent of the revenues.

- Products in class B account for 20 percent of the revenues.

- Products in class C account for 10 percent of the revenues.

The ABC class of a product needs to be stored in a calculated column because you want to use it to perform analysis on products, slicing information by class. For example, Figure 10-8 shows you a simple PivotTable that uses the ABC class on the rows.

ABC Class	NumOfProducts	Margin
A	215	$1,411,868.11
B	285	$404,299.99
C	2,017	$202,448.10
Total	**2,517**	**$2,018,616.20**

FIGURE 10-8 The ABC class is used in this report to show products and margins based on their class.

As often happens with ABC analysis, you can see that only a few products are in class A. This is the core business of Contoso. Products in class B are less important, but they are still vital for the company. Products in class C are good candidates for removal because there are many of them and their revenues are tiny when compared with the core products.

The data model in this scenario is very simple. You need only sales and products, as shown in Figure 10-9.

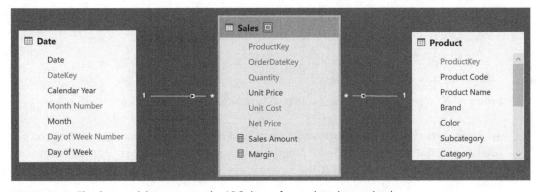

FIGURE 10-9 The data model to compute the ABC classes for products is very simple.

This time, we will change the model by simply adding some columns. No new table or relationship will be needed. To compute the ABC class of a product, you must compute the total margin of that product and compare it with the grand total. This gives you the percentage of the overall sales for which that single product accounts. Then, you sort products based on that percentage and perform a rolling sum. As soon as the rolling sum reaches 70 percent, you have identified products in class A. Remaining products will be in class B until you reach 90 percent (70+20), and further products will be in class C. You will build the complete calculations using only calculated columns.

First, you need a calculated column in the Product table that contains the margin for each product. This can be easily accomplished using the following expression:

```
Product[TotalMargin] =
SUMX (
    RELATEDTABLE( Sales ),
    Sales[Quantity] * ( Sales[Net Price] - Sales[Unit Cost] )
)
```

Figure 10-10 shows the Product table with this new calculated column in which the data is sorted in descending order by TotalMargin.

Product Name	TotalMargin ↑
Adventure Works 26" 720p LCD HDTV M140 Silver	$81,856.27
Contoso Telephoto Conversion Lens X400 Silver	$53,464.04
Fabrikam Refrigerator 24.7CuFt X9800 White	$51,574.26
A. Datum SLR Camera X137 Grey	$51,459.16
Litware Refrigerator 24.7CuFt X980 Brown	$29,756.33
Litware Refrigerator 24.7CuFt X980 White	$28,256.56
NT Washer & Dryer 27in L2700 Blue	$26,591.59
Proseware Projector 1080p DLP86 Black	$25,065.45
NT Washer & Dryer 24in M2400 Green	$24,472.50
SV 16xDVD M360 Black	$20,989.22
Contoso Projector 1080p X980 White	$19,648.68

FIGURE 10-10 TotalMargin is computed as a calculated column in the Product table.

The next step is to compute a running total of TotalMargin over the Product table ordered by TotalMargin. The running total of each product is the sum of all the products that have a value for TotalMargin greater than or equal to the current value. You can obtain it with the following formula:

```
Product[MarginRT] =
VAR
    CurrentTotalMargin = 'Product'[TotalMargin]
RETURN
    SUMX (
        FILTER (
            'Product',
            'Product'[TotalMargin] >= CurrentTotalMargin
        ),
    'Product'[TotalMargin]
    )
```

Figure 10-11 shows the Product table with this new column.

Product Name	TotalMargin ↑	MarginRT
Adventure Works 26" 720p LCD HDTV M140 Silver	$81,856.27	$81,856.27
Contoso Telephoto Conversion Lens X400 Silver	$53,464.04	$135,320.31
Fabrikam Refrigerator 24.7CuFt X9800 White	$51,574.26	$186,894.56
A. Datum SLR Camera X137 Grey	$51,459.16	$238,353.72
Litware Refrigerator 24.7CuFt X980 Brown	$29,756.33	$268,110.06
Litware Refrigerator 24.7CuFt X980 White	$28,256.56	$296,366.62
NT Washer & Dryer 27in L2700 Blue	$26,591.59	$322,958.20
Proseware Projector 1080p DLP86 Black	$25,065.45	$348,023.65
NT Washer & Dryer 24in M2400 Green	$24,472.50	$372,496.15
SV 16xDVD M360 Black	$20,989.22	$393,485.38
Contoso Projector 1080p X980 White	$19,648.68	$413,134.06

FIGURE 10-11 MarginRT computes a running total over the rows that are sorted by TotalMargin.

The final point is to compute the running total sales as a percentage over the grand total of margin. A new calculated column easily solves the problem. You can add a RunningPct column with the following formula:

```
Product[MarginPct] = DIVIDE ( 'Product'[MarginRT], SUM ( 'Product'[TotalMargin] ) )
```

Figure 10-12 shows the new calculated column, which has been formatted as a percentage to make the result more understandable.

Product Name	TotalMargin ↑	MarginRT	MarginPct
Adventure Works 26" 720p LCD HDTV M140 Silver	$81,856.27	$81,856.27	4.06 %
Contoso Telephoto Conversion Lens X400 Silver	$53,464.04	$135,320.31	6.70 %
Fabrikam Refrigerator 24.7CuFt X9800 White	$51,574.26	$186,894.56	9.26 %
A. Datum SLR Camera X137 Grey	$51,459.16	$238,353.72	11.81 %
Litware Refrigerator 24.7CuFt X980 Brown	$29,756.33	$268,110.06	13.28 %
Litware Refrigerator 24.7CuFt X980 White	$28,256.56	$296,366.62	14.68 %
NT Washer & Dryer 27in L2700 Blue	$26,591.59	$322,958.20	16.00 %
Proseware Projector 1080p DLP86 Black	$25,065.45	$348,023.65	17.24 %
NT Washer & Dryer 24in M2400 Green	$24,472.50	$372,496.15	18.45 %
SV 16xDVD M360 Black	$20,989.22	$393,485.38	19.49 %
Contoso Projector 1080p X980 White	$19,648.68	$413,134.06	20.47 %

FIGURE 10-12 MarginPct computes the percentage of the running total over the grand total.

The final touch is to transform the percentage into the class. If you use the values of 70, 20, and 10, the formula for the ABC class is straightforward, as you see in the following formula:

```
Product[ABC Class] =
IF (
    'Product'[MarginPct] <= 0.7,
    "A",
    IF (
        'Product'[MarginPct] <= 0.9,
        "B",
        "C"
    )
)
```

The result is shown in Figure 10-13.

Product Name	TotalMargin ↑	MarginRT	MarginPct	ABC Class
Adventure Works 26" 720p LCD HDTV M140 Silver	$81,856.27	$81,856.27	4.06 %	A
Contoso Telephoto Conversion Lens X400 Silver	$53,464.04	$135,320.31	6.70 %	A
Fabrikam Refrigerator 24.7CuFt X9800 White	$51,574.26	$186,894.56	9.26 %	A
A. Datum SLR Camera X137 Grey	$51,459.16	$238,353.72	11.81 %	A
Litware Refrigerator 24.7CuFt X980 Brown	$29,756.33	$268,110.06	13.28 %	A
Litware Refrigerator 24.7CuFt X980 White	$28,256.56	$296,366.62	14.68 %	A
NT Washer & Dryer 27in L2700 Blue	$26,591.59	$322,958.20	16.00 %	A
Proseware Projector 1080p DLP86 Black	$25,065.45	$348,023.65	17.24 %	A
NT Washer & Dryer 24in M2400 Green	$24,472.50	$372,496.15	18.45 %	A
SV 16xDVD M360 Black	$20,989.22	$393,485.38	19.49 %	A
Contoso Projector 1080p X980 White	$19,648.68	$413,134.06	20.47 %	A

FIGURE 10-13 The result of the ABC class is the calculated column, ABC Class.

Because ABC Class is a calculated column, it is stored inside the database, and you can use it on slicers, filters, and rows or columns to produce interesting reports.

As this example shows, you have the option of storing in the model some complex calculations by using calculated columns and executing them systematically. It takes some time to recognize whether a calculation is better achieved by using a calculated column or a measure, but once you master this, with practice, you will unleash the power of calculated columns.

Note You can find more information on ABC analysis at *http://en.wikipedia.org/wiki/ABC_analysis*.

Conclusions

In this chapter, we moved one step forward from standard relationships by analyzing some segmentation techniques that made extensive usage of the DAX language. The important points in this chapter are as follows:

- Calculated columns can be used to create relationships by building calculated relationships. The power of calculated relationships is that you can base the relationship on any kind of calculation, not only simple joins based on equality, like the ones supported by the engine out of the box.

- If the relationship cannot be created because it is dynamic, because it depends on the filter and slicers used in the report, you may be able to leverage virtual relationships. Virtual relationships appear like standard relationships to the user, but they are computed on the fly. Performance can potentially suffer, but the flexibility you gain is well worth it.

- Calculated columns are a great addition to the modeling feature of a Tabular solution. Using calculated columns, you can perform very complex segmentation with a few calculated columns that are computed at model refresh time. Thus, they are a marriage between speed and flexibility that let you create extremely powerful models.

We hope that these few examples helped you gain a new perspective on how a little creativity can aid you in building great models.

CHAPTER 11

Working with multiple currencies

In this chapter, we will analyze some models that have in common the need to handle multiple sales in multiple currencies. As you will learn, whenever you need to handle multiple currencies, the number of problems increases by a lot. In fact, there are many decisions you will need to make to accommodate for multiple currencies in terms of the size of the model, flexibility, and performance.

We first introduce the problem of currency conversion, showing the challenges and problems you might face when developing models in different scenarios. Then, as in previous chapters, we build some examples of data models involving currency conversion. There are different ways of modeling the same scenario, and we analyze them to identify the pros and cons of each.

Understanding different scenarios

As mentioned, currency conversion hides some complexity that is already in the definition of the problem. In fact, a large company is likely to receive and to pay money in different currencies, and, as we all know, the value of a currency changes over time. This makes it important to convert from one currency to another to compare volumes of money in different currencies. Let us focus on a simple example. Suppose Contoso received EUR 100 on January 20 from a customer. How do we convert this value into USD, given that USD is the main currency of Contoso? There are the following ways:

- **You immediately transform EUR to USD when the money is received**   This is the simplest way to handle currency conversion because basically, you have a single currency to handle.

- **You deposit EUR into a current account and then use it to pay in EUR when needed**   This makes it hard to build reports in different currencies because the value of sales changes every day, depending on the current value of the currency.

- **You deposit EUR into a current account and perform a currency conversion at the end of the month (or at any given point in time except the original transaction)**   In this case, you must handle multiple, varying currencies for a limited amount of time.

Note   There might be policies that make any one of these three basic options impossible. The reason we cited these three different ways is not to give you an exhaustive list of options. Instead we wanted to show at least three legitimate ways of managing currency conversion.

By defining the point in time when conversion should happen, you are thinking about how to store the data. But, once the data is stored, you might want to build reports on top of it. If you perform conversion in the main currency, then the reporting problems are somewhat mitigated. However, if you want to be able to report in different currencies, then you might need to store transactions in EUR and report them in USD, Yen, or any other currency. This makes it necessary to be able to perform online conversion—that is, conversion of currency in real-time when the query is executed.

When it comes to currency conversion, you need to spend a lot of time understanding exactly what the requirements are because the resulting data models are very different. There is no single model that can handle all the possible scenarios. Moreover, from a performance point of view, currency conversion is very challenging. This is probably the main reason you should try to keep it as simple as possible, by avoiding handling models that are more complex than strictly needed.

Multiple source currencies, single reporting currency

Suppose the source data contains orders in different currencies, and you want to produce a report containing information with a single type of currency. For example, you collect orders in EUR, USD, and other currencies, but, to be able to compare sales, you want to convert them all to a single currency.

Let us start with a quick look at the model we use for this scenario, shown in Figure 11-1. Sales has a relationship with Currency, which indicates that each sale is recorded with the currency in which it happened.

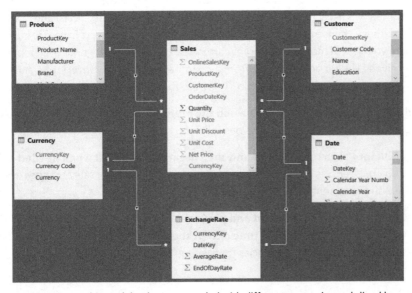

FIGURE 11-1 In this model, sales are recorded with different currencies and sliced by currency.

The first question with such a model is, what is the meaning of Unit Price, Unit Discount, and all the other currency columns stored in Sales? If you saved the values in the original currency, as is likely the case, then you are in trouble as soon as you author a simple calculation like the sales amount. If you use a formula like the following one, the result might not be what you expected:

```
Sales Amount := SUMX ( Sales, Sales[Quantity] * Sales[Net Price] )
```

We used the same formula for Sales Amount in most of this book, but when used with currencies, it stops working. Figure 11-2 shows the result of a simple report based on this formula, where the totals at the column level make no sense. This is because they are summing values in different currencies, which leads to useless numbers.

Currency	CY 2007	CY 2008	CY 2009	Total
Armenian Dram	181,160.03	98,721.99	133,696.43	413,578.45
Australian Dollar	181,974.84	128,466.53	155,045.00	465,486.37
Canadian Dollar	136,916.66	159,722.90	159,992.10	456,631.66
Danish Krone	151,100.25	84,134.31	130,819.13	366,053.69
EURO	170,560.82	124,161.46	158,567.36	453,289.64
Hong Kong Dollar	120,129.99	130,518.12	161,045.14	411,693.25
Indian Rupee	174,326.71	123,890.69	139,402.73	437,620.13
Thai Baht	123,623.76	159,501.98	106,073.85	389,199.58
US Dollar	219,422.89	113,417.08	97,892.87	430,732.85
Total	1,459,215.95	1,122,535.05	1,242,534.61	3,824,285.61

FIGURE 11-2 In this report, the total at the column level is summing different currencies.

The report correctly shows the values and the row totals because they refer to a single currency. When it comes to the column level, however, these numbers are a nonsense. You simply cannot sum together Euro, Danish Krone, and US Dollar unless you perform a conversion and define a target currency to use for the sum.

Because of the presence of data in different currencies, you should protect these measures from showing meaningless values. Use the HASONEVALUE function to guarantee that the result is returned if and only if a single currency has been selected. In the following code, we cover this first need:

```
Sales Amount :=
IF (
    HASONEVALUE ( Currency[Currency] ),
    SUMX ( Sales, Sales[Quantity] * Sales[Net Price] )
)
```

Using this new measure, the report loses the total on the columns, where the sum should not be displayed, as shown in Figure 11-3.

Currency	CY 2007	CY 2008	CY 2009	Total
Armenian Dram	181,160.03	98,721.99	133,696.43	413,578.45
Australian Dollar	181,974.84	128,466.53	155,045.00	465,486.37
Canadian Dollar	136,916.66	159,722.90	159,992.10	456,631.66
Danish Krone	151,100.25	84,134.31	130,819.13	366,053.69
EURO	170,560.82	124,161.46	158,567.36	453,289.64
Hong Kong Dollar	120,129.99	130,518.12	161,045.14	411,693.25
Indian Rupee	174,326.71	123,890.69	139,402.73	437,620.13
Thai Baht	123,623.76	159,501.98	106,073.85	389,199.58
US Dollar	219,422.89	113,417.08	97,892.87	430,732.85
Total				

FIGURE 11-3 By protecting the code, you avoid showing the totals when they cannot be computed.

Even without the totals at the column level, this report is not very useful. A report is generally used to compare numbers, but the values shown in this table cannot simply be compared. It would be even worse to build a chart on top of this data because, at that point, it would seem natural to do a comparison. If you need to compare these values, then you need to either use the currency as a filter and then slice by some other column or normalize all the values to a common currency.

The easiest way to do this is to create a calculated column in the Sales table that computes the amount in the currency you want to use for your reports. For now, let us make things simple and imagine that we want to produce reports in USD. You can create a calculated column in Sales that computes the rate to USD of the current day for the current currency. In the demo, we used the following code, which you might need to adapt for your scenario:

```
RateToUsd =
LOOKUPVALUE (
    ExchangeRate[AverageRate],
    ExchangeRate[CurrencyKey], Sales[CurrencyKey],
    ExchangeRate[DateKey], RELATED ( 'Date'[Date] )
)
```

Once RateToUSD is in place, you can use it to compute Sales Amount USD by simply multiplying the value of the sales amount by the exchange rate. Thus, Sales Amount USD is computed by the following DAX code:

```
Sales Amount USD =
SUMX (
    Sales,
    Sales[Quantity] * DIVIDE ( Sales[Net Price], Sales[RateToUsd] )
)
```

With the measure, you can now show a report that lets you compare sales in different years and currencies with meaningful values, as shown in Figure 11-4.

Currency	CY 2007	CY 2008	CY 2009	Total
Armenian Dram	$546.23	$322.85	$226.76	$1,095.83
Australian Dollar	$151,722.84	$112,736.93	$44,261.88	$308,721.65
Canadian Dollar	$127,000.26	$152,197.14	$84,405.27	$363,602.67
Danish Krone	$27,499.38	$17,389.56	$15,441.66	$60,330.60
EURO	$235,090.17	$187,431.98	$107,056.88	$529,579.04
Hong Kong Dollar	$15,386.65	$17,131.00	$9,188.17	$41,705.83
Indian Rupee	$4,303.89	$2,944.15	$2,027.75	$9,275.79
Thai Baht	$3,829.75	$5,015.39	$2,036.08	$10,881.23
US Dollar	$219,422.89	$113,417.08	$62,749.16	$395,589.14
Total	**$784,802.08**	**$608,586.08**	**$327,393.61**	**$1,720,781.77**

FIGURE 11-4 When values are converted to the report currency, you can safely compare them and produce totals.

This technique is pretty simple to implement. The logic about the exact date when the conversion should happen is configured in the calculated column. If you have different needs, you can change that definition and obtain the right result. For example, if you need to get the exchange rate of the day after, you can simply modify the LOOKUPVALUE function to search for that exchange rate. The main limitation of this technique is that it works fine if you have a single currency for the reports. If you have many of them, you will need a separate measure (and calculated column) for each of them.

 Note The `Sales Amount USD` measure has a format string that shows a dollar symbol in front of it. The format string of a measure is static, meaning you cannot change it dynamically. The technique of using a separate measure for each reporting currency is widely adopted, and we suggest you follow it to make the user experience better.

Before leaving this first scenario, it is worth noting that the number it computes is not completely correct. In fact, if you compare Figure 11-4 and Figure 11-3, you will see that the value for 2009 is lower in Figure 11-4. (This is evident if you look at the US Dollar row.) When complex calculations are involved, as in this case, spotting errors is not trivial. In fact, the problem is evident in the US Dollar row, which should always convert one-to-one. However, it is also present in all the other currencies, although much less evident. Double-checking your values is always a good practice. So where is the issue? If you look at the data in the Sales table, you will notice several hundreds of rows that have a blank RateToUsd column, as shown in Figure 11-5. Here, we sorted by RateToUsd to show the blank rows first.

OrderDateKey	Quantity	Unit Price	Unit Discount	Unit Cost	Net Price	CurrencyKey	RateToUsd
20090930	1	9.99	0	5.09	9.99	3	
20090930	1	9.99	0	5.09	9.99	3	
20090930	1	9.99	0	5.09	9.99	3	
20090930	1	9.99	0	5.09	9.99	3	
20090930	1	9.99	0	5.09	9.99	3	
20090930	1	9.99	0	5.09	9.99	3	
20090930	1	9.99	0	5.09	9.99	3	
20090930	1	9.99	0	5.09	9.99	3	
20091001	1	9.99	0	5.09	9.99	1	
20091001	1	9.99	0	5.09	9.99	1	
20091001	1	9.99	0	5.09	9.99	1	
20091001	1	9.99	0	5.09	9.99	1	
20091001	1	9.99	0	5.09	9.99	1	
20091001	1	9.99	0	5.09	9.99	1	

FIGURE 11-5 The RateToUsd column is empty for several rows.

The problem here is that the exchange rate is not available for all the dates, so the LOOKUPVALUE function does not return any number. As with many other scenarios related to currency conversion, you need to define what to do in such a case. If the conversion rate for a given day is not available, then the numbers reported are wrong, and you cannot afford such a scenario. In the following code, we decided to take the latest conversion ratio if the current day's rate is not available:

```
RateToUsd =
LOOKUPVALUE (
    ExchangeRate[AverageRate],
    ExchangeRate[CurrencyKey], Sales[CurrencyKey],
    ExchangeRate[DateKey], CALCULATE (
        MAX ( 'ExchangeRate'[DateKey] ),
        'ExchangeRate'[DateKey] <= EARLIER ( Sales[OrderDateKey] ),
        ExchangeRate[CurrencyKey] = EARLIER ( Sales[CurrencyKey] ),
        ALL ( ExchangeRate )
    )
)
```

With the new RateToUsd in place, the report shows meaningful values, as shown in Figure 11-6.

Currency	CY 2007	CY 2008	CY 2009	Total
Armenian Dram	$486.21	$264.96	$358.82	**$1,109.99**
Australian Dollar	$145,926.59	$103,017.99	$124,331.41	**$373,276.00**
Canadian Dollar	$121,959.54	$142,274.37	$142,514.17	**$406,748.08**
Danish Krone	$28,586.93	$15,917.52	$24,749.91	**$69,254.37**
EURO	$240,162.23	$174,828.51	$223,274.57	**$638,265.31**
Hong Kong Dollar	$15,496.84	$16,836.92	$20,774.92	**$53,108.68**
Indian Rupee	$3,602.25	$2,560.05	$2,880.59	**$9,042.89**
Thai Baht	$3,630.17	$4,683.72	$3,114.83	**$11,428.72**
US Dollar	$219,422.89	$113,417.08	$97,892.87	**$430,732.85**
Total	**$779,273.67**	**$573,801.13**	**$639,892.09**	**$1,992,966.89**

FIGURE 11-6 With the new calculated column, conversion happens smoothly for all the periods.

Single source currency, multiple reporting currencies

Now that you learned about converting multiple currencies into a single currency, we can go further and analyze a different scenario, where you have a single currency in the source data and you want to be able to produce reports in a different currency.

As with the previous scenario, you must make some decisions in this case, too. For example, if you collected an order in USD on the first of January 2005 and you prepare a report in December 2006, what exchange rate should you use? You can choose between the exchange rate that was active at the moment of the order or the latest available exchange rate. The model, in both cases, is the same, even if the DAX code to compute the values is different. Thus, you have the option to develop both calculations in the same model. The model is shown in Figure 11-7.

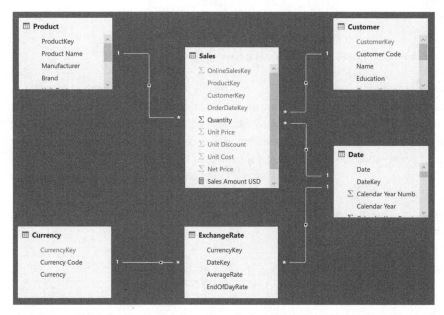

FIGURE 11-7 This is the data model to convert a single currency in multiple reported currencies.

The model looks very similar to the one shown in Figure 11-1, but there are some important differences. First, there are no longer any relationships between Sales and Currency. This is because all the sales are now recorded in USD. (We decided to use this currency for this demo, but it might be any other currency.) Thus, the currency does not filter Sales. This time, the Currency table is used to define the reporting currency. In other words, even if the sales are stored in USD, by choosing a different currency, the user should be able to see the values in any other currency.

You want to compute the value in a dynamic way. That is, you want the user to be able to select the currency at report time. You cannot leverage on a calculated column, however. Instead you must author some more complex DAX code in a measure. The named measure needs to do the following:

1. Check that a single currency is selected to avoid the grand-total issue we encountered in the previous section. As you might recall, the grand total for a report with multiple currencies is not accurate, and we do not want to display it.

2. Iterate on each date in the current selection; compute the value of sales and the currency rate for each date; and make the conversion in the desired currency. This iteration is necessary because the exchange rate changes every day. You cannot compute the conversion until you fix the day, which is what the iteration does.

The second point is further complicated by the fact that, on some days, the exchange rate might not be available. Thus, you will need to search for the latest exchange rate every day. Most of the time, this process will lead you to the exchange rate of that day. On some days, however, you will need to use a prior date. The following code, although somewhat complex, accomplishes all these steps:

```
Sales Converted =
IF (
    HASONEVALUE ( 'Currency'[Currency] ),
    SUMX (
        VALUES ( 'Date'[Date] ),
        VAR CurrentDate = 'Date'[Date]
        VAR LastDateAvailable =
            CALCULATE (
                MAX ( 'ExchangeRate'[DateKey] ),
                'ExchangeRate'[DateKey] <= CurrentDate,
                ALL ( 'Date' )
            )
        VAR Rate =
            CALCULATE (
                VALUES ( ExchangeRate[AverageRate] ),
                ExchangeRate[DateKey] = LastDateAvailable,
                ALL ( 'Date' )
            )
        RETURN
            [Sales Amount USD] * Rate
    )
)
```

Using this measure, you can build reports that, starting from a single USD currency, generate results in many different currencies, as shown in Figure 11-8.

Currency	CY 2007	CY 2008	CY 2009	Total
Armenian Dram	497,313,199.88	343,111,620.09	453,595,182.50	1,294,020,002.47
British Pound	728,743.44	597,671.41	789,621.94	2,116,036.79
Danish Krone	7,922,101.44	5,558,070.18	6,722,243.97	20,202,415.59
EURO	1,063,036.09	745,278.13	902,419.03	2,710,733.25
Swedish Krona	9,842,772.38	7,119,212.92	9,772,519.79	26,734,505.09
US Dollar	1,459,215.95	1,122,535.05	1,242,534.61	3,824,285.61
Total				

FIGURE 11-8   In this report, the value in the Currency column is the reporting currency. All orders are converted to the given currency.

Unfortunately, the formula is far from being simple and readable. This is problematic for several reasons, not least being the fact that you might need the same code snippet in other measures to (for example) convert the cost or the revenues in a similar way.

The most complex part is the search for the correct exchange rate. As is often the case, your best option here is to work at the data-model level. This time, instead of changing the model, you can build a new ExchangeRate table that provides an exchange rate for any date in the Sales table by searching for the latest exchange rate for that date, the same way you do in the measure. In doing so, you do not completely remove the complexity from the model. Instead you isolate the complexity in a calculated table to be able to use it whenever needed. In addition, isolating this calculation in a calculated table greatly improves the measure behavior because the slow process in the formula is the search for the correct exchange rate.

Note   This option is available only if you are working with SQL Server Analysis Services 2016 or Power BI because it makes use of calculated tables. If you are using a version of DAX that does not support calculated tables, then you need to perform a similar operation in the ETL process.

The following code generates the ExchangeRateFull table, which contains the exchange rate for every pair of date and currency:

```
ExchangeRateFull =
ADDCOLUMNS (
    CROSSJOIN (
        SELECTCOLUMNS (
            CALCULATETABLE ( DISTINCT ( 'Date'[Date] ), Sales ),
            "DateKey", 'Date'[Date]
        ),
        CALCULATETABLE ( DISTINCT ( Currency[CurrencyKey] ), ExchangeRate )
    ),
    "AverageRate",
    VAR CurrentDate = [DateKey]
    VAR CurrentCurrency = [CurrencyKey]
    VAR LastDateAvailable =
```

```
        CALCULATE (
            MAX ( 'ExchangeRate'[DateKey] ),
            'ExchangeRate'[DateKey] <= CurrentDate,
            ALLNOBLANKROW ( ExchangeRate[DateKey] )
        )
    RETURN
        CALCULATE (
            DISTINCT ( ExchangeRate[AverageRate] ),
            ExchangeRate[CurrencyKey] = CurrentCurrency,
            ExchangeRate[DateKey] = LastDateAvailable
        )
)
```

With this new calculated table in place, the model is very similar to the previous one, as shown in Figure 11-9.

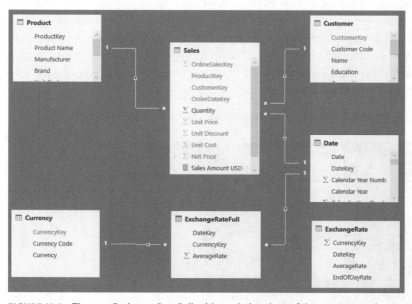

FIGURE 11-9 The new ExchangeRateFull table took the place of the previous ExchangeRate table.

Moreover, the code of the measure becomes much simpler to write, as you can see in the following measure definition:

```
Sales Converted =
IF (
    HASONEVALUE ( 'Currency'[Currency] ),
    SUMX (
        VALUES ( 'Date'[Date] ),
        [Sales Amount USD] * CALCULATE ( VALUES ( ExchangeRateFull[AverageRate] ) )
    )
)
```

As mentioned, the complexity is not gone. We only moved it into a calculated table, thus isolating it from the measures. The advantage of this approach is that you will spend less time debugging and writing the measures (and you might have plenty of them). Moreover, because the calculated table is computed at data refresh time and stored in the model, the overall performance will be much better.

In this case, we simplified the code not by changing the model structure; the last model is identical to the previous one. Instead, we changed the content of the table, which forced the relationship to be at the correct granularity.

Multiple source currencies, multiple reporting currencies

If your model stores orders in multiple currencies and you want to be able to report in any currency, then you face the most complex scenario. In reality, however, it is not much more complex than the one with multiple reporting currencies. This is because, as you might expect, complexity comes from the need to perform a currency conversion at query time by using measures and precomputed tables. Moreover, in the case of multiple currencies on both sides (storage and reporting), the exchange rate table needs to contain many more rows (one row for each pair of currencies for every day), or you will need to compute the exchange rate in a dynamic way.

Let us start by looking at the data model shown in Figure 11-10.

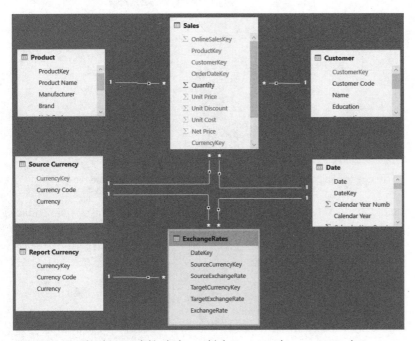

FIGURE 11-10 The data model includes multiple source and target currencies.

Note the following things about this model:

- There are two currency tables: Source Currency and Report Currency. Source Currency is used to slice the currency that records the sales, whereas Report Currency is used to slice the currency used in the report.

- The ExchangeRates table now contains both the source and the target currency because it lets you convert any currency into any other currency. It is worth noting that the ExchangeRates table can be computed (through DAX code) from the original table that converted every currency to USD.

The following code generates the ExchangeRates table:

```
ExchangeRates =
    SELECTCOLUMNS (
        GENERATE (
            ExchangeRateFull,
            VAR SourceCurrencyKey = ExchangeRateFull[CurrencyKey]
            VAR SourceDateKey = ExchangeRateFull[DateKey]
            VAR SourceAverageRate = ExchangeRateFull[AverageRate]
            RETURN
                SELECTCOLUMNS (
                    CALCULATETABLE (
                        ExchangeRateFull,
                        ExchangeRateFull[DateKey] = SourceDateKey,
                        ALL ( ExchangeRateFull )
                    ),
                    "TargetCurrencyKey", ExchangeRateFull[CurrencyKey] + 0,
                    "TargetExchangeRate", ExchangeRateFull[AverageRate] + 0
                )
        ),
        "DateKey", ExchangeRateFull[DateKey],
        "SourceCurrencyKey", ExchangeRateFull[CurrencyKey],
        "SourceExchangeRate", ExchangeRateFull[AverageRate],
        "TargetCurrencyKey", [TargetCurrencyKey],
        "TargetExchangeRate", [TargetExchangeRate],
        "ExchangeRate", ExchangeRateFull[AverageRate] * [TargetExchangeRate]
    )
```

This basically performs a cross-join of the ExchangeRateFull table with itself. First, it gathers the exchange rate to USD of both currencies, on the same date. Then it multiplies the exchange rates to obtain the correct exchange rate of any currency with any other one.

This table is much larger than the original one (we grew from 25,166 rows in ExchangeRateFull to 624,133 rows in the final table), but it lets us create relationships in an easy way. The code can be written even without the creation of this table, but it is utterly complicated.

When it comes to writing the code that computes the amount sold, you basically mix the two previous scenarios into a single one. You must slice sales by date and currency to obtain a set of sales that share the same exchange rate. Then you need to search, in a dynamic way, for the current exchange rate, taking into account the selected report currency, as in the following expression:

```
Sales Amount Converted =
IF (
    HASONEVALUE ( 'Report Currency'[Currency] ),
    SUMX (
        SUMMARIZE ( Sales, 'Date'[Date], 'Source Currency'[Currency] ),
        [Sales Amount] * CALCULATE ( VALUES ( ExchangeRates[ExchangeRate] ) )
    )
)
```

Using this model, you can, for example, report orders in different currencies in both EUR and USD with a currency conversion on the fly. In the report shown in Figure 11-11, for example, currency conversion happens at the date of the order.

Currency	Currency	CY 2007	CY 2008	CY 2009	Total
EURO	Armenian Dram	43,373,742.38	19,173,119.06	34,759,303.63	97,306,165.08
	Australian Dollar	159,842.98	99,235.98	148,748.47	407,827.44
	Canadian Dollar	109,409.84	115,736.45	135,707.60	360,853.89
	Danish Krone	613,644.73	276,219.86	511,179.97	1,401,044.57
	EURO	90,109.34	55,623.72	82,799.02	228,532.08
	Hong Kong Dollar	686,597.21	672,497.85	906,915.35	2,266,010.41
	Indian Rupee	5,173,111.76	3,568,148.79	4,880,686.52	13,621,947.08
	Thai Baht	2,927,959.72	3,421,109.47	2,657,193.07	9,006,262.26
	US Dollar	158,649.44	75,565.55	71,791.82	306,006.81
	Total	**53,293,067.41**	**27,457,256.73**	**44,154,325.47**	**124,904,649.61**
US Dollar	Armenian Dram	60,370,506.29	30,189,302.89	47,865,914.70	138,425,723.89
	Australian Dollar	218,812.35	148,993.71	204,242.14	572,048.20
	Canadian Dollar	148,139.37	169,625.07	185,952.40	503,716.84
	Danish Krone	830,847.78	413,258.38	705,403.35	1,949,509.52
	EURO	123,896.88	82,818.64	114,555.62	321,271.15
	Hong Kong Dollar	937,908.50	996,945.47	1,248,510.82	3,183,364.80
	Indian Rupee	7,079,309.87	5,281,242.15	6,743,294.80	19,103,846.83
	Thai Baht	3,997,511.72	5,117,644.99	3,657,183.94	12,772,340.64
	US Dollar	219,422.89	113,417.08	97,892.87	430,732.85
	Total	**73,926,355.67**	**42,513,248.38**	**60,822,950.66**	**177,262,554.72**
Total					

FIGURE 11-11 The values are converted in EUR and USD from the original currency.

Conclusions

Currency conversion requires models of increasing complexity depending on the requirements. The following main points were made in this chapter:

- You can achieve simple conversion from multiple currencies to a single currency (or a very small number of different currencies) through simple calculated columns.

- Converting to multiple reporting currencies requires a bit more complex DAX code and some adjustments on the data model because you can no longer leverage a calculated column. The conversion needs to happen in a more dynamic way.

- The dynamic conversion code can be made simpler by ensuring that the exchange rate table contains all the needed dates, which you can achieve by using a simple calculated table.

- The most complex scenario is when you have multiple source currencies and multiple reporting currencies. In that case, you need to mix the previous techniques and create two currency tables: one for the source currency and another for the reporting currency.

Data modeling 101

The goal of this appendix is to explain the data-modeling concepts that are used throughout the book and that are often discussed in articles, blog posts, and books. It is not an appendix to read from the beginning to the end. Instead, you can take a quick look at this appendix if, while reading the book, you find a term or a concept that is not clear or you want to refresh your memory. Thus, the appendix does not have a real flow. Each topic is treated in its own self-contained section. Moreover, we do not want this to be a complex appendix. We provide only the basic information about the topics. An in-depth discussion of them is beyond the scope of this book.

Tables

A *table* is a container that holds information. Tables are divided into rows and columns. Each row contains information about an individual entity, whereas each cell in a row contains the smallest piece of information represented in a database. For example, a Customer table might contain information about all your customers. One row contains all the information about one customer, and one column might contain the name or the address of all the customers. A cell might contain the address for one customer.

When building your model, you must think in these terms to avoid some common pitfalls that can make the analysis of your model a nightmare. Imagine, for example, that you decide to store information about an order in two rows of the same table. In one row, you store the amount ordered, along with its order date. In the other row, you store the amount shipped, again with its shipment date. By doing so, you split one entity (the order) into two rows of the same table. An example is shown in Figure A-1.

Order No	Customer	Date	Type	Amount
1	Contoso	01/01/2017	Order	100.00
1	Contoso	01/15/2017	Ship	60.00
1	Contoso	01/15/2017	Ship	40.00
2	Imageware	01/16/2017	Order	90.00
3	Imageware	01/20/2017	Order	45.00
4	Contoso	01/22/2017	Order	25.00

FIGURE A-1 In this table, information about a single order is divided into multiple rows.

This makes the table much more complex. Computing even a simple value like the order amount becomes more complex because a single column (Amount) contains different kinds of information. You cannot simply sum the amount; you always need to apply a filter. The problem with this model is that you have not designed it the right way. Because the individual order information is split into several rows, it is difficult to perform any kind of calculation. For example, computing the percentage of goods already shipped for every customer becomes a complex operation because you need to build code to do the following:

1. Iterate over each order number.

2. Aggregate the amount ordered (if it is in multiple lines), filtering only the rows in which the Type column equals Order.

3. Aggregate the amount shipped, this time filtering only the rows in which Type equals Ship.

4. Compute the percentage.

In the previous example, the error is that if an order is an entity in your model, then it needs to have its own table where all the values can be aggregated in a simple way. If you also need to track individual transactions for shipments, then you can build a Shipments table that contains only shipments. Figure A-2 shows you the correct model for this dataset.

Orders

Order No	Customer	Order Date	Amount
1	Contoso	01/01/2017	100.00
2	Imageware	01/16/2017	90.00
3	Imageware	01/20/2017	45.00
4	Contoso	01/22/2017	25.00

Shipments

Order No	Date	Amount
1	01/15/2017	60.00
1	01/15/2017	40.00

FIGURE A-2 The correct representation of orders and shipments requires two tables.

In this example, we only track shipments. However, you might have a more generic table that tracks the transactions of the order (orders, shipments, and returns). In that case, it is fine to store both types of transactions in the same table by tagging them with an attribute that identifies the type of operation. It is also fine to store different types of the same entity (transactions) in the same table. However, it is not good to store different entities (orders and transactions) in the same table.

Data types

When you design a model, each column has a data type. The *data type* is the type of content in the column. The data type can be integer, string, currency, floating point, and so on. There are many data types that you can choose from. The data type of a column is important because it affects its usability, the functions you can use on it, and the formatting options. In fact, the data type of a column is the format used internally by the engine to store the information. In contrast, the format string is only pertinent to how the UI represents the information in a human-readable form.

Suppose you have a column that should contain the quantity shipped. In that case, it is likely that an integer is a good data type for it. However, in a column that needs to store sales amounts, an integer is no longer a good option because you will need to store decimal points, too. In such a case, currency is the right data type to use.

When using plain Excel, each cell can contain values of any data type. When using the tabular data model, however, the data type is defined at the column level. This means all the rows in your table will need to store the same data type in that column. You cannot have mixed data types for one column in a table.

Relationships

When your model contains multiple entities, as is generally the case, you store information in multiple tables and link them through relationships. In a tabular model, a relationship always links two tables, and it is based on a single column.

The most common representation of a relationship is an arrow that starts from the source table and goes to the target table, as shown in Figure A-3.

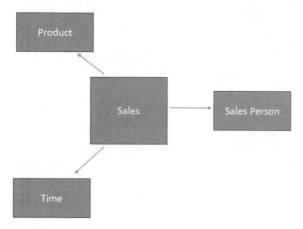

FIGURE A-3   In this model, there are four tables that are linked through relationships.

When you define a relationship, there is always a one side and a many side. In the sample model, for each product, there are many sales, and for each sale there is exactly one product. Thus, the Product table is on the one side, whereas Sales is on the many side. The arrow always goes from the many side to the one side.

In different versions of Power Pivot for Excel and in Power BI, the user interface uses different visualizations for relationships. However, in the latest versions of both Excel and Power BI, the engine draws a line that tags the ends of the line with a 1 (one) or * (star) to identify the one or the many side of the relationship. In Power BI Desktop, you also have the option of creating one-to-one relationships. A one-to-one relationship is always bidirectional because for each row of a table, there can be only zero or one rows in the other table. Thus, in this special case, there is no many side of the relationship.

Filtering and cross-filtering

When you browse your model through a PivotTable or by using Power BI, filtering is very important. In fact, it is the foundation of most—if not all—calculations in a report. When using the DAX language, the rule is very simple: The filter always moves from the one side of a relationship to the many side. In the user interface, this is represented by an arrow in the middle of the relationship that shows how the filter propagates through the relationship, as shown in Figure A-4.

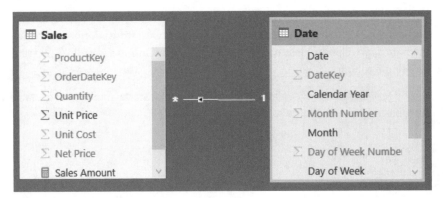

FIGURE A-4 The small arrow inside the line of the relationship represents the direction of the filter.

Thus, whenever you filter Date, you filter Sales, too. This is why, in a PivotTable, you can easily slice the sales amount by the calendar year: a filter on Date directly translates to a filter on Sales. The opposite direction, on the other hand, does not work by default. A filter on Sales will not propagate to Date unless you instruct the data model to do so. Figure A-5 shows you a graphical representation of how the filter is propagated by default.

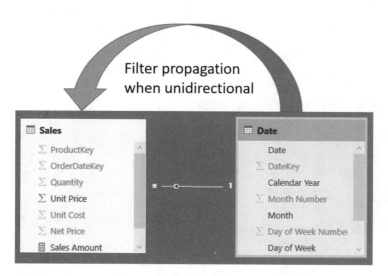

FIGURE A-5 The large arrow indicates how the filter is being propagated when unidirectional filtering is on.

You can change the direction of the filter propagation (known as *cross-filter direction*) by modifying the setting of the relationship. In Power BI, for example, this is done by double-clicking on the relationship itself. This opens the Edit Relationship dialog box, shown in Figure A-6.

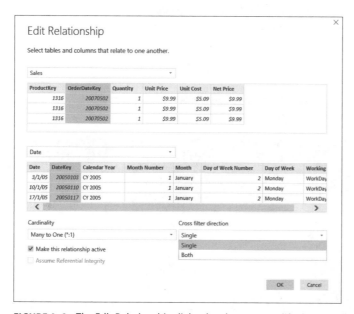

FIGURE A-6 The Edit Relationship dialog box lets you modify the cross-filter direction.

By default, the cross-filter direction is set to Single—that is, from one to many. If needed, you can change it to Both so that the filter also propagates from the many side to the one side. Figure A-7 shows a graphical representation of how the filter propagates when you set it to be bidirectional.

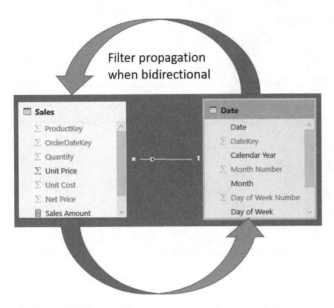

FIGURE A-7   When in bidirectional mode, the filter propagates both ways.

This feature is not available in Power Pivot for Excel 2016. If you need to activate bidirectional filtering in Power Pivot for Excel, you must activate it on demand by using the CROSSFILTER function, as in the following example, which works on the model shown in Figure A-8:

```
Num of Customers =
CALCULATE (
    COUNTROWS ( Customer ),
    CROSSFILTER ( Sales[CustomerKey], Customer[CustomerKey], BOTH )
)
```

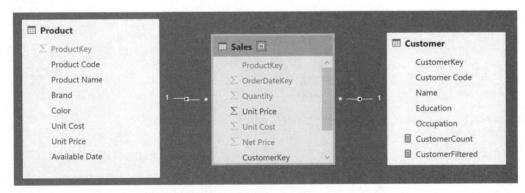

FIGURE A-8   Both relationships are set to their default mode, which is unidirectional.

The CROSSFILTER function enables bidirectional filtering for the duration of the CALCULATE statement. During the evaluation of COUNTROWS (Customer), the filter will move from Sales to Customer to show only the customers who are referenced in Sales.

This technique is very convenient when you need, for example, to compute the number of customers who bought a product. In fact, the filter moves naturally from Product to Sales. Then, however, you need to use bidirectional filtering to let it flow to Customer by passing through Sales. For example, Figure A-9 shows two calculations. One has bidirectional filtering activated and the other uses the default filter propagation.

Brand	CustomerCount	CustomerFiltered
A. Datum	18,869	189
Adventure Works	18,869	392
Contoso	18,869	815
Fabrikam	18,869	173
Litware	18,869	199
Northwind Traders	18,869	151
Proseware	18,869	125
Southridge Video	18,869	855
Tailspin Toys	18,869	594
The Phone Company	18,869	76
Wide World Importers	18,869	133
Total	**18,869**	**18,869**

FIGURE A-9 The two measures differ only for the direction of the cross-filter. The results are completely different.

The definitions of the two measures are as follows:

```
CustomerCount := COUNTROWS ( Customer )

CustomerFiltered :=
CALCULATE (
    COUNTROWS ( Customer ),
    CROSSFILTER ( Customer[CustomerKey], Sales[CustomerKey], BOTH )
)
```

You can see that CustomerCount uses the default filtering. Thus, Product filters Sales, but Sales does not filter Customer. In the second measure, on the other hand, the filter flows from Product to Sales and then reaches Customer, so the formula counts only the customers who bought one of the filtered products.

Different types of models

In a typical model, there are many tables linked through relationships. These tables can be classified using the following names, based on their usage:

- **Fact table**   A *fact table* contains values that you want to aggregate. Fact tables typically store events that happened in a specific point in time and that can be measured. Fact tables are generally the largest tables in the model, containing tens of millions or even hundreds of millions of rows. Fact tables normally store only numbers—either keys to dimensions or values to aggregate.

- **Dimension** A *dimension* is useful to slice facts. Typical dimensions are products, customers, time, and categories. Dimensions are usually small tables, with hundreds or thousands of rows. They tend to have many attributes in the form of strings because their main purpose is to slice values.

- **Bridge tables** *Bridge tables* are used in more complex models to represent many-to-many relationships. For example, a customer who might belong to multiple categories can be modeled with a bridge table that contains one row for each of the categories of the customer.

Star schema

When you look at the diagram of your model, if it is built based only on fact tables and dimensions, you can put the fact table in the center with all the dimensions around it—an arrangement known as a *star schema*, as shown in Figure A-10.

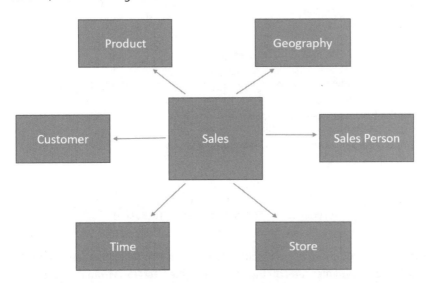

FIGURE A-10 A star schema emerges if you put the fact table in the middle and all the dimensions around it.

Star schemas have a lot of great features: They are fast and easy to understand and manage. As you read in this book, you will see that they are—with good reason—the foundation of most analytical databases. Sometimes, however, you need to structure your model in different ways, the most common of which are described in the next sections.

Snowflake schema

Sometimes, a dimension is linked to another dimension that further classifies it. For example, products might have categories, and you might decide to store the categories in a separate table. As another example, stores can be divided in business units, which again, you might decide to store in a separate table. As an example, Figure A-11 shows products that, instead of having the category name as a column, store a category key, which, in turn, refers to the Category table.

Product

ProductKey	Product	CategoryKey
1	Apple	1
2	Orange	1
3	Bike	2
4	Helmet	2

Category

CategoryKey	Category
1	Fruit
2	Sport

FIGURE A-11 Categories are stored in their own table, and Product refers to that table.

If you use such a schema, both product categories and business units are still dimensions, but instead of being related directly to the fact table, they are related through an intermediate dimension. For example, the Sales table contains the ProductKey column, but to obtain the category name, you must reach Product from Sales and then Category from Product. In such a case, you obtain a different schema, which is known as a snowflake, as shown in Figure A-12.

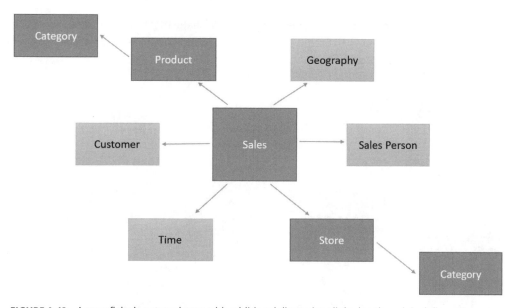

FIGURE A-12 A snowflake is a star schema with additional dimensions linked to the original dimensions.

Dimensions are not related among themselves. For example, you can think of the relationship between Category and Sales as a direct relationship, but it is passing through the Store table. For no reason is a relationship allowed to link Store with Geography. In such a case, in fact, the model would become ambiguous because there would be multiple paths from Sales to Geography.

Snowflake schemas are somewhat common in the business intelligence (BI) world. Apart from a slight degradation of performance, they are not a bad choice. Nevertheless, whenever possible, it is better to avoid snowflakes and stick to the more standard star schema because the DAX code tends to be easier to develop and less error-prone.

Models with bridge tables

A bridge table typically lies between two dimensions to create many-to-many relationships between the dimensions. For example, Figure A-13 shows how an individual customer might belong to multiple categories. Marco belongs both to the Male and Italian categories, whereas Kate belongs only to the Female category. If you have a scenario like this, then you design two relationships starting from the bridge and reaching, respectively, Customer and Category.

Customer			Bridge Customer Category			Category	
CustomerKey	Customer		CustomerKey	CategoryKey		CategoryKey	Category
1	Marco		1	1		1	Male
2	Alberto		2	1		2	Female
3	Kate		3	2		3	Italian
4	Ed		1	3			
			2	3			

FIGURE A-13 A bridge table lets an individual customer belong to different categories.

When your model contains bridge tables, it takes a new shape that has never been named in the BI community. Figure A-14 shows an example where we added the capability for a customer to belong to multiple customer categories.

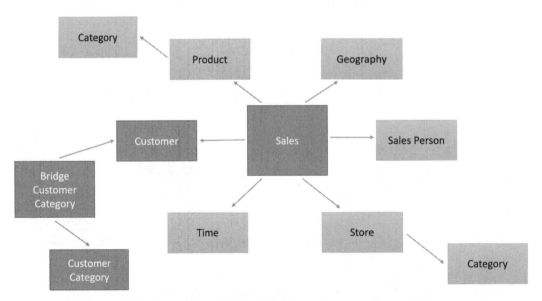

FIGURE A-14 A bridge table links two dimensions, but it is different from a regular snowflake.

The difference between the regular snowflake schema and this one with a bridge table is that this time, the relationship between Customer Category and Sales is not a straight relationship that passes through two dimensions. In fact, the relationship between Customer and the bridge is in the opposite direction. If it was going from the Customer to the bridge, then it would have been a snowflake. Because of its direction (which reflects its intended usage) it becomes a many-to-many relationship.

Measures and additivity

When you define a measure, an important concept is whether the measure is additive or not against a specific dimension.

Additive measures

A measure is said to be *additive* when it aggregates by using a simple sum. For example, the amount sold is additive against products, meaning that the total sold results from the sum of sales of individual products. As another example, Sales is additive against all dimensions because the total sold over a year results from the sum of the sales of individual days.

Non-additive measures

There is another category of calculations that is known as *non-additive*. Distinct count, for example, is a non-additive calculation. If you perform a distinct count of the product sold, then the distinct count over one year is not the sum of the distinct counts over individual months. The same applies to customers, countries, and any other dimension (apart from the product). Whenever you need to compute a non-additive measure, you must perform a full scan of the table for each level of the hierarchy that you are browsing because you cannot aggregate values from their children.

Semi-additive measures

The third category of calculations is *semi-additive*. Semi-additive measures are the most complex measures because they are additive against some dimensions and non-additive against others. Typically, the dimension that acts as an exception is time. For example, a Year-to-Date calculation is non-additive because the value you show for one month (for example, March) is not the sum of the individual days. Instead it is the value of the last day of the month. Figure A-15 shows an example of these three kinds of measures.

Calendar Year	Month	Sales Amount	Sales YTD	Distinct Products
CY 2007	January	$101,097.12	$101,097.12	38
	February	$108,553.20	$209,650.32	45
	March	$119,707.83	$329,358.16	52
	April	$121,085.74	$450,443.90	56
	May	$123,413.41	$573,857.31	58
	June	$121,707.44	$695,564.75	50
	July	$139,381.00	$834,945.75	52
	August	$87,384.31	$922,330.06	47
	September	$155,275.94	$1,077,606.00	52
	October	$99,872.65	$1,177,478.64	52
	November	$122,522.86	$1,300,001.50	51
	December	$159,214.45	$1,459,215.95	60
	Total	**$1,459,215.95**	**$1,459,215.95**	**426**

FIGURE A-15 The report shows the three types of additivity: additive, semi-additive, and nonadditive.

DAX offers a set of functions to handle semi-additivity over time. Functions like DATESYTD, TOTALYTD, LASTDATE, and CLOSINGBALANCEQUARTER help you author semi-additive measures when time is the non-additive dimension. Handling semi-additivity over different dimensions requires more complex FILTER functions because there is no predefined function to handle non-additivity on dimensions that are not related to time.

Index

A

B

C

T

Free ebooks

From technical overviews to drilldowns on special topics, get *free* ebooks from Microsoft Press at:

www.microsoftvirtualacademy.com/ebooks

Download your free ebooks in PDF, EPUB, and/or Mobi for Kindle formats.

Look for other great resources at Microsoft Virtual Academy, where you can learn new skills and help advance your career with free Microsoft training delivered by experts.

Microsoft Press

Hear about it first.

Get the latest news from Microsoft Press sent to your inbox.

- New and upcoming books

- Special offers

- Free eBooks

- How-to articles

Sign up today at MicrosoftPressStore.com/Newsletters

 Microsoft

Visit us today at

microsoftpressstore.com

- **Hundreds of titles available** – Books, eBooks, and online resources from industry experts

- **Free U.S. shipping**

- **eBooks in multiple formats** – Read on your computer, tablet, mobile device, or e-reader

- **Print & eBook Best Value Packs**

- **eBook Deal of the Week** – Save up to 60% on featured titles

- **Newsletter and special offers** – Be the first to hear about new releases, specials, and more

- **Register your book** – Get additional benefits

 Microsoft